My Road to Mo

To my dear friend, Matt

Thanks for the memories,
many of which enriched this
book!

Enjoy!

Love,

Matt

My Road to Mo

A memoir about falling in love... with a girl,
cycling and the California coast.

MATTHEW KOEHLER

ISBN (paperback): 978-1-7373938-0-1
ISBN (ebook): 978-1-7373938-1-8

First Edition

To my love, Maureen:

So we may always remember,
this is a story of our beginning.
I love you more now than I did then.
And I loved you dearly, even in the beginning.

To my sister, Stacie:

Thank you for choosing Disneyland.

CONTENTS

PREFACE

I met my wife, Maureen, in Disneyland on July 17, 1994, Disneyland's 39th birthday. I was nineteen, she was twenty.

Those simple sentences tell a story all by themselves . . . but there's more to it, of course. All the fun stuff is in the details. People ask me all the time about our story, and when I give them the simple rundown, they always want to know more about how our chance meeting came to be at the "Happiest Place on Earth," and on such a special day. What's interesting is . . . it's all my sister's fault. I'll admit, it's a heartwarming story, one I love to share, so I usually indulge these curious souls, filling them in on how it all came to be. Over the years, Maureen and I have shared our story with so many people that the memories of that special moment are as vivid today as they were the day after we met.

Just as memorable for me was the 430 mile, 3-day bicycle ride I took to visit Maureen at UC Irvine about three months after we met. I traveled south, unsupported, from Capitola to UC Irvine, following as much of the California coastline as possible, just to visit with her for a while. The journey was an eventful one, packed full of unforgettable challenges, chance encounters with interesting people, and breathtaking views of the iconic Pacific coastline.

My purpose for writing this book was two-fold. First, in 2018 Maureen and I celebrated our twentieth wedding anniversary. I felt the need to give her a gift she would never expect, something so personal and special that forgetting about it someday would be impossible. I succeeded, presenting it to her at the exact location in Disneyland where we had met twenty-four years earlier. Secondly, the story is so loved by our family and friends that I wanted to put it down in writing for all to read, and to have something tangible to add to our family history.

This is the story of our beginning, from my perspective. It shares with you the happiness and hopefulness of a new, budding relationship and explores my personal experience with falling in love . . . and not just with the most amazing woman ever, but also with cycling and the California coastline.

Matthew Koehler

Santa Rosa, California, 2021

i

PART ONE

The Meeting
Disneyland – July 17th, 1994

CHAPTER ONE

My socked feet slipped easily across the polished white tile as I swayed nervously, standing wide-stanced in the house entryway. A little apprehensive about the revelation I was about to make, I rehearsed the script in my head one last time before opening my mouth to speak.

"Hey Mom, Dad," I said inquisitively.

"Yes?" Mom said, her voice rising from somewhere in the kitchen.

"Yeah?" Dad replied, presumably from the dining room. His response started softly but quickly became loud.

"Can you come out here for a moment, please?"

"Sure, just a second," Mom replied in between the banging of cooking pots. The reverberating clang of steel hitting steel reminded me of the always-too-loud crashing cymbals of my high school marching band.

I heard Dad push his chair back from the dining room table. It was late afternoon, and he was catching up on yesterday's news with the morning paper. The sound of chair legs squeaking across the dining room floor filled the house and brought my concentration back to the case at hand.

Mom was closest to where I was in the entryway, so she appeared first, drying her hands on her pants as she walked. Taking short steps, she moved strangely fast down the hallway. Her eyes were wide, her body language questioning. Dad followed close behind.

"Everything okay?" Mom asked as she walked, her gaze never leaving mine.

"Oh, yeah. Everything's fine. No bad surprises, don't worry."

"Oh, okay." she replied softly, sounding relieved.

"Could you both stand over here with me for a moment?"

I gestured next to me with my right hand as they got closer, like I was ushering them into an empty church pew.

"Just stand right here," I said, smiling. My hand gesture directed traffic to the corner of the entryway nearest the front door.

They both did as I asked and stood alongside me on the tile floor, both with quizzical looks on their faces.

"What?" Mom asked, nervously crossing her arms across her chest. An inquisitive, toothy smile filled her face as her eyebrows lifted, slightly wrinkling the thin skin of her forehead.

"Stacie's in her bedroom, right?" I asked.

"She was a little while ago. Listening to music I think."

"Okay. Well, her birthday's coming up and I've got a couple gift ideas that might make that sister of mine, let's just say, a little bit excited." I said, whispering in a voice only they could hear.

"Oh yeah? Did you get her something already?" Dad asked.

"Not really. Not yet, anyway," I said.

"What is it?" Mom probed.

"You'll see. Just wait a minute. She has to choose. I'll call her out here now."

I peered down the hallway and cupped my hands over my mouth. Shouting loudly, I brought the heart of the house alive with noise.

"Stacie!"

She answered almost immediately from her bedroom, located almost at the end of the L-shaped hallway.

"Yeah?"

Similar to Dad's response from the dining room earlier, her voice started low and rose sharply. It probably started out as a yell but reached my ears as a muffled whimper.

"Can you come out here for a moment, please?" I replied, speaking louder than normal so she could hear me. And, in our family, that's pretty loud.

"Okay. Coming. Just a second."

I sensed trepidation in her voice. Not much, just a little. That wasn't unexpected. I usually went to her if I had something to talk about. It was rare that I called out for her, so I presumed she might be thinking something was amiss. The faint squeak of a door hinge and the dull thuds of bare feet striking carpet preceded her appearance at the bend in the hall. She paused at the corner and glanced into the dining room. Seeing nobody there, she turned and faced the front door, where all three of us were standing. When she saw me at the other end, she stood fast on the threshold between the hallway carpet and dining room linoleum. The sun shined in through the dining room windows where Dad had been reading the paper a few minutes before, filling the room with warm summer sunlight and bathing the right side of her body in various shades of orange and yellow.

"Yeah? What's up?" she asked.

"Come over here, please." I said. "I need to ask you something."

Stacie slipped out of the sunglow and walked slowly down the hallway. No more thuds, her feet were now sliding across the carpet.

Her gaze naturally migrated in Mom and Dad's direction as they came into her view. The stern expression on her face indicated confusion and discrete curiosity.

Stacie came to a stop a couple feet in front of me, still standing on the hallway carpet. With her on the carpet and me on the tile, it must have looked like we were about to square off in a boxing match. In between darted glances she fired off to Mom, Dad, and me behind eyeglasses and beneath a furrowed brow, she spoke to the obvious.

"What? Is something wrong?"

"Oh no, not at all," I said and then paused.

Stacie leaned forward, flipped her palms outward, and raised them from her sides to waist level. This brought her face so close to mine that she could only focus on one of my eyes at a time, even while looking through the large lenses of her glasses. Her eyes shot back and forth, searching mine for clues.

"Then what's going on?" she inquired.

I placed my hands on her shoulders and pushed her back to an upright position.

"So." I paused. "I need to know the answer to a question only you can answer."

I stared at her while a half-smile formed on my face.

"Okay," she replied.

Her body still exuding frustration and her face still frozen in confusion, she shot sideways glances at Mom and Dad before settling in on my face again.

"What?" she said in an elevated tone, impatient.

"I need to know what you would like for your birthday," I said.

She paused for a second and the furrow on her brow deepened.

"Um." Her brow relaxing some and her eyes wandering, she scanned the ceiling for an answer. "I don't know. I haven't really thought about it all that much, really."

I dipped my chin in disbelief and gave her an unconvincing smirk.

"Really? Come on, Stace. What fourteen-year-old girl doesn't know what she wants for her birthday?"

"Well, alright. I guess I have thought about it. Maybe just a little bit. Do you need to know right now?"

"Yeah. It's kinda important, actually," I said, my half-smile growing full. "But it really doesn't matter what's on your list. I have two presents for you to choose from. Neither of which are going to be on your birthday wish list anyway."

"Then how do you know I want either of them?" she replied smartly.

Finally feeling better about the questioning, the built-up frustration and confusion left her face. But a slight tension of suspense remained. Keeping her hip cocked out to the side, she playfully crossed her arms over her chest and waited for the interrogation to continue.

"Let's just say I have a feeling what my soon-to-be fifteen-year-old sister would like for her birthday this year, more than anything else."

Stacie continued to relax. She could read me like a book and knew something awesome was coming her way. She uncrossed her arms and pressed her hands together in front of her waist. The nervous confusion plastered on her face quickly morphed to suspenseful excitement now that the possibility of hearing bad news was off the table. She tried hard to hide it but wasn't succeeding.

I peered at my parents over my right shoulder, grinning, and could see they were just as anxious.

"Okay. What, Matt? Tell me already! What are my choices?" she asked, her eyes widening.

"Well, Stacie, for your birthday this year I will either . . ." — pausing for effect, I watched her eyes intensely lock on to mine — ". . . buy you the contact lenses you wa-"

She cut me off with a shriek and jumped in the air a couple inches.

"Hold on a second," I said, raising my hands, palms up, making the universal slow-down sign. I started laughing but quickly got it under control. "You're going to want to hear the second choice, trust me." More pausing for effect.

Stacie took in a deep breath. Holding it in behind clinched teeth and an open-mouth smile, she started bobbing at the knees. I continued in an elevated and insinuating tone.

"OR . . . take you on a two-day trip to Disneyland. Your choice."

My initial thought was that she would immediately go for the contact lenses, or at least give both choices some agonizing thought. She hated wearing glasses and wanted contact lenses so badly, had wanted them for years. But in 1994, they weren't covered under our parent's insurance plan, and they were too expensive to pay for out-of-pocket, especially for something that could get lost or misplaced so easily. So, she had no choice but to stick with the glasses.

The decision was instantaneous. Her eyes glistened with happiness, an ear-to-ear smile forcing them into thin slits.

"Forget the contacts. I want to go to Disneyland!" She screamed.

Stacie leaped from her excitement-induced-bent-knee-squat, crossed the carpet-tile barrier in mid-air, and slammed her body into mine. Her feet hit the floor, and she wrapped me up in a giant bear hug. I had to take a step back to keep us from crashing to the floor.

"Oh, wow!" she squealed. "Thank you! I'm so excited."

She pulled away, eyes tearing up behind the large round lenses of her glasses. For the moment she was able to hold them back from streaming down her face, but soon she would need to wipe them away, or let them fall.

*　　　*　　　*

Stacie's my only sister, and we share a special bond, a close brother-sister relationship. This may have had something to do with her excitement. Or, maybe it was just the fact that she now had a confirmed trip to

Disneyland. I mean, who doesn't want to spend the day in Disneyland? This trip was going to give us some rare time together, just her and me. But I wasn't the only crazy human she was forced to share her childhood with. Two other brothers complete our sibling circle. I just happen to be the oldest one.

Stacie enjoys meaningful kindships with all three of us, each one unique. What the three of them share between themselves is surely just as special as our relationship. All I know is that Stacie and I just naturally seemed to get along, as they say, like peas and carrots. She is the youngest of four children and five years my junior. Despite the age difference, we always got each other.

I attended the last two years of high school with my brother Mark and my senior year with both Mark and Shaun. But Stacie entered high school in September of 1993, three months after I graduated. This also happened to be the same month I entered Marine Corps Boot Camp.

While running around the Marine Corps Recruit Depot and Camp Pendleton for thirteen weeks, getting yelled at by USMC drill instructors learning how to be an American badass (at least that's what the USMC recruiter told me I'd be doing), Stacie entered high school without her biggest brother.

Our separation forced me to miss out on a lot of time hanging out with her during her high school tenure, time I was fortunate to have shared with Mark and Shaun. I thought doing something outrageous, like taking her on a trip to Disneyland in celebration of her fifteenth birthday, would make it a special moment to remember, a perfect opportunity to make up for lost time. I never imagined her decision would lead not only to a lifetime of memories, but the single most life-changing moment of my life.

*   *   *

"So, I'm guessing it's Disneyland then, huh?" I asked confirmingly, peering through her glasses, glasses that she would need to wear indefinitely now.

"Yes. Yes. Yes!" She screamed again. "When do we go?"

"How about next weekend?" I said.

She sank into my arms, her slender frame pulling me down a few inches toward the floor.

"Oh, come on. Why can't we go right now?"

"Ha ha! We can't do that. I need to make hotel reservations and everything. I didn't want to book all the reso's and then have you go with the contact lenses. Besides, it will give you some time to get everything ready to go. Maybe the anticipation will make it an even better experience. Some people say the anticipation of having a good time is half the fun."

"Ahhh. No way," she said, pouting in protest. "But alright. If we have to."

An exaggerated clown-frown draped down her face. And then, almost like it was taking too much effort to keep that frown in place, she turned it upside down, stood up, and jumped out of my arms.

"Oh my gosh," she said, jumping around, her bare feet slapping on the tile. "I can't believe this. I'm so excited." Ironically, all the jumping around caused her glasses to slip down her nose and almost fall off her face.

"Me too. I would have understood if you chose the contact lenses though. They would stop you from having to worry about those things falling off your face," I said, pointing at her glasses as she pushed them back up the ridge of her nose. "But I'm glad you decided on Disneyland. I'm excited for the trip."

"Gosh, I haven't been since I was like, five. I hardly remember it," she reminisced.

"Yeah, it's been a while for me too."

Tired of standing by as a spectator watching this all unfold, Mom chimed in after the excitement died down a bit.

"Wow, Matt, that's really nice. You two will have a great time."

"Thanks. I don't see how we couldn't. If we can't have a good time in Disneyland, it's our fault, right?" I replied.

Stacie turned to our parents. "Did either of you know about this?"

"No. Not at all." Dad said through a breathy giggle, pulling his hands out of his pockets and crossing his arms over his chest. He seemed pleasantly amused.

"This is the first we heard about it," Mom added.

"Yeah. They didn't know a thing, Stace," I said. "Everyone found out at the same time." I turned to Dad. "You mind if I borrow the Tempo for the trip?"

"Fine with me," Dad replied, shrugging. "Just make sure you get the oil changed and check all the fluids before you go," he added.

"No problem," I said.

CHAPTER TWO

The next week was a buzz of excitement. Stacie was beside herself and became increasingly giddier as the weekend drew near. As a result, the atmosphere around the house was more energetic than usual, and thick with anticipation.

I called 411 and wrote down the names and phone numbers for several affordable hotels surrounding Disneyland. After contacting several of them, I settled on a room at the Best Western, conveniently located right across the street from Disneyland's front entrance, and booked us for the nights of July 15, 16, and 17. This particular hotel stood out, mainly because of its location, and for the simple fact that it had a swimming pool. The convenience of simply walking across the street to enter the park instead of having to worry about driving and parking every morning was a huge bonus too. Parking at Disneyland was expensive, and I'd rather spend that money on something else.

Our Disneyland visits were booked for the July 16 and 17. I chose to add Disney's Magic Mornings pass to our tickets as well. This pass granted participants one hour early access to Disneyland where several main attractions would be open early and we'd have the opportunity to enjoy "breakfast with the characters" in Tomorrowland. It's a great way to give yourself a little extra time to enjoy all the wonderful things Mickey and friends have to offer. I mean, if you're going to Disneyland and don't visit very often, as was the case for us at this time in our lives, you might as well get the whole experience, right?

*   *   *

Reservations booked. Now to share the news with Stacie.

I was finishing up my telephone conversation with the hotel when Stacie walked into the kitchen. More like floated really, gliding effortlessly across the linoleum floor in socked feet with the refrigerator in her sights. As I returned the phone to its cradle on the wall, Stacie pulled a half-empty can of Pepsi out of the fridge, the first half consumed four hours ago with her breakfast. I leaned back against the counter and slid eight fingers into the front pockets of my jean shorts, resting both thumbs inside currently belt-less loops. She took a long draw from the can and I patiently waited for her to finish, entertaining myself watching the refrigerator door slowly close behind her. She turned to face me after the door thumped shut and pulled back from the can.

"Ahhhh!" she crooned.

"Dude, it's like, lunchtime," I informed her. "Didn't you open that can at breakfast?"

"Yeah. So?" she replied, shaking her head from side to side, enjoying the last few moments of pleasure only soda can provide.

"Isn't it flat?"

"A little bit, but not really. I like it like this though. I can drink it fast without hurting my throat," she said, taking another swig.

She drained the can dry, head cocked to the ceiling and shaking out every last drop into her wide-open mouth. Holding the empty can out in my direction she opened her eyes wide. Baring her teeth through a wicked smile, she slowly crushed the can between her fingers.

"Raaahhh!" she snarled.

I snickered.

"Is that supposed to intimidate me, you weirdo?" I asked, raising my eyebrows in animated surprise, genuinely amused by the theater.

"What, you're not scared? Grrrr!"

Stacie crushed the can with even more vigor now.

I humored her efforts with a laugh.

"Oh, sister. You funny! Don't hurt yourself, now."

Stacie couldn't hold the grimace on her face once I started laughing. Her toothy growl turned into a toothy grin, and her eyes shrunk into slits of happiness. She dropped her hands and walked over to the sink, opened the cabinet underneath, and threw the empty can in the trash. After closing the door, she turned back to me.

"Well, we're all set," I said.

"Yeah? With what?" she answered.

"What do you mean, with what? I just finished booking our hotel reservations. And I have our Disneyland reservations all worked out and paid for too."

"Oh! Awesome! I can't wait," she replied in a sing-song voice.

"Me too, Stace. You almost ready to go?"

"Um, yeah . . . weirdo!" she replied, waving her head around like one of those baseball bobbleheads, her voice thick with sarcasm. "Just say when, and we're outta here."

"That would be Friday. Three more days and off we go."

"Woo hoo!" Stacie screamed.

She was so excited her bags were packed two days before we left.

CHAPTER THREE

The day finally came. Road trip time! And we were ready, ready to "get outta Dodge" and have a good time. Attempting to avoid most of the Bay Area commuter traffic, we left an hour before daybreak on Friday, July 15.

The first hour of driving was pleasantly uneventful as we headed north on Highway 680 to 580E. We beat the early-morning traffic and made it to the infamous Highway 5 in record time, where we cruised several miles per hour over the speed limit for a majority of the next six hours, slowed only by intermittent "elephant races," where one big rig attempts to pass another but does so very slowly, if at all, frustratingly holding up traffic for a while.

Notoriously considered a long and boring drive, uninspiring to most travelers, Highway 5 proved to be just that, at least to a couple teenagers with Disneyland on their minds. It takes a little introspection and respect for the land traversed by this highway to have any real appreciation for it. Eighteen thousand square miles, seven million acres, of some of the most fertile land in the world reside in this valley. The remanence of an ancient sea, it's flat, arid and deceivingly unexciting to the passing tourist. But its value rests not in the views, but in productivity. Producing eight percent of the country's agriculture, the Central Valley is an integral part of the United States economy.

These facts are interesting and all, and makes Highway 5 a noteworthy thoroughfare, but its admirable vanity escaped us at the moment. We made the best of the drive regardless, stopping along the way only for lunch and to restock our snack stash at various "country stores" when pulling off the highway for fuel. We passed the hours singing along with some of our favorite grunge bands and swapping her high school stories for my Marine Corps boot camp adventures. We must have listened to both Pearl Jam albums at least twice.

After a long self-guided tour of the fruitful California Central Valley, a grueling climb up and over the Tejon Pass, more commonly known as "The Grapevine," and an epic stop-and-go struggle through the Los Angeles freeway traffic, the exhausting drive finally came to an end. We pulled into the Best Western Hotel around 6 p.m. and it felt exhilarating to shut off the engine for the final time. I wouldn't fire it up for another three days. We only needed our feet for transportation now.

Worn out and tight from being seatbelt-shackled in the car for most of the day, we felt a special kind of relief as we hopped out of the car's small bucket seats and stretched out our legs in the hotel parking lot under the hot Southern California sun. Afterward, we walked into the lobby to check in to our room. I walked up to the front desk to get all of the reservation details worked out while Stacie stared out the window and across the street. There was plenty to see, but the Matterhorn, sticking up like a dark thumb in the early evening sky over Disneyland's plant-covered fence, attracted most of her attention.

Check in didn't take long, and our room keys soon found a home in my pocket. We walked back to the car, removed our bags from the trunk, and carried them up to the second floor and into our room. We each had our own bed, and Stacie chose the one closest to the window, claiming it as her own by jumping up and down on it a few times. Who was I to argue?

"Well, we finally made it, Stacie. Man, that Highway 5 is a drag."

"Yep. But we're here!" she shouted.

"True enough," I said through a deep breath. "Sure glad we left early enough so we have time to chill out and get situated. I think we'll fly next time, what do you think?"

"Sure, whatever."

I dropped my bag and fell back onto the bed with a thud, bouncing once before settling into the mattress and rattling the headboard against the wall in the process. I stretched my arms out, kicked off my shoes, closed my eyes, and let out a sigh.

Stacie didn't seem too exhausted, however.

"I'm. So. Excited. We. Are. Finally. Here!" she said, uttering one word in between each jump on the bed, rattling her headboard too.

"They're going to call the cops if we keep banging on the walls," I said, playfully grimacing.

She stopped jumping and hopped off the bed, landing with a rumbling thud that would have woken up anyone sleeping in the room below, and skipped over to the window. With one fast swipe of her hands, she pushed the partially separated curtains all the way open, causing the loosely hanging tracks to slap together.

"I wish we could go tonight," she said, scanning the street below and peering over the fence into Disneyland as the curtain swayed to a stop. "Look, I can see the Matterhorn!"

Without looking, I continued my staring contest with the inside of my eyelids and said, "Well, we can't do that. But what we can do is take a dip in the swimming pool . . . or we could get some dinner if you're hungry."

There was a short pause before she replied, and I remember thinking, *She seems so happy about this trip. It sure is going to be a great weekend.* There wasn't any reason I would have thought differently. So far, everything was moving along swimmingly.

"I'm not hungry yet. But let's go to the pool!"

Sliding the back of my head across the smooth, white comforter linen, I opened my eyes and turned my head in her direction. She was still gazing out the window.

"All right. Get your swimsuit on. Let's go."

We slipped into our swimsuits and leisurely strolled on down to the pool. I unlocked the gate, and before I could even close it behind me, Stacie had tossed her towel to the side and jumped into the deep end. I picked it up and laid claim to a couple chairs next to an open table, tossing our towels, sunglasses, and my white Stetson cowboy hat on the cushions.

Late as it was, the slowly sinking sun still hung heavy in the evening sky, keeping the temperature far north of warm, something that took a little getting used to for us NorCal natives. Hard to believe it was 7 p.m. already as the day still felt so young.

We were far from alone on our pool adventure as the patio was spattered with several families and a few lone sunbathers. Gaggles of children splashed around in the blue water, screaming with delight and doing quite an adequate job of keeping the edge of the pool soaking wet. A few adults, presumably the children's parents, seemed content hanging out in the shaded Jacuzzi next to the pool. God knows why. It was too hot for that sort of thing. The thermometer, hanging in the shade next to the "No Lifeguard On

Duty, Swim At Your Own Risk" sign, was pinned just shy of 90 degrees.

From the muddled conversations bellowing out from the "Jacuzzi clan," it wasn't a stretch to assume many of them were taking a "pre-fireworks show" break from their Disneyland adventures. Young children can only take so much, you know. The day always starts out with plenty of excitement and all-encompassing bewilderment, but hours of overstimulation, too much sugar consumption, and heat will take its toll on the young ones, sometimes even the old ones. At some point in the day, the crash comes. Disneyland's a crazy place—a crazy, happy, and lovely place. A place that takes something from you, but gives you so much more in return. No worries though; after a rejuvenating dip in the pool, a cold drink, and possibly a nap, most are ready for another round of magic, fun, and fireworks. Disneyland at night is a whole different experience than what you get during the day. You don't want to miss out on that either.

After the amusing assessment of the "pool area humanoids," I accompanied Stacie into the pool and we enjoyed the refreshing coolness of chlorinated water against our sun-warmed skin. After goofing around for a while, I got out to dry off and enjoy the final moments of the day laying out under the cloudless blue sky. Stacie remained in the pool like the fish that she was.

Laying out on the sunbaked concrete made my back feel as warm as the sunray-hammered front part of my body. I lay there, unmoving, my ten-gallon Stetson shielding my face from the sun, allowing the SoCal desert air to dry my skin. It was the perfect way to wind down from a long day of driving.

Soon thereafter, Stacie finally had her fill of the pool and we retired to our room. We took showers and changed back into our clothes. Even though it was the end of the day and it would have been easy to just flip on the TV and chill out for a while, we couldn't bring ourselves to do it. It was too early for bed. Too restless to sit still in the hotel room, we decided to take an aimless walk down the street under the slowly developing twilight sky.

The heat of the day quickly waned with the approaching blanket of darkness and we enjoyed a lackadaisical walk up the street, people-watching as we went. Feeling like fish swimming upriver, we gracefully wove in and out of a seemingly never-ending deluge of strollers, each one cradling a child in one of two Disneyland-induced states of consciousness—either passed out cold or screaming at the top of their lungs because they wanted to be passed out, but couldn't because of the extreme amount of sugar running through their veins.

To be honest, most of the parents looked as tired as their children.

Disneyland—it can have that kind of effect on you. It's a fascinating place, a place offering such an elevated level of stimulation that it straight-up wears you out. Grown-ups aren't immune to its charm either; let's be real here. You're exhausted at the end of it all, having spent the day getting your money's worth of experiences only Disneyland can provide.

Pausing at an intersection just up the street from the hotel, we waited in the middle of the oversized sidewalk for the red crossing light to flip green. From here we witnessed the colorful array of lights dancing in the darkening sky above Disneyland and listened to the faint sounds of music and joyful screaming rising from inside the park. It was the last night of anticipation for us, and we tempted ourselves standing in its aura. The next day would be our day.

The crossing sign finally flashed green and we continued walking up and down Harbor Boulevard for the next thirty minutes or so, passing a litany of restaurants along the way: Denny's, IHOP, Mimi's Café, and McDonalds, just to name a few. We thought a little snack would settle us nicely for the night, so we stopped into McDonalds on our way back to the hotel for a quick bite.

There was no need for a big meal; we would be eating breakfast with the characters in less than twelve hours, after all. Picking at our late-evening snack, we talked about what might lay in store for us in the morning. We agreed to wake up before dawn and be one of the first people in line for the Magic Mornings breakfast.

Mindful that nighttime had settled in and the sun was currently making its way around the other side of the planet, we finished our sorry excuse for a dinner and headed back to the hotel to get some sleep and ready ourselves for its arrival tomorrow, when it would lead us in through the main gates of the "Happiest Place on Earth."

Back in our room, we laid out our clothes for a speedy change in the morning, called the front desk for a wake-up call, turned off the lights, and laid our heads down on our pillows.

"Night, sis," I said.

"Good night, Matt," she replied.

The mental fatigue from the hundreds of miles I'd driven helped me fall asleep immediately. I didn't stay awake long enough to see if Stacie slipped off to Neverland just as quickly, but she didn't wake me up after I drifted off, so I assumed she wandered off without much effort.

CHAPTER FOUR

I wouldn't put Stacie in the category of "early riser," unless you happen to be visiting Disneyland that day. Contrary to her usual wake-up regimen, she had no problem springing out of bed when the front desk called our room at 6 a.m. with our requested wake-up call, the ringing of the phone acting on Stacie like the spring release of a toaster. There was no "Just a few minutes longer" or "Can you have them call us back in thirty minutes?" No hitting the snooze button on the alarm clock either. No shaking her out of bed. No turning the lights on until she was blinded awake. No way, not today. She was up at the first ring. Before I even finished thanking the front-desk attendant for the wake-up call, Stacie was already on her way to the bathroom to get ready, rubbing her eyes as she stumbled around in the dim room. The park opened at 7 a.m. for the Magic Mornings participants, an hour earlier than the general admission, and we wanted to be standing at the gate no later than 6:45. Stacie wasn't going to be late for that.

I was just as excited, so we didn't waste time. Dressed and out the door by 6:30, we made a beeline across Harbor Boulevard to Disneyland's main entrance.

I opted to wear my cowboy hat for the day. Funny, I didn't see anyone else wearing one. An observant person might have seen this as a clue that wearing such a large wide-brimmed hat might be cumbersome in such a place as Disneyland, where elbowroom is a luxury. Plenty of people sported the traditional baseball cap, and even a few brave souls walked up to the line under the protection of full-brim sun hats, but I was the only one with a cowboy hat.

We waited outside the main gate for about fifteen minutes, watching the place fill up with other Magic Mornings participants. Like the previous night's walk down Harbor Boulevard, we were surrounded by a similar herd of toddler-cradling strollers. This time, however, the children were full of nervous energy and awe, wide awake with anticipation. The air was filled with their excited questions: "Look, Mom!" "When are we going to see Mickey?" "Will Ariel talk to us at breakfast?" "Can I have some cotton candy?" "Will we see Snow White today?" "Why are we not moving?" Yes, quite a contrast from ten hours earlier.

Stacie brought me out of my bubble of thoughts and observations with an elbow to my upper arm.

"I can't wait to get inside! This is so exciting."

"Me too," I replied.

"I'm starving. You?" she asked.

"Of course. Pfft. Am I ever not hungry?" I replied. Just the thought of breakfast made my stomach growl. Definitely the best way to kick this whole shindig off, and it couldn't come soon enough. No sooner was I thinking about breakfast, when another thought came to mind. "Hey, did you grab any sunscreen on your way out of the hotel room?"

"No. I think it's still in the car, actually. Do you really think we're going to need some?" Stacie asked.

"Who knows?" I replied. "Probably not, but maybe. Well, if we need it, we'll get some. No worries."

I shrugged off the sunscreen issue and turned my attention towards the front gate. Stacie's gaze followed. The anticipation was weighing on her. I could sense it as she kept rising onto her tippy-toes to look over all the bobbing heads for any signs of life beyond the "gates to the Magic Kingdom."

"Man, when are they going to let us in?" Stacie said with excited impatience.

"I think it's almost time . . . OH! Hey, here they come!" I said. Standing on my toes now with my chin in the air, I peered through the bars of the main entry gate from under the molded brim of my white Stetson hat and over the heads of about fifty Disneyland die-hards.

From around the corner, on the right side of the train station inside the main gate, about a dozen Disney cast members appeared, escorted by a small clan of Disney characters. They casually made their way to the entrance turnstiles, all of them strutting their character's appropriate gait, waving wildly as they approached the turnstiles. Tiny cheers erupted from the children around us. Some of the parents, while pushing their "children transportation units," bent over and pointed with one of their hands, directing their stroller-trapped kids' gazes toward some of the Disney characters they would soon be sharing breakfast with.

As the crowd grew larger, so did the number of Disney cast members. They formed a semi-permeable boundary around everyone outside of the main gates, directing traffic into long uniform lines, preventing the formation of a large mob rushing the turnstiles.

Shortly thereafter, the gates opened with a bang of metal on metal, and the patiently waiting guests started shuffling through. Smiling ticket-takers stamped tickets with the day's date and the turnstiles clicked over with each passing guest. A minute later we arrived at the front of the line, the first of many lines we would wait in throughout the weekend, and I handed over our tickets. The friendly cast member stamped them July 16, 1994, handed them back to me, smiled, and gestured us into the park, reminding us to have a wonderful day.

Once inside the park, several Disney cast members, along with a few random Disney characters, directed us down the right-side entrance on to Main Street USA, around the main train station and under the train track overpass. The currently parked train engine above seemed to be huffing steam in unison with the welcoming Disney music playing from hidden speakers among the flowers. As the music played on, our Disneyland escorts carefully guided the growing crowd down Main Street USA. If so inclined, one could enter a variety of stores to take care of some early-morning shopping, or, as with us, continue into Tomorrowland where breakfast was being served.

Stacie and I didn't even need to entertain a conversation about where we wanted to start our morning. We were starving and walked right by all of the open shops. Meandering our way into the heart of the park toward Sleeping Beauty's Castle, we tried to take it all in. As we walked past the sweet shop and bakery, our noses, almost involuntarily, lifted into the air as we filled our lungs with scent of sugary pleasantries, catching the faint smells of chocolate and caramel, followed by the almost irresistible aroma of freshly baked cinnamon rolls and ice cream.

"Oh my gosh! This has to be the best-smelling street in the world!" Stacie said between deep breaths, still sniffing at the air as we ambled down the middle of the street between the cable car tracks. "Ahh! I can't believe we're finally here! So exciting."

"Yeah, tell me about it." I took in another lungful. "If we weren't on our way to breakfast, we would definitely be stopping for some of that goodness."

Although tempted to change course, we continued down Main Street into Tomorrowland. The scents faded away just as quickly as they'd emerged the further we walked into the park.

A short time later we arrived at the Terrace Restaurant and stood in line for our breakfast. After receiving our trays, piled high with pancakes, eggs, bacon, and potatoes, we found a table and began shoveling food into our faces. Not five minutes after sitting down, halfway finished with our meal already, did all the characters show up. They spread themselves out among the tables so quickly it seemed like they instantly appeared from nowhere and everywhere at the same time.

Children erupted into cheers and laughter, and the parents echoed their enthusiasm. Toddlers not strapped into strollers or high-chairs dropped their eating utensils, and with mouths full of pancakes and milk, ran around hugging their favorite Disney friends, like they'd personally known them for years. Parents followed suit, cameras in hand, snapping photos of their children rubbing their syrupy hands all over Goofy, Chip, Dale, Donald Duck, Minnie Mouse, and Mickey, smiling like it was the best day of their lives. The accompanying cast members did their best to control the mayhem. We didn't immediately stand up, perfectly content observing the craziness from the comfort of our chairs. We weren't as invisible as we may have thought, though. A few of the characters came by to say hi, greeting us with silent waves of their oversized hands. We were even treated to a couple of high-fives by Donald Duck as he swiftly made his way between the tables, attempting to avoid the sticky fingers attached to the entourage of laughing children chasing him around the dining area. Minnie Mouse even came by our table and admired my cowboy hat! She pointed at it and then put her large four-finger hands over her head, laughing quietly behind a permanent smile. Like a proper cowboy, I tipped my hat in acknowledgement and she moved on to the next table.

"See, Stacie, cowboy hats get all the girls' attention," I said.

Stacie rolled her eyes and smiled.

"Well, maybe it works on human-size mice that have issues with their vocal cords," replying snidely through a mouthful of food.

*   *   *

Stacie and I hadn't been in the park for thirty minutes, and we were already having a wonderful time. Stacie was all smiles while we ate. Was it an omen that we were starting off our Disneyland trip in Tomorrowland? Maybe. If I only knew the drastic turn my life would take just thirty-six hours later. My "tomorrow," as it were, was going to be one to remember. I just didn't know it yet. Neither one of us knew how life-changing Stacie's birthday decision would be.

We finished with breakfast and decided to leave the Magic Mornings craziness behind. Already in Tomorrowland, we had access to some of the coolest rides in the park right away. So, we made our way across the quad to Space Mountain and experienced an incredibly rare event. We wove our way to the front of the line without stopping. We ended up waiting a total of about five minutes to hop on our first roller coaster of the day, and most of that time was spent getting strapped into our "spaceship."

Our stomachs still full of breakfast, we nevertheless managed to find room in our "dessert leg" for an early morning serving of moon cheese, a unique variety only Space Mountain could serve up. (If you rode Space Mountain before they modified it, you know what I'm talking about). After a turbulent tour through outer space at light speed, we exited Space Mountain and came face to face with a fast-moving crowd of excited people making a beeline for the ride's entrance.

"Well, I guess the park's open," I said.

"Yep. Sure looks like it," Stacie replied.

"Where do you want to go now?" I asked her.

"Pirates of the Caribbean!" Stacie responded without hesitation.

"Sounds great, let's go. We should be able to get right on at this time of day."

We moved quickly to the other side of the park, weaving in and out of the river of people walking in the opposite direction, pausing at the Walt Disney and Mickey Mouse statue in front of Sleeping Beauty Castle for a photo. We passed the Tiki Room, Jungle Cruise, and the Swiss Family Robinson Treehouse, and walked right by the currently under construction Indiana Jones Ride.

"Hey, Stacie," I said inquisitively as we walked past. "Do you remember how angry Mom was at Grandpa and Grandma K for letting me watch *The Raiders of the Lost Ark?* I had nightmares for a week because of the spider scene and when that guy's face melted off after they watched the angels fly out of the ark."

"No way. Really?"

I laughed. "Yeah, I got so scared. I thought for sure that If I ever saw an angel my face would melt off too. Funny, huh? I wonder what parts of the movie they're going to include on this ride when it's done?'

"I don't know. It will probably have some other storyline, something just for the ride. I guess we'll just have to come back and find out after they finish building it," Stacie said, with a not-so-subtle hint of hopefulness in her voice. "How's that sound?"

I said nothing and just stared ahead. That was, until I felt an elbow jab into my upper left arm a few seconds later.

"Hey!" Stacie said.

"Okay, okay. Deal." I said, smirking. "If I must. Hey, did you see that Dole Whip stand back there?" I asked, continuing our walk toward Pirates and hammering my left thumb over my shoulder.

"Yeah."

"Have you ever had one?" I asked.

"Don't think so. I haven't been here in, like, forever! Why, they pretty good?"

"As long as you like pineapple. You'll love them if you do."

"I love pineapple," she said.

"Then we need to get one of those before we leave. Deal?"

"Deal," Stacie agreed. We sealed the agreement with a high-five.

"Just don't tell me you want to watch the Tiki Room show," I added.

"Why not?"

"I can't stand it. Too much clicking and clacking going on with the animatronics. Drives me crazy," I said, crinkling my nose.

"Really? Why?"

"I don't know. It's just weird. I know it's a throwback to Disneyland's early days, and people find it endearing and entertaining, but I can't stand it. Tough for me to explain. I think it's the only thing in Disneyland I'm not a fan of, even though I'm pretty sure I'm in the minority on that one. A lot of people seem to like it. Go figure."

"Hey, As long as we get some of that Dole Whip, I'm cool."

"Sweet. I can handle that. And if you REALLY want to watch it, I think I can make it through. It is your birthday present, after all. Just let me know."

"Okay. But I think there are a ton of things we can do instead of that."

"Awesome . . . Hey, hold on a sec." I stopped after passing the Swiss Family Robinson Treehouse and turned back toward the Jungle Cruise. The path through Adventureland wasn't that crowded yet, and we could still see all the way to the other end. I pointed down the path and, still holding my finger extended, looked at Stacie. "Instead of the Tiki Room, you want to go have dinner tonight over there and watch that Aladdin show? It's a dinner show called *Aladdin's Oasis*."

"Yeah!" She replied excitedly. "That should be fun."

"Sweet. When we head back this direction I'll go see if we need reservations."

We continued our trek around the corner and descended a small ramp into a new land. At the end of the sloping path, New Orleans Square came to life with southern charm and French-inspired Louisiana mystique. Centering the entire area was the Rivers of America, where you could enjoy a short, leisurely trip down the great Mississippi aboard the Mark Twain steamboat, or paddle around Tom Sawyer's island inside canoes. There was even a pirate ship stashed away around one of the bends in the river.

After pausing for a short while at the bottom of the ramp to enjoy the soulful serenade of a barbershop quartet, all four dressed to the nines in matching pinstripe outfits of different colors, we continued our travels through the Bourbon Street–themed area. We absorbed the ambiance of the square for a bit, then walked right up to the front of the line at the Pirates of the Caribbean, just like we had done at Space Mountain a short time ago.

"Man, I wish we could walk to the front of the line like this on all the rides today," I said as we waited for the next boat to pull up.

"That would be nice, huh? Don't think that's going to happen, though," Stacie said, raining on my parade.

"Yeah, the park's going to fill up pretty fast," I said. "It is Saturday, after all, in the middle of July. You know, we have the Magic Morning booked for tomorrow, too. What do you want to do first thing tomorrow?"

"I don't know. Let's worry about that tomorrow. Probably Space Mountain again," Stacie replied. "I love the roller coasters."

"Me too. The faster the better. Best thing about Space Mountain is that you can't see where you're going. Adds to the excitement."

The short line moved forward, then paused again.

"But I'm always nervous sticking my hands up in the air on that ride," I continued. "Afraid I'm going to hit something, ya know? You?"

"I'm pretty sure they got that all figured out, don't ya think?" Stacie replied reassuringly. "It wouldn't do them any good to have people getting their hands broken."

"I suppose. That might cause a bit of a public relations problem, huh?" I agreed.

"Maybe just a little bit."

Our boat pulled up shortly thereafter. After the passengers exited out of the boat, the gate attendant guided us on with the sweep of his hand. Stacie and I took up the entire first row. After the rest of the guests clambered onto our hidden-track-guided dinghy, the ride operator reminded us to "stay seated and keep our hands and arms inside the boat at all times." The brakes released with a quick gust of air, and we were set free to slowly float through the swamp.

Serenaded by a porch-propped, banjo-plucking bayou dweller, fireflies dancing and flickering in the air around him, we slowly creeped passed the currently empty Blue Bayou restaurant and toward an unseen waterfall that would lead us into the depths of a pirate adventure.

The trip down the short waterfall propelled our boat into the pirate lair below, and we continued our slow float along the underground river, weaving past the remains of long-dead pirates sprawled out on beaches, riverside markets where brides were sold to the highest bidder and watched towns set ablaze after a pirate raiding party. We sailed through the middle of a sea battle, and glided past collapsing dungeons where trapped prisoners tried to convince a dog with keys dangling from its mouth to come help them escape. Picked-over bones and hopeful whistling failed to entice the K9 however, and our boat left them all behind.

All this filled me with a sense of amazement, yet again, at how masterful Disney is at pulling you out of whatever world you are living in and subtly escorting you into a make-believe world of their own design, just for your temporary entertainment. They do it better than anyone else. Brilliant.

*   *   *

The day was young, but time went by quickly and before we knew it, half the day had disappeared. We spent the remains of the day riding our favorite attractions, watching our favorite shows, and eating more food than we probably should have. We made sure to enjoy every minute of the seventeen hours Disneyland was open to us, including a trip to the Dole Whip counter and visits with some wacky Disney characters in Toon Town.

We imitated the Small World animatronic characters while waiting in the long line for Splash Mountain and screamed our lungs out in exaggerated fear when the hanging corpse appeared above us in the Haunted Mansion. All part of a fulfilling day in the Magic Kingdom.

The dinner show at Aladdin's Oasis was a crowded affair, complete with the mind-opening experiencing of trying out a new cuisine neither one of us were familiar with, all while enjoying an interactive dinner show with many of the characters from the movie. It was Stacie's first time eating hummus, too. Aladdin even came by our table for a short visit, and, if my intuitions were correct, may have flirted with Stacie a little bit. But at least he left our breadbasket alone.

*   *   *

The day was grand, lovely and memorable. At the end of it all, after the sun had long set and the smell of spent gunpowder from the fireworks show over Sleeping Beauty's Castle had faded, we slowly made our way back to the hotel. Thank goodness we got a room across the street and close to the entrance. The short walk was a welcome end to a day spent mostly on our feet.

Having opted not to indulge in a "pre-fireworks-show break" many families take during the long summer days, our feet paid a price; a price paid in soreness and swelling. But our cups were full and our hearts happy. I do have to admit, though, I was way beyond done with wearing that damn cowboy hat. Having to take it off at every ride and find a place to stash it, or leave it at the exit with the hope that no one would take it before I got back to retrieve it, was annoying. It would be staying in the hotel room tomorrow; I was sure of that. We felt like zombies, content but exhausted . . . and we didn't even have kids to worry about. This gave us a higher level of appreciation for the parents we'd made fun of the day before while walking the streets after our relaxing dip in the pool.

After climbing the stairs to the second floor, we shuffled into our room. I threw my Stetson on the desk, and we both kicked off our shoes and collapsed on our beds.

"Thanks, Matt. That was a fun day," Stacie said, leaning her head to the side and looking over at me from her bed.

"Sure thing sis. It was a fun day, wasn't it?" I cocked my head in her direction and smiled. "You going to be ready to do it all again tomorrow?"

"You bet."

"Well, Disneyland opens back up, for us anyway, in seven hours. We should probably get some sleep and a shower, yeah?"

"Definitely," she said.

"Why don't you go first. I want to get my clothes laid out and everything good to go, and stash that cowboy hat in the closet. It will not be joining us tomorrow."

"Okay. And good call on the hat."

We prepped for "Disneyland, Day Two" and were in bed before 1 a.m., asleep before our heads hit the pillow.

CHAPTER FIVE

D ay Two began the same as Day One, with the phone on the nightstand between our beds ringing loudly at 6 a.m. with our friendly wake-up call. I rolled over to answer it. As I did, Stacie propped herself up on her elbows, but remained under the covers. We were excited about the day ahead, but our exuberance for getting up so early was subdued, compared to the vibrancy of yesterday. Neither of us would admit it, but I think both of us were secretly coveting a few extra hours of sleep. Not at the expense of time in Disneyland, though. *You can sleep when you're dead!* Right?

If we put ourselves at a ten on the energy meter for Day One, we were now running at a nine. It's reasonable to say that every consecutive day in Disneyland will consume one bar of energy on that scale. The place is that all-consuming, and stimulating. Applying that rationale to an epic Disneyland escapade, Day Eleven would either turn you into a Disney zombie, or you would need to sleep the day away. Hanging out by the pool for a couple of hours during the heat of the day may move the meter back toward the ten mark a little bit, however. So, that was always an option . . . for the weak.

After hanging up the phone, I slid out of my covers and sat on the edge of my bed facing Stacie, who was now sitting up in hers, evident by the faint silhouette she cast against the curtains behind her. I reached over to the lamp on the nightstand behind the phone and flicked the switch. It shined like a miniature sun in the dark room, and I watched through squinted eyes as Stacie fell back into her pillow and buried her head in her hands with the sudden luminescence.

"Hey," I said softly, rubbing the corners of my eyes clear of the crusty gunk that had accumulated there overnight.

"Hey," she replied softly, speaking into her hands, her muffled voice restrained, as if originating from the depths of a deep cave.

"Wazzup!?" I said loudly, my attempt at startling her into wakefulness.

"Hmmm," she grumbled quietly.

"Hungry?" I asked.

She lifted her hands from her face and slowly brought herself up to a seated position. Her bedhead-induced frizzy blond hair fell across her face as she scooted to the edge of her bed, supporting her slouching frame with her hands while squinting through tiny slits in her eyes.

"Yep," she whispered, then cleared her throat.

"Tired?"

"Nope." She answered affirmatively, bringing her voice to a normal range to accentuate the point.

"Liar," I replied. I smiled, my eyes also burning from the bright light.

"No, really." Stacie took a deep breath. "I'm good."

"You sure? We could just sit by the pool all day today, if you want. Ya know, if you're too tired and all . . ." I joked.

She leaned her head back, flicking her hair out of her face.

"Are you kidding?" she asked softly but without reservation. "No way. I just need a few minutes, that's all."

"And a Pepsi," I snickered.

"That would help."

"Your hair is crazy," I informed her, glancing at the rat's nest of tangles on her head.

Stacie ran her hands through her frizzled hair. Well, she tried to anyway. She just ended up pulling at knots.

"I know. It's always like this in the morning if I don't let it dry before going to bed."

"You should walk around Disneyland with your hair like that all day today," I said. "I double-dare you."

"No way! Just because you have a Marine Corps haircut and it looks the same in the morning as it did when you went to bed doesn't mean you can make fun of my hair."

"I double-dog-dare you."

"Ehhhh. Stop," she whimpered.

I laughed.

"Well, you can make your life a little easier and get the same haircut as me, ya know. Just think of all the time you would save getting ready in the morning, and all those extra minutes of sleep," I said with a grin.

Stacie dropped her hands back onto her lap.

"Right. I don't think so. Come on," she said eagerly. "Let's get ready."

We slid out of our beds and took turns getting ready in the bathroom. As with the day before, we were out the door by 6:30 a.m. and waiting in front of the gate at 6:45, minus one cowboy hat. Today I only had my Oakley Razor Blade sunglasses to protect me from the bright sun. Those would be much easier to manage.

For the most part, the day started off in true *Groundhog Day* fashion. Cast members and characters came out to meet us at 7 a.m. as a new, just-as-excited, gaggle of children and parents waited alongside us, behaving as the day before. After getting our tickets stamped we were led through the gates, saying hi to the same few Disney characters that greeted us the day prior. Shortly thereafter, we were escorted back to Tomorrowland for breakfast. Again, the characters appeared out of nowhere, and the children soon forgot about their breakfast and ran around all over the place, chasing their new friends with their sticky fingers in the air.

We even got a few high-fives from some of the characters again. I think Dale gave me the first one of the morning, or maybe it was Chip. I don't know. One of those two anyway, I can never keep them straight. Donald Duck even hit me up with an elbow-to-elbow greeting, "Bash-Brothering" me as if he was Mark McGuire and I was Jose Canseco. Who knew Donald Duck was into baseball, and an Oakland Athletics' fan to boot?

After eating, we indulged in another early-morning trip through outer space, via Space Mountain of course, then took a meandering stroll around the park, taking a little time to "smell the roses," so to speak. We were in the mood to not only ride the main attractions, but take in some of the lesser-known attractions as well; especially since the park was decorated so festively.

It was July 17, Disneyland's thirty-ninth birthday. In celebration of the special day, the park was splashed with happy birthday decorations, and cast members sported special pins and badges commemorating the event. They advertised birthday cupcakes would be provided to all guests after a celebration took place on Main Street later in the day, complete with a ceremony in front of Sleeping Beauty Castle led by then Disney CEO Michael Eisner. I always thought he was a good pick, if only because I thought he looked a little bit like Mickey Mouse.

This probably meant that the park would be crazy crowded, but that shouldn't be a surprise to anyone. Not to me, anyway. It was July, after all, peak season for Disneyland. I did not know about the whole birthday thing when booking our trip reservations, however. That was a surprise. It turned out to be a fortunate coincidence, a coincidence that will always be a special one for me, Stacie, and Mo, and maybe even Disneyland.

*   *   *

As anticipated, come midday Disneyland was swarming with so many humans it was impossible to maneuver without rubbing shoulders or zig-zagging to avoid a collision; and it was hot. Consequently, Frontierland and Critter Country, where all the water-related rides were located, were the most populated lands that day. Stacie and I spent most of the afternoon there, paddling around Tom Sawyer's Island in the canoes, descending into the air-conditioned depths of the Pirates of the Caribbean again, and hoping to get wet after splashing down from the final descent of Splash Mountain. We were not disappointed and walked around with damp shorts most of the afternoon.

We enjoyed a leisurely lunch under the canvas-covered patio next to Café Orleans, drinking virgin Mint Julips between spoonfuls of Jambalaya. After eating we gave some thought to watching the Lion King parade along Main Street, so we walked over to the parade route and scanned the area for a good place to sit. Finding curbside seats available only on the sunny side of the street, where we would spend the next hour baking under the relentless heat of the afternoon sun, we decided against it, opting instead to take in a few of the other shows around the park. Speaking of shows, it was important that we closely kept track of the time. We didn't want to miss our opportunity to claim the best seats in the house for the most spectacular nighttime show Disneyland had to offer.

CHAPTER SIX

F antasmic!, an awe-inspiring nighttime performance showcasing giant fans of water as movie screens, live actors, lights, pyrotechnics, and plenty of imagination, was the one show we couldn't miss. The trip wouldn't have been the same if we skipped it. It's performed over, and in, the Rivers of America, using part of Tom Sawyer's Island as a stage. This grand show debuted two years earlier and was an instant success, with per-show attendance averaging about 11,000 people, completely smashing Disneyland's estimation that 6,500 guests would show up for each performance. Its popularity was such a surprise that part of New Orleans Square needed to be redesigned to accommodate the extraordinary number of guests that wanted to see the two nightly performances.

Stacie and I wanted to make sure we landed great seats for the 9 p.m. show, the first one of the evening. About an hour and a half before the show's scheduled start, we made our way back to New Orleans Square and found what we thought would be one of the best spots to watch the show. It was around 7:30 p.m. but still surprisingly bright outside.

We sat down on the cobblestone riverbank just right of center stage and directly in front of the entrance to the Pirates of the Caribbean, about 10 feet back from the fence that kept people from falling into the Rivers of America. We took a seat on the pavement, spreading our legs wide to solidify our temporary claim to this tiny bit of riverfront territory. The sun's heat had been beating against the shade-deprived stones all day, and the backs of our bare legs burned as we slowly, gingerly, settled into position on the hard ground, silently grimacing.

We sat for a while, slathering on sunscreen, arguably our most important purchase of the day, under the relentless early-evening sun, keeping guard over our spots as other people gradually filled in the surrounding prime-real-estate plots with blankets and strollers. *Blankets. In Disneyland? Baw!* Any other time I would have laughed at such a ridiculous notion. But the burning sensation on the back of my legs made me reconsider. No matter, though; the burning slowly subsided, and we both settled in for the wait. As long as we didn't move, all was good. *Yeah, try sitting on concrete for hours without having to move. It's only a matter of time until you need to shift around.* Stacie and I relaxed and talked about the day, finishing up the soda we were sharing. And, with all that liquid consumption, the inevitable was sure to follow. It didn't take long before some of that soda needed to come out the other end.

"I need to go to the bathroom," Stacie said, pulling her glasses off her face and wiping away a few beads of sweat from her brow. "And I should probably go now before too many people get here and sit down."

"Really?" I said, tilting my head down and looking at her over the top of my sunglasses. "Now?"

Stacie fired back with her own sarcasm.

"I wouldn't talk, Mr. Tiny-Tanks."

"Ouch! Okay, okay." There's some truth to that. I'll admit it. "Alright. I'll stay here and reserve our spots. You should use the one by the Dole Whip cart. I think it's the nearest one."

"Okay. I'll be right back," she said.

Stacie slipped her glasses back on, stood up, and took off in a fast walk toward the Tiki Room.

I leaned back, resting my hands on the pavement in an effort to prevent people from creeping into our area while Stacie was away, spreading my short legs out as wide as I could without ripping the crotch of my snug-fitting jean shorts. *Now would be the perfect time to have a blanket,* I thought, comically.

Thousands of people meandered around me, some rustling about, impatiently waiting for the show to begin. Others walked up and down the riverfront, apparently more interested in a different attraction or form of entertainment. An invisible fog of conversation hovered in the air, and everyone standing looked like giants from my seated position. Well, not the children; we saw each other eye-to-eye, so they didn't look like giants at all. For the sake of my hands, I kept a constant watch over both shoulders to avoid the unintentional stomp or "stroller roll-over."

While staring off into the distance over my right shoulder, the familiar sound of slapping shoes rose up from behind me, cutting sharply through the subtle conversational hum I was quickly adjusting to. It sounded like someone was attempting a full stop after running full speed right at me. It was loud enough to attract my attention and, without thinking too much about it, I whipped my head around to see what was going on. Just as my head made it all the way around to my shoulder, I watched as a woman went from a running gait to frozen still in an instant, just a couple feet behind me. I flinched and instinctually lifted my left hand from the pavement as all the muscles in my upper body tightened. After she came to a stop, the threat of being trampled quickly waned and the tension in my body relaxed. I was safe, for now at least. I watched from my vulnerable position as she staked her claim by taking a wide stance, squatting halfway down to the ground and spreading her arms out wide into the open air at her sides. It became obvious she wasn't going anywhere, so I laid my hand back down on the same spot as before. *What the hell, man?* I thought. *Geez. She almost ran right into me.*

We caught a quick glance of each other, making brief eye contact before she whipped her head around with dizzying speed, gazing over her shoulder like she was being followed, her pulled-back hair following in a blur. I shouldn't have stared, but I couldn't bring myself to look away as quickly as she did. Not that I was really paying attention or anything, but I took note of her bright and colorful outfit: white sneakers; red, white, and blue striped jean shorts; and a tight red tank top. Her wavey brown hair, partially pulled back into a messy ponytail, settled softly against her shoulders. Another chance to look away before things got awkward presented itself while she was still peering over her shoulder, but I still couldn't bring myself to unlatch my gaze. I didn't want to turn back and stare at Tom Sawyer's Island again. Nothing over there was half as interesting as this girl. For the moment she had my full, undivided attention, and so far, we hadn't even spoken a word to each other. A blush of sunburn blanketed the surface of her exposed arms and legs, evidence that she had been hanging out under the sun all day, just like us. In the bright evening sun and radiant heat, her cheeks appeared flushed, too, like she'd been moving quickly from one attraction to another.

"Over here!" she shouted, still glaring off into the mob of people over her left shoulder. "I found a good spot!"

Her voice boomed over the growing volume of a ballooning crowd, and I pulled my eyes away from her, following her gaze through the tinted lenses of my Oakley Razor Blade sunglasses. I watched two other girls and one guy quickly weave through the crowd to join her. Soon afterward, I didn't need to worry about passersby stepping on my hands anymore. With all her friends huddled around, shuffling about for real estate among the masses, this girl, who'd just entered my life like thunder, dropped her arms and finally began to relax. The group of four quickly claimed their own piece of land and situated themselves right behind where Stacie and I were sitting.

They talked among themselves as they got as comfortable as the situation would allow. When a break in their conversation presented itself, I took the opportunity to strike up our own conversation, or attempt to anyway. I shifted my body around to the right, into a position that allowed me to converse without having to strain my neck, keeping my legs straight as I maneuvered to retain my claimed territory. Stacie should be back soon and she will need her space back.

Should I? I pondered. *Do I dare?* A short pause festered an internal battle of conscience and soon something, or someone, answered the question for me. An angel on my shoulder? Maybe. The devil in my pocket? Not likely. More like a drill instructor, really. *Yes, yes, you do dare. Talk to her, you chicken-shit!* Yes, yes. That's more like it . . . that's more my style . . . or at least the style I was used to at this point in my life having just graduated from Marine Corps boot camp.

"Hi," I said. "That was quite an entrance."

I smiled, then waited. Had I interrupted something important? Was talking to some strange guy sitting all by himself in Disneyland the last thing she wanted to do today? I guess I'd find out soon enough wouldn't I?

She turned away from her friends and faced me, flicking her chin in such a way that tossed her hair over her left shoulder. Her breathing was still elevated, presumably from all the running, and little beads of perspiration dotted her forehead.

"Hi," she said, wiping away a glistening sheen of sweat from beneath her bangs with one quick flick of her hand. "Yeah, that's the kinda girl I am. I don't do quiet very well," she said, then snickered.

"This seems to be the spot to watch the show, huh?" I teased, adding emphasis to "the," indicating that all of us happened upon, either accidentally or purposefully, the perfect location to watch the performance. "Everyone seems to want to sit here. Look at all these people trying to cram into this place."

"Oh, yeah. This is one of the best spots," she responded, still settling herself into a reasonably comfortable position, getting as comfortable as she could on the hot ground. All three of her friends were still fidgeting about as well, spreading out a bit to claim some "move-around" space.

"Awesome. Well, that's good to hear. This is my first time seeing this show. You?"

"Na. I've seen it a few times. It's good." she replied.

I nodded to show my interest.

"Sweet. I'm looking forward to it. I've heard good things."

I smiled again, and she smiled back. At this point one of her friends called out to her and she became immersed in conversation with them for a while.

My inner voice came alive.

Woah, woah, woah, Matt. This girl's hot! But I had to watch it. I promised Stacie this was going to be a trip for us only. "Picking up on girls" was out of the question. It was her birthday present, after all.

Speaking of Stacie, I turned around and scanned the area for her whereabouts, as she should have been coming back soon. I was getting a little nervous about the encroaching crowd and my ability to fight for our spots. My legs had already been kicked and stepped on a few times by people trying to fit into some of the tight spaces next to the fence along the riverbank. Hordes of people were staking claim to the prime areas around me as well, and I wanted Stacie to be sitting down where my legs were currently splayed out. I really didn't want to dampen the mood having to deal with anyone trying to slip in and lay claim to her spot. That would just lead to confrontation, and I hate that. A few seconds later she appeared from behind a couple of people near the River Belle Terrace and came jogging over. *Awesome. Just in time.*

"All better?" I asked as she walked up and reclaimed her spot.

"Yep. All good. Geesh, it's crowded here today. I had to wait in line for like five minutes just to use the bathroom," Stacie said.

"Yeah, I bet. I'd be surprised if it wasn't at capacity. I mean, look at all these people. Happy birthday, Disneyland, huh? Good thing we got our spots when we did," I replied.

I moved my legs out of the way and Stacie got comfortable next to me.

"Yeah, no kidding," she said as she lowered herself down to the pavement.

Stacie and I sat for a short while, both of us wishing we could jump over the fence and go for a swim in the river. The water looked refreshing and cool. But we would just need to settle for the slowly dropping temperature to cool us down. Small groups of people sitting around us were immersed in their own not-so-private conversations, including the group that sat down behind me. And that brought her back to the front of my mind.

This girl, the pretty one that stomped up behind me, was laughing and talking to one of the girls sitting next to her. The other two, a girl with blond hair and a guy, were engaged in their own conversation. I couldn't help but eavesdrop. The boy and girl were speaking loudly for all to hear anyway, deep in conversation about politics, so I didn't feel awkward about listening in. I overheard the girl talking about her work as a volunteer, or something like that, for Bill Clinton's 1996 presidential re-election campaign. I found that interesting, so at the risk of exposing my eavesdropping shenanigans, I asked her what it was like working on one of those campaigns. She turned and happily included me in their discussion, admitting most of the work was pretty boring. Lots of research and meetings, cold-calling and flyer mailings.

The conversation soon evolved into a much more interesting discussion, at least for me, and we all quickly became absorbed in exuberant conversation about Disneyland and Disney movies. Well, at least five of us did. The guy in the group really didn't say much.

After several minutes, Maureen, Michelle, Tristan, and Brian finally introduced themselves. I was relieved at the natural evolution of this, as I was thinking of a non-intrusive way to introduce myself without seeming creepy, weird, or obvious.

"I'm Maureen," the stomping girl said with a smile, "but you can call me Mo, everyone does."

"Alright, sounds good. I'm Matt. And this is my sister, Stacie," I replied. "It's nice to meet all of you. Where you from?"

This was a friendly enough question, asked within earshot of the entire group, one that could be answered by any one of them, but it was obvious by the locked gaze I had on Mo that her response was the only one I cared about at the moment. She obliged, and we set off on our own conversation.

"Northern California, but I'm getting ready to start my senior year at UC Irvine," she said.

Mo brought her knees up to her chest and wrapped them up with her arms. She clasped her right hand over her left and I was able to make out a gold Claddagh ring glimmering brightly in the sun.

Of course she's Irish, I said to myself. *Ah, man, you in trouble, dude. Irish girls. Tough to resist. Tread lightly, Matt.*

"UC Irvine? That's cool," I said. "What are you studying?"

"Musical theater and dance."

"I can see that," I said. "You seem like the dancing type. I mean, the way you ran over here and claimed your territory was quite dramatic." I smiled.

"That's me, Ms. Dramatic." She returned the smile. "What about you?"

"Me? Well, I just finished up Marine Corps basic training and I'm trying to figure out where I want to go to college. There are a couple universities down here in Orange County that I'm looking in to."

"You're a Marine?" she asked.

The expression on her face didn't change, and the tone in her voice didn't come across as judgmental. But I wasn't quite sure either.

"Yep. I'm in the reserve program at the moment. Stationed in Hayward."

"That's great. I have a few family members that served in the military too," she added. "My grandpa is an actual Pearl Harbor survivor."

"As in, he was there when the attack happened?"

"Yeah. He was on the USS Tennessee. A battleship."

"Woah. Glad he made it out okay," I said, feeling weird about my response. If he didn't make it out okay, I wouldn't be talking to her. But whatever, I was just filling space with words.

"Me too," she said.

"Both my grandpas served in World War II as well. My dad was in Vietnam. I'm the first Marine in the family, though. Part of the reason why I chose that branch of the service." I lifted my chin in pridefulness. "The few the proud. Ya' know?"

"Huh. Ah, I get it." She smirked playfully. "So, you're stationed in Hayward? That's in the East Bay. Near Cal State Hayward, yeah?" she asked, inquisitively.

"Yeah," I replied. "But way down the hill from the university. I actually live in Fremont."

"That's just across the bay from where I live. Well, kinda. I live in Cotati." She raised her chin under a questionable stare, looking for any sign of territorial recognition. None materialized.

"Cotati?" I said, unfortunately dumbfounded. "Where's that?"

"Yeah, I get that response a lot. It's a small town, just north of Petaluma, in Sonoma County."

I still had no clue. *Did she say Peta-llama, or Petaluma? I think it was Petaluma.* I knew where Sonoma County was. My family had taken many camping trips in Northern California over the years, but the town of Petaluma didn't ring a bell either.

"Ah, shoot. I'm still at a loss," I said, embarrassed. "I'm sorry."

I finished with an uncomfortable grimace. She answered with a shy smile.

"It's okay. Not many people out of the area know of it. They usually drive right by on their way to the wine country. It's north of San Francisco, about thirty minutes or so," she explained.

"Ah, okay," I said.

"So, you're coming to Orange County for school?"

My head seesawed back and forth a couple times. "Thinking about it. I've checked out a couple universities so far. Pacific Lutheran University in Thousand Oaks and Concordia University in Irvine top the list at the moment."

"Concordia? What are the chances? That's just up the road from my school."

"Right? Funny, huh?"

"Those are Christian Universities, right?" Mo asked.

"Yeah. They're both Lutheran Universities. I'm thinking about going into the ministry," I replied.

"Oh." She paused. "That's interesting."

I suddenly realized Stacie was being left out of the conversation and felt guilty about it immediately. I turned to her. She was sitting on her left hip with her legs slightly bent, supporting her upper body with her left hand on the pavement under her shoulder and slightly behind. I lifted my left hand and placed it on her right shoulder.

"So, Stacie here is going to be fifteen in a couple weeks. This Disneyland trip is her big birthday present from her biggest brother."

"Happy Birthday!" Mo said with a smile.

"Thanks," Stacie replied, sitting up and placing her hands in her lap.

Mo looked surprised and amused at the same time. "Wait. This is your sister? And you took her to Disneyland for her fifteenth birthday?"

"Yep. Well, she chose to come. She could have picked a different present, if she wanted. I gave her two options, contact lenses or this Disneyland trip. Personally, I think she made the best choice." I smiled at Stacie, and she returned the gesture.

"Well, yeah! Of course she did," Mo said enthusiastically. "Who wouldn't choose a trip to Disneyland? That pretty much out-does any other present. I would have chosen the same."

Stacie chimed in. "Right? That's what I thought. Easy decision."

*   *   *

Cordial conversation continued between the six of us as we waited under the fading sun for Fantasmic! to begin. Everything evolved so naturally, and as the temperature began to drop, and the sun disappeared behind Tom Sawyer's Island, the next hour was filled with vibrant get-to-know-you chit-chat. Slowly, as fate would have it, most of the talking evolved to a point where Maureen and I seemed to be the only ones engaged.

The more we talked, the more we found out how much we had in common. We loved Disney movies and were big fans of Disneyland. We were both athletes. We had similar tastes in music. *Pearl Jam, baby!* We both came from families with military backgrounds. She didn't like tomatoes, but I could look past that for the moment. I wasn't familiar with her hometown, but it was still in Northern California, only about eighty miles north of my stomping grounds. *I can deal with that. A short drive, really.*

I paused and looked over at Stacie. She had that I-know-what's-going-on-here look in her eyes. I wasn't fooling anyone, especially my only sister. I grimaced and turned back to Maureen.

"So, did you come here just for Disneyland's birthday today?" I asked.

"No, not really. I only came down to hang out with my friends here during my summer break from school. Just a coincidence really. You?"

"Oh no. Just coincidence for us too," I replied.

*   *   *

The longer we talked, the more infatuated I became. She was pretty, so very pleasing on the eyes. Radiant might be the best way to put it. And she seemed so genuinely happy and full of life. We lived relatively close to each other, and had similar interests. Even though we'd just met, it quickly became apparent that she was different from girls I'd dated in the past. I was captivated, intrigued, and, yes, interested.

45

Hmmm, I thought to myself. *How can a girl like this be single?* But I didn't dare ask. There are certain things a guy doesn't ask a girl when they first meet, and that's one of them. If she was in a relationship, I was sure to know, or she would have let me know. Girls know if you're interested. Guys really can't hide their interest very well. They wear it on their sleeve, that's for certain.

Well, if you're looking to make yourself look like a dork by introducing cheap pickup lines into the conversation, then go for it, dumb dumb. I wasn't going there, no way. Besides, what if she wasn't single? I mean, I assumed that she was, but shit, we'd just met an hour ago. Having a question like that come bellowing out of my mouth would just make things awkward, regardless of the answer. So, I kept my mouth shut for once. Remember, I promised Stacie that I would not be picking up on any girls this trip anyway, and I was, *ahem*, committed to sticking to my promise. Really . . . I promise.

But she's so pretty!

CHAPTER SEVEN

O ur conversation, and those of everyone else around us, was soon interrupted by energetic music and colorful lights, setting the scene for the opening scene of Fantasmic! The crowd of patient spectators erupted into cheers as their attention was attracted to Tom Sawyer's Island, where Mickey Mouse kicked off the show. Stacie and I turned away from Mo and the gang, sitting up straight for the best possible view and awkwardly angling our heads upward like meerkats keeping guard over their den, maneuvering for the best possible position between the ocean of swaying heads in front of us.

For the next twenty minutes we entered the world of Mickey's imagination. Everything in our field of view—the Rivers of America, Tom Sawyer's Island, floating stages, a pirate ship, and the Mark Twain—were all intertwined to create a performance that made you feel like you were inside the show. Not just a spectator, but part of it.

Dancing monkeys and happy-ever-after Disney movie couples, like Beauty and the Beast and Price Eric and Ariel, danced together as they floated down the river on appropriately themed rafts. A thirty-foot-tall dragon spit fire and set the river ablaze, a fight scene on a pirate ship between Peter Pan and Captain Hook played out in the rafters high above the deck of the ship, and a choreographed fireworks display from *The Sorcerer's Apprentice* kept us awestruck and entertained by magic only Disney could provide. When the show ended, we all stood up, clapping, cheering and begging for an encore.

"Wow, Stacie. What a show, huh?" I said, both of us still clapping.

"That was amazing!" she replied.

We stood unmoving as chaos ensued, our bodies sore and muscles tight from sitting uncomfortably on the hard pavement for the past several hours. It was dark now, and the temperature had cooled off some. People that had just watched the show were leaving the area and a new set of show-goers hurried in like hungry wolves to a kill, devouring our now-available prime spots. Temporarily trapped by all the commotion, the six of us grouped together within the ensuing craziness. We couldn't go anywhere until the crowd thinned . . . or so I thought.

I turned to Mo. "So, what are you all doing next?"

For all the talking we had done over the past hour and a half or so, I realized this was the first time we were facing each other while standing. I also realized that at some point during the show she had slipped a sweatshirt on over her red tank top. *There, there, Matt. Relax. Now your eyes won't be tempted to wander into places they shouldn't; and that, my dear friend, might keep you out of trouble.* She looked to be a few inches shorter than me, but it was tough to tell exactly by how much. Her eyes were almost at the same level as mine, and they twinkled under the light of the streetlamps shining dimly along the river, which had just switched on after the conclusion of the show. The soft light shining out from the restaurant windows behind her made the frizzled ends of her hair glow gold.

"Haunted Mansion. Want to join us?" Maureen replied.

"Sur—" I cut myself off and cleared my throat. It wasn't obstructed, but I had a moment of clarity and needed to buy some time.

I turned to Stacie.

"What do you think, Stace? Up for the Haunted Mansion again?"

"Yeah," she said assuringly. "I'm always good for that. Let's go."

I gave Mo a single left-shoulder shrug.

"Sounds good. Let's go for it." I looked around at what appeared to be a thinning crowd. "As soon as it thins out a bit more, I guess."

We continued getting bumped and gently pushed by the waves of people quickly moving around. Leaving now would be like running upstream and would likely result in a little "people pinball" cutting through the mayhem. Moving through this made me uncomfortable, but it didn't detour Mo one bit.

"No way," Mo said. Taking control of the situation, she grabbed Michelle's hand and screamed out to all of us, "Follow me!"

Following her lead, we all started bobbing and weaving through the turbulent sea of people, bumping shoulders with a few of them. Our six-person train quickly snaked through the crowd, and in a matter of a couple hundred feet, the Fantasmic! mayhem was behind us and we were all standing a couple of steps from the entrance to the Haunted Mansion.

"That wasn't so bad," I said.

"You can't wait for everyone to move around here. You just have to go for it," Mo said.

It was dark now, and the front of the mansion took on its intended spooky appearance. We waited in the fast-moving line and laughed at all of the pun-y tombstones lining the path. A short time later we entered the Haunted Mansion's main entryway together.

After the caretaker's warning that this was our last opportunity to escape, the doors slammed shut behind us. No takers; we were in for the long haul. A moment later the room began to stretch. We all played the part of the scared houseguest and waited for the hanging dead guy to appear. As tradition dictates, we screamed in exaggerated fear when the lights went out and the lightning-illuminated corpse, swinging in a hangman's noose from the rafters, appeared above us, freaking out some of the Haunted Mansion virgins and small children standing among us. We took a short walk down a creepy hallway lined with shape-changing artwork and statues, whose gaze never left our own, and soon arrived at the start of the actual ride. At this point we needed to choose our doom-buggies. Much to my subdued excitement, Michelle suggested that Stacie ride with her and I ride with Mo.

Thanks, Michelle. You rock!

Stacie was cool with the ride-share. I made sure of that before we got going. And so, Mo and I had our first moment "alone" together. Suffice to say, I wouldn't put it in the category of the most romantic alone time, but hey, I wasn't complaining. Besides, it was still Disneyland, and it wasn't like we were a couple or anything like that . . . yet.

Mo and I continued sharing a few things about ourselves as our doom-buggy made its way through the ride, firing off a few hand-waves at Michelle and Stacie as we passed by the dinner party of dancing ghosts. Upon exiting, Mo shared with me her mom's favorite part of the ride, the tiny hologram witch at the end. She offers you one last piece of advice as you ride the escalator up to the exit, reminding you of something very important. "Don't forget your *death* certificate. Hmm, hmm, hmm."

Despite the warning, we all survived and met up at the exit, safe and sound. No death certificates necessary.

"So, where to next? Probably enough time for one more ride before the park closes," I proposed.

"I vote for Splash Mountain!" Stacie said.

That made perfect sense. Splash mountain was right next door to the Haunted Mansion. We could get in line quickly and didn't have to slog through the thousands of people waiting for the next Fantasmic! show to begin. Everyone agreed, so off we ran.

We waited a while for this one, which was fine with me. It gave Mo and me more time to get acquainted. It's a rare event when you get to walk right on to Splash Mountain, unless it's one of those days when it's cold or raining in Anaheim, California, an equally rare event indeed. This was not one of those days, and for the first time ever, I really didn't give a shit. It was almost closing time, and the park seemed as packed as it had been at mid-day, maybe even more so. Some people only come to Disneyland after darkness sets in, and it seemed this might be one of those evenings where nocturnal Disney enthusiasts close down the park after many of the daytime sun-bathers clock out for the day.

Disneyland takes on a life of its own, slowly changing as the day unfolds. Predictably entertaining under the light of day, everything changes as the sun goes down. The park transitions into a nighttime wonderland of outdoor adventures, where creative light-centric theatrics take control. Light parades, like the well-loved "Main Street Electrical Parade," replace the daytime ones. Fireworks shows light up the starless sky over Sleeping Beauty's Castle, itself painted brightly with large strokes of pastel luminescence. Main Street is bathed in a warm, inviting light glowing from the many 19th century streetlamps lining its path, pushing tired children into slumber and subtly guiding their accompanying adults into the welcoming stores as they slog their way toward the exit.

*   *   *

Splash Mountain is a popular ride, to say the least, especially when it's hot out. Today had been just that, so it was no surprise to any of us that the line was long. Considering the situation Stacie and I had landed in, there would be no complaining from me. The uniqueness of the ride gave everyone a chance to cool off some with the guarantee of getting wet. The only question was, how wet? The amount of weight you had in your "log canoe" and the distribution of said weight also made a difference. If you're looking for a soaking, make sure you front-load the log and have the people in the back secure their cameras, because a deluge is coming their way.

Like a Slinky, we gradually pulsed our way to the start of the ride. The further we progressed into the mountain, the more muffled the sounds from the second *Fantasmic!* show became, slowly fading into the background. It didn't take long for the "Zippidy Do Da" music to drown out the entire thing. We split ourselves up when we got to the front and lined up to step into the log. Michelle and Mo rode in the front, Stacie and I in the middle, and Tristan and Brian balanced everything out in the rear.

After being set free by the gate holding us back, the log gently meandered along the watery track, lightly banging against the sides at every turn. We sang along to all the songs and wondered out loud how much water was actually going to end up in our little log come touchdown. Halfway down the long slide, just before launching our log into to the ride's grand finale under a shower of water spray, our picture was taken. All of us were aware of the camera's location, so we knew exactly when we needed to put on our "Splash Mountain" face. Nobody disappointed.

Our log stopped next to the entry/exit gates at the end of the ride and we all climbed out, each one of us slightly wet from the splashdown. The drenching was less than expected, most of us only having to endure wet shorts and damp socks as we scuttled off toward the exit. On our way out, we checked out the photo taken of us midway down the slide. Stacie liked it so much that she asked if I would buy one as a memento of the day. And so I did.

And so it was, a perfectly timed memento of the weekend for me and Stacie, and the first, albeit unintentional, photograph of my and Maureen's relationship. How often does something like that happen, and on Disneyland's birthday to boot? Um, never! How many other signs does a person need to see, how many more neon lights need to buzz and flash, to know our meeting was meant to be, right from the start?

Disneyland closed soon after our adventure on Splash Mountain finished up. There wasn't enough time for another ride. So, we casually shuffled our way down Main Street USA toward the park exit.

"Well, I hope you had a wonderful time, sis," I said.

"I did, Matt. Thank you. I'll never forget it," Stacie replied as we followed the tram rail down the middle of the street, leading us toward the train station and out of the park. I put my arm around Stacie's shoulders as all six of us walked through the clicking turnstile for the final time.

Our trip was done. A birthday to remember, and the spark of a new relationship. What a weekend. This one would set the bar for all the rest. I don't remember the details of my own fifteenth birthday, but I will always remember Stacie's.

CHAPTER EIGHT

S omewhat awkwardly, we all huddled-up near the ticket booths after making it past the gates where Stacie and I had started the day sixteen hours earlier. *Now what? Where do we go from here?* I broke the silence to see if anyone was up for some late-night eating.

"I know it's late, but are you all hungry?" I asked.

With no hesitation, Brian spoke up.

"No, not really. I need to get back home."

"All right," I said. "Well, it was wonderful to meet you."

"Wait a minute," Maureen said, looking over at Michelle. "I don't need to be anywhere. We can do something."

"Sounds great," I said. "Our hotel is across the street if you want to hang out for a bit. We're at The Best Western."

Brian and Tristan decided they were going to head on home, while Michelle and Mo would come and hang out with us at our hotel for a while.

"I'm not feelin' it," Brian said. "No offense, I just want to go home. I'm tired."

"Me too," said Tristan. "It's late."

"Okay. Sounds like a plan to me," Mo said. "We'll drop you two off at home, then Michelle and I will come back and hang out."

"Perfect," I said.

I'm an "early to bed, early to rise" kind of guy. It was already late, and having spent the last sixteen hours in Disneyland, I was pleasantly exhausted and looking forward to crashing. But knowing Mo was going to come back to hang out reinvigorated my wavering motivation and got me all excited that the night wasn't over yet. That being said, I was a little worried they may decide the effort wasn't worth it once they got where they were going. What could I do that would encourage them to come back? I really wanted to see Mo again, so I did my best to play on her conscience.

"Here, take this. It's our spare hotel room key. Our room number on it, just in case you forget. But please don't lose it. The hotel will charge me, like, fifty bucks to replace it."

She took it and snickered.

"Okay. Don't worry. We'll be back. And we won't lose your key, I promise," Mo said through a smile.

"Sweet, see you in a little while then," I said excitedly.

With that, we all waved at each other and went our separate ways, Mo and the gang toward the parking lot, Stacie and I across the street to our hotel. As we walked we unraveled what happened over the past several hours.

"Holy crap. What happened there, Stacie?" I said, as we slogged our way across the street, my hands buried deep in the still-damp pockets of my jean shorts.

"I don't know, Matt. You tell me."

"I don't know either. Sorry about all that. There is something special about her though, I can feel it," I said, shrugging sheepishly.

"You think so?" Stacie said, snickering at my child-like infatuation.

"I don't know. I'm probably just being dumb. What do you think?"

Stacie answered without words, just a shoulder shrug.

"It's weird though. I have a crazy feeling about her. Isn't she pretty?" I asked, following with a bit of pathetic laughter.

"Oh, Matt, you're such a romantic," Stacie said, batting her eyes.

"She had to be an Irish girl, too, didn't she? Those girls are irresistible."

"And how do you know she's Irish?"

"Well, I don't, really. But I noticed a Claddagh ring on her finger. And look at her skin. She has as many freckles as Grandpa K."

"Ah. I see. But he's German," she pointed out.

"And Irish," I exclaimed.

Stacie stopped at the intersection and pushed the button to signal the walk sign. After releasing the button, she stared up at me. I pulled my hands from my pockets and crossed my arms over my chest. I looked down at her and noticed that I wasn't looking as far down as I used to. *She's getting taller,* I thought. A thin-lipped, toothless smile spread across her face, and her eyes were laughing at me.

"What?" I said, then I turned away, laughing shyly.

"Nothing. It's cute to see you like this."

Now, she was laughing at me. I turned back to defend myself.

"Ah, come on. I've had other girlfriends before."

"So, she's your girlfriend already? Does SHE know that?"

I dipped my head and let out a playful sigh. I had nothing to say for a second. She got me.

The crosswalk light turned to "walk" and we started across the street. The perfect distraction to gather my thoughts.

"It's kina cute, though," she continued. "I've never been there in the beginning."

"The beginning?" I answered, quizzically. "How do you know this will turn into anything?"

"I don't. But if it does, I'm going to take all the credit!"

"Ha ha! Alright. Stacie, if this goes anywhere, I'll let you have it. I'll consider that a win for both of us."

"Sweet."

Stacie seemed cool with the whole thing, but I still had a bit of guilt sitting in my gut.

"Sorry, Stacie, I really didn't try on this one. It just . . . happened," I said, crinkling my nose.

"Yeah, I know. I was there, remember? Shoot, don't worry about it, bro. She seems like a nice girl. And yes, she's pretty. Don't get all attached like you usually do though, at least until you know it's the real thing."

I fired back. "I don't get attached. What are you talking about?"

"Oh, come on," Stacie barked through a laugh. "Bah! Don't kid yourself."

"Crazy that I invited her to our room, huh? Was it stupid to give her my key?"

"Yeah, that was a little weird," she said. "Why did you do that? It's not like we weren't going to be in the room anyway."

"What if she forgot our room number and then decided not to bother coming back? At least that was printed on the keychain."

"You could have written it down, ya know, on some paper," Stacie replied snidely.

"Dang it. I just want her to come and hang out," I said, thinking I might have just made a big mistake. "Oh well, guess we'll have to wait and see."

*   *   *

Stacie and I finally made it back to the hotel room. In anticipation of Maureen actually showing up, and because I smelled like I'd been walking around Disneyland for the last sixteen hours—as was the case—I took a shower and put on a clean pair of clothes. Stacie followed suit and in a matter of about thirty minutes we were clean, packed up, and ready to go home. Even our clothes were laid out for the next day.

About thirty minutes later I watched from the balcony railing as a green Geo Storm pulled into the hotel parking lot. *Could this be her?* I asked myself. I watched it swerve into one of the parking spaces and listened to the air go quiet after the engine shut down. Both doors popped open a few seconds later and two girls stepped out of the car. *They came!* Maureen and Michelle shut the car doors in unison with a single thud.

"Hey! Up here," I called.

"Hi!" they said as they started walking across the parking lot.

I turned to Stacie through the open door. "Hey, Stacie. They're here."

"Really?" she said and came to the stairwell to say hi.

We leaned on the railing and waited for them to finish climbing the stairs. After reaching the second story landing, I invited them into our room and we all went inside.

"Thanks for coming," I said.

Maureen passed me the hotel room key I gave her earlier, looking me right in eyes. "Of course."

"Thanks," I said.

"You're welcome," she replied, softly.

She might as well have spoon-fed me a jar full of butterflies, because my stomach was suddenly full of them. There was something electric about this girl. I found her wonderfully attractive, and it seemed deeper than her pretty face and sexy body. A sensation of thrilling newness came over me, like this was the beginning of . . . something. It felt like we both looked right into each other. I tried to hide it, but I was smitten.

"You look a bit surprised to see us. We told you we'd come back. You still hungry?" Mo asked.

"No. not at all. And sure, yes, let's get some grub," I answered awkwardly. I was a bit hungry, but even if I wasn't, I would have said the same thing. Even at 1 a.m., I was able to throw down some food if it meant that I would be able to learn a little more about her. "There's a Denny's next door," I said, pointing at the wall in the direction of the restaurant. "Want to go there?"

"Sounds good to me," Mo said.

She looked over at Michelle for input.

"That's fine. Let's go," she said.

"Great," I said and looked to Stacie for approval. "You cool with that?"

"Yeah. Sure."

We walked next door to Denny's. It only took a minute or two. The hostess seated us right away at a booth in the far corner of the mostly empty restaurant. Mo and Michelle sat on one side of the table, and Stacie and I sat on the other. We all seemed to take in a sigh of relief sitting down after a long day of fun.

Mo slouched down in her booth, kicking her legs up next to me on my booth, crossing her feet at the ankles.

"Oh, look at that," I said, like I had just found a dollar bill on the ground. I dropped my left hand from my menu and reached down to put my hand on her lower leg.

"Oh, I wouldn't do that if I were you. I haven't shaved in a while," Mo said, giggling. Michelle and Mo glanced at each other and the giggling turned to laughter.

A large grin spread across my face. "That's okay, I haven't shaved my legs in a while either," I responded.

The laughter fizzled and her eyes filled with an are-you-fucking-with-me stare.

"You shave your legs?" Mo asked with surprise.

"Sometimes. Yeah. Doesn't everybody?" I replied, my voice dripping with false confidence.

Mo just kept looking at me, waiting for me to admit I was kidding. I wasn't.

"I do a lot of cycling, so I shave my legs for that," I continued.

"No, you don't. Really? Why?" she inquired, amused. Now she was glancing under the table, looking for proof. All it took was a slight tilt of her head as she was already halfway there, being in the slouched position. *Why didn't she notice already?* I wondered. *I mean, shoot, I was wearing shorts all day.* After checking my ego, I continued. *Relax, man. You only met her, like, five hours ago.*

"Well, you know . . . aerodynamics," I said, smiling.

"You're kidding," she responded, dropping her menu to the table and dipping her chin in disbelief, or wonderment, who knows? Maybe a little bit of both. She was now looking at me suspiciously.

"A little. I thought it was stupid the first time I did it, but after putting in a lot of miles without a carpet of hair on my legs, I got used to the way it felt riding hairless. Feels good. So I keep doing it. And, it makes cleaning out mountain-bike-crash injuries so much easier."

"That's crazy. I don't think I've ever met a guy that shaves his legs, except swimmers."

"Well, that's how it all started, funny enough. I was on the high school swim team my senior year and I refused to shave the entire season. Some of the varsity girls relentlessly bugged me all season to do it. So finally, at our district finals, the last swimming meet I would ever participate in, I broke down and let them shave my legs."

"You let THEM shave YOUR legs? I'm guessing that didn't go very well."

"Yeah. Big mistake. Three of them were shaving my legs at the same time, while I just stood there, bleeding from multiple nicks. I couldn't believe I let them do it. Every time they nicked me with the razor they would burst out in fits of laughter. While they laughed, I bled. And they did a horrible job, to boot. I had to redo the whole thing again when I got home. My dad thought I was crazy, while my mom just thought it was funny."

"I bet it felt good in the water after that, though."

"Huh," I laughed. "Not really. I dove in that chlorinated water to rinse off the blood and naps of shaved hair still stuck to my legs. It stung so bad that I let out a screaming lungful of air under the water. Everyone enjoyed a healthy laugh at my expense after I climbed out of the pool. But hey, I scored some points with the team. It was all in good fun."

"Oh, man. Lesson learned, huh?"

"Yeah, I should have just let Stacie do it, or at least show me how to do it the right way, without all the bleeding."

I slouched in my booth and kicked my left leg up on Mo's booth, right between her and Michelle. "See, it's not all that weird. And you can see I got stubble, too," I said, smiling.

Immediately following our entertaining "unshaved legs" conversation, a waitress came by and took our order. It was late, and I wasn't hungry at all. I was only there for the conversation. Regardless, we all had a few bites and headed back up to the hotel room.

We all found a spot to sit on the hotel beds and continued to talk for a while, until my CD binder caught Mo's attention.

"Those all your CD's?" she asked.

"Yep. Sure is," I replied, feeling weirdly apprehensive. *What if we don't like the same music?*

Mind if I check them out?"

"Sure."

She grabbed the binder and put it down on the floor. Lying down in front of it, she propped herself up on her elbows and started flipping through the sleeves. Each one held four CD's.

"You have a lot of country music in here," she said as she flipped through the first several sleeves.

"Yeah. I like some of the new country. Montgomery Gentry, Garth Brooks, Clint Black, you know," I said.

"Nope, I don't," she said, looking up.

"Look, I even have a hat. Check it out." I walked over and pulled my white Stetson out of the closet, laying it down next to my luggage on the floor.

"No way," she said, eyes wide. "Do you wear that all the time?"

"No, no no. Not all the time. I wore it in Disneyland yesterday, though."

Stacie laughed.

"Yeah. That was a mistake, right Matt?"

"Not the best decision of the day, that's for sure," I agreed.

I leaned over and picked up the hat.

"Oh wow," Mo said, laughing as she watched me put it on and then take it off. "We probably would not have talked at *Fantasmic!* today if I met you wearing that."

"No? You don't like it?" I said, slapping a fake frown across my face as I put the hat back in the closet.

"I don't blame her," Stacie said, still laughing.

"Not really. It's just not my thing," Mo said. "I know that might sound weird coming from someone who lives in farm country, but that's just me."

"That's cool. I spent some time in Texas recently for Marine Corps training and everyone wears one of these out there. I kinda got into the whole country thing during my time there and picked up this hat. I like it, but it does present some challenges on the Disneyland rides. Now that I know that little bit of information, it won't be joining me in Disneyland anymore, or any other amusement park for that matter."

She continued flipping through the translucent sleeves full of genre-organized CD's and got a little more excited when arriving at the middle of the binder where Pearl Jam, Nirvana, Stone Temple Pilots, and other grunge bands lived. Her eyes perked up.

"Now, THIS is better," she said. "Much more my style."

"The first part of the binder has the country music. The middle part has the grunge, and the back has the rock," I said.

She finished flipping through the binder and closed it. Getting back up to her feet, she let us know it was time for her and Michelle to head back home.

"Well, I think we need to be getting back now," she said, placing the binder back on the table next to the TV. "It is getting late."

"Okay. We have a long drive tomorrow, too. So I guess we should get some sleep."

Mo grabbed the hotel-provided pen and paper off the table, now lying next to my CD binder, and wrote down her name and phone number.

"If you want to hang out, give me a call," she said as she finished writing.

She held out the paper and I happily took it from her. "I'll be back up north in a couple days," she added, smiling, not only with her lips but with her eyes. *What is it with this girl?*

"Oh, I will," I said. "Looking forward to it."

We all gave each other hugs and said our goodbyes. Mo and Michelle walked down the stairs and got into Mo's green—no . . . teal—Geo Storm. I was corrected on that mistake earlier. Stacie and I hung out on the balcony for a bit and waved them off.

"What just happened there?" I asked Stacie as we walked back into the hotel room.

"Yeah, crazy," Stacie said, throwing herself on the bed.

"Again, I'm sorry, it was not my intention to meet any girls this weekend. I know I promised you . . ."

Stacie cut me off, snickering. "Matt, stop. It's fine, really. Let it go. I like her. She's funny, and cute. I can't believe they came all that way back here just to hang out though."

"Well, they had one of our keys. They had to come back, right?" I asked.

Stacie turned her head towards me and laid her hands on her belly.

"Maybe. They didn't have to. But I would have felt guilty if I had someone's hotel key and didn't bring it back. So, yeah, maybe that helped," she said.

"I think I'll go see her next weekend, if she's around."

"I think you should. But don't forget to shave your legs!" She laughed.

"Ha! Good one!" I said.

Stacie and I crashed soon after that. The next morning, we woke up much later than the previous two and got on the road back to Northern California soon after that. In between all the country songs, grunge music, and rock ballads we entertained ourselves with on the way home, I thought about this girl I just met. *Hopefully we can see each other again,* I thought.

*   *   *

I called a few days later, and we arranged to meet up the following weekend. I traveled to Sonoma County for the first time, not counting the times we drove through it on our way to Hendy Woods for camping trips when I was a kid.

We spent our first full day together hanging out at Windsor Waterworks. As the name implies, it's a waterpark in Windsor, just north of Santa Rosa. The following day we had a wonderful time hanging out in San Francisco, taking in the sights on Pier 39 and Fisherman's Wharf. That's all it took to reel me in. I knew then this was the girl for me, and I never wanted to let her go. And I still feel the same way today.

July, 1994. It was one of the best months of my life. And so my journey of love began.

Me posing at the fountain in Toontown. (July 16th)

Stacie hanging out with Mickey Mouse. (July 16th)

Saying hi to Mickey Mouse in his Toontown house. (July 17th)

Peering through Mickey's telescope,
possibly looking for my future wife. (July 17th)

Stacie and I taking a canoe ride around Tom Sawyer's island on the
Rivers of America. (July 17th)

Maureen (on right), with her cousin Michelle (far left) and a couple
friends, posing with Mickey Mouse mere hours before we met. (July 17th)

Our very first photo together. Splash Mountain. Stacie was thinking
ahead when she asked for this one!

Me and my buddies enjoying a day in the Pacific Ocean somewhere in Santa Cruz. (Summer of 1993)

Good times in Santa Cruz with my friends Matt, Jen and Jeff. (Summer of 1993)

Mo at Windsor Waterworks on our first day together after meeting in Disneyland.

Same day. Mo turned the camera around on me.

Traffic at the Golden Gate Bridge on the way into San Francisco.

Convinced a fellow tourist to capture a photo of us on Pier 39.

Mo looking off into the sunset with her favorite leather jacket. Alcatraz Island is in the background.

Matthew Koehler

PART TWO

Getting on the Road

Matthew Koehler

CHAPTER ONE

M o and I spent what remained of the summer watering our budding relationship, exchanging trips across "The Bay"—Northern California speak for the San Francisco Bay—to hang out with each other. She'd come visit me in Fremont a few days during the week after I got off work, and I would go hang out at her house in Sonoma County on the weekends. We shared stories about our childhood "stomping grounds" and became intimately familiar with each other's unique attributes—likes, dislikes, dreams, aspirations—things like that. We loved every minute of it and spent the remainder of the summer swimming in a pool of youthful innocence and boundless dreams.

Alas, if only that summer was as endless as our visions for the future. It all ended abruptly in late August when Mo had to leave for the fall semester of her senior year at UC Irvine. I missed her the minute she left, and I immediately started tossing ideas around in my mind about how I could get down to visit her, as soon as possible. I settled on a bike ride from Santa Cruz to Irvine pretty quickly and began planning for it right away. I gave myself a month to plan, train and get all the gear together for a 3-day trek down the California coast. *It shouldn't be too hard, right? Easy-peasy.* I was in the best shape of my life, addicted to cycling, and motivated by love! Nothing would stand in my way. True to that sentiment, nothing did.

After turning down Mo's suggestion of driving down to visit her instead, I took the month of September to prepare. I planned the route and laminated maps, rode my bike everywhere—to and from work, two-hour training rides after work, to the grocery store, everywhere—regardless of weather conditions, and purchased all of the gear I would need for the trip but didn't currently own.

Before I knew it, it was October, September having gone by in a blur. It was time to go. I had already convinced my brother Mark to drive me from our home in Fremont to Capitola, where I was to begin the journey.

And, so it begins.

*   *   *

With a gentle push of my fingertips I slowly opened Mark's bedroom door, careful not to let it slam into the wall. Truthfully, I didn't need to be quiet about it. The only reason I was there was to wake him up anyway. Making a racket would have only sped up the process. But I didn't need to startle the entire house either. Many of my family members are light sleepers, including Mark, and brewing up a bunch of noise would likely pull everyone out into the hallway to shut me up. That would just delay my trip.

I leaned against the door frame with my left shoulder and stood silently in the room's early-morning darkness. My muscles felt heavy and sluggish, but my mind was alert. *Maybe it's the nerves*, I thought. I wasn't worried about it though, my body would catch up once the sun started to rise, it always does.

This part of the day is my favorite. The time of day when morning is near, the moment in time when darkness releases its grip on the world; well, this part of the world anyway. You know that moment right before dawn, when the air is heavy, still, and cool? Yeah, that's the best time, the most welcoming window of time the day has to offer. It's a fascinating time, don't you think? I do. It isn't nighttime anymore, but it isn't quite daytime yet either. Only the clock knows the truth. But, does it really? If you think about it, it is just a human invention, used only to constrain and explain what has come to be known as something not quite as linear as we originally thought it was. *Humph. Something to contemplate, I guess. Later though, okay?* What I can tell you for certain is that dawn is a time of transition, when anticipation and renewal take control. *Oh, Matt, give it a rest, Man. Stop with all the deep thinking and get on with what you need to do today.*

With this introspection in mind, I sank my hands deep into the front pockets of my acid wash Silver Tab Levi's and gave my eyes some time to adjust to the dark void.

It was Saturday, October 8, 1994. A little over a year earlier, in September, Mark couldn't wait for me to leave the house, or at least my room.

74

That same month I shipped off to Marine Corps boot camp, after which he immediately claimed the territory as his own. I didn't even clear everything out of my room before he started moving his stuff in. It wouldn't be fair of me to hold a grudge over his excitement at my forthcoming absence, however. So I didn't, and it was all good. Shoot, I would have been just as thrilled in his place. After all, he spent the first sixteen years of his life sharing a bedroom with our youngest brother, Shaun. Shaun's a great guy, we all know that, but everyone covets their own space, a place to make and call your own. And now, with my departure, Mark finally had it. Likewise, so did Shaun. As for me? I was living rent-free at MCRD San Diego. *Thank you, federal government.* That's what many would calculate as a triple win!

Still quietly standing in the doorway, I reminisced about all the years I called this bedroom my own. It's interesting how fast my adolescent life had become a basketful of memories. Only a couple months out of high school and I was off to start the next phase of my life, in the Marine Corps no less. The everyday moments and significant events of my past were now mere seeds. Seeds from which future stories would grow. They would be watered by time, only to be harvested later to be shared with those that enjoy the subtle art of storytelling. As the years pass and my ever-expanding story garden grows crowded, details once clear as mountain air in the wake of a storm will become murky and uncertain, like that same mountain air before the storm.

Humans are storytellers by nature. This social attribute is an important one, as most memories are fragile; over time building up a patina of obscurity that dilutes the vibrancy of the original experience. Even so, not all will be forgotten. Sharing keeps them polished. The significant ones, sealed deep in the vaults of our minds, live longer lives than others. Details wither, but the "big picture" always remains. Over time though, even after questioning your own version of the memories you harbor—like whether you were wearing red Converse All Stars or dirty white ones, or if you really did run non-stop up the Mission Peak trail with thirty pounds of rocks in your backpack—the story remains the same.

Part of my story, my contribution, is written in these pages. If it makes just one person smile, it's done its job.

*   *   *

Far removed from my tenure here, I felt strangely out of place standing in the doorway of my old room. Memories now fill the space—plentiful, warm, and comforting for the most part. We moved frequently during my childhood until my parents finally settled us into "the Tonopah house" in 1989. I was in sixth grade when we moved in and consider it my "childhood home," as most of my memorable childhood experiences happened while living there. I'm grateful these memories follow me, and I hoped Mark would make some of the same. After all, today I was leaving on a journey destined to plant a whole new garden of memories along the way, and he was helping me get to the start of it all.

*　　　*　　　*

It didn't take long for abstract shapes to appear, transforming the dark room into a shallow cave of shadowy silhouettes. The moonlight, accentuated by the amber glow of a nearby streetlight, crept in through a thin sliver of space between the wall and the window shade. The outline of the bed appeared first, its square-cornered frame accented by the faint red light emitting from the digits displayed on Mark's alarm clock. The time blinked forward a minute as I watched: 4:28 a.m. At the same time, slowly taking shape in my periphery, the borders of his dresser became clear. My pupils now fully dilated; the familiarity of the room's layout became comfortably apparent. Even the posters on the wall started to morph into recognizable images. Planes, trains, and automobiles graced the sheets of glossy poster board. The outline of Mark's head buried in his pillow soon came into view as well. He was a light sleeper, and I was a little surprised that my entry hadn't stirred him awake. He lay silent and unmoving, sleeping soundly on his back with his head turned to the left, facing the wall and away from the center of the room.

A teenager known for his high energy, he was in a rare state at the moment, lying perfectly still with the exception of the rhythmic rising and falling of his chest with each shallow breath. His position under the covers made it appear that he was purposely avoiding the inevitable buzz of the alarm clock.

Time to go. I stood upright, balancing out my weight with one quick push off the door frame with my shoulder. As my weight settled over both feet, one of the floorboards beneath the carpet let out a muffled creak. Mark didn't stir, not even a bit. To tell you the truth, I was surprised. Clearly, he was way under, in a deep sleep for sure.

Such a shame, I thought, somewhat sadistically. I was about to interrupt whatever dream he was taking part in. He was only seventeen, and that means he was most likely dreaming about girls, fast cars, or airplanes. My vote went to the former, and I cracked a thin smile at the thought of it.

After listening in on a few more breaths and watching the clock display click over to 4:29, I decided it was time. I needed to get going and thought it better to get him out of bed myself instead of letting the annoying buzz of the alarm clock do it for me in another minute.

Mark was a bit of a clean freak and kept his room tidy, clothes folded and always in their proper place. So I didn't have to worry about stepping on anything or kicking some random item on the floor as I slid my bare feet across the carpet in the dark. Even so, I shuffled carefully along the left side of his bed and stopped just shy of where his head lay. I leaned over, pulled my left hand out of my pocket, and turned off the alarm on his bedside clock. The switch let out a soft "click" when I flipped it. To my surprise, that's all it took to spring Mark from his slumber. So much for sleeping deeply. *Wakey, wakey, Sleeping Beauty!*

"What? Hey! What are you doing?" Mark said drearily.

He sucked in a deep, involuntary breath, clearly startled by the unexpected awakening. Who would have thought that such a subtle movement would be all it took? It was weird, though, because the floorboard made more noise than the flick of the switch. His head quickly rotated away from the wall and was now facing to his right, in my direction. Almost following in the same rotation of his head, his right arm swung in a precisely aimed arc, landing squarely on the clock, perfected after years of slapping the snooze bar way earlier than he wanted to. If the room had been brighter and his eyes focused, he would have woken to the rude realization that his first image of the new day was the crotch of my jeans. Not a good way to end the type of dream I presumed he was having. Like I said . . . light sleeper.

"Hey, relax, man. It's just me," I whispered. "Keep it down, you'll wake everyone up. Come on. Get up. It's time to go."

"Ah, man. Is it 4:30 already? No way." He grunted as he held himself propped up in his bed with his right arm while rubbing his left eye with the palm of his left hand. His voice was crusty and dry. It had a grumble to it, common when you've been breathing through your mouth most of the night and you try speaking through vocal cords that feel dry as desert dirt in the middle of an August afternoon.

I bent over and leaned in close to his face, so I could speak quietly. Even in the dark I could hear him rubbing his hand through his hair. *Oh, Mark. You and your hair!* He sure loved his perfectly styled head of strawberry-blond locks. Don't even think about touching it, unless you were looking for a fight. Trust me. Many childhood squabbles started with just those kinds of shenanigans.

"Yeah. I'm going to finish packing your car with my stuff while you get ready. Where's your keys?"

Mark licked his lips and cleared his throat of the frog that had taken refuge there while he slept. He glanced at the alarm clock, making sure I wasn't pulling his leg about the time.

"Um, on my desk. Don't turn the light on yet."

In one seamless and impressive movement, Mark, a moving shadow at the moment, sat up and quickly flicked the covers off his lower body. He stood up and sprung out of bed just as quickly, and I watched his shadowy silhouette lumber into the hallway and out of sight, stepping on the same creaking floorboard I did when I walked into the room. Off to the bathroom, I presumed.

*   *   *

My hands fumbled around on his desk and located his keys in a matter of seconds. I took them with me and left the bedroom without turning the lights on, and quietly made my way down the shadow-laden hallway toward the front door. Last night I'd perched my bicycle against the wall next to the double doors, along with all my gear packed neatly into two matching panniers. We hardly ever used one of those doors, the one that had to be opened after you opened the main one.

Anyway, Jezebel was her name, and she was beautiful. At least I thought so. I had a habit of naming my bikes back then and always gave them girl names. I would be riding them all the time, after all, and giving them anything other than a girls name would feel awkward, especially as a teenage boy in the nineties.

Jezebel. She was a 1994 Trek 2200 road-touring bike. Quite a beautiful piece of machinery, if I do say so myself. Ice indigo blue, with carbon fiber tubes. It even had a clear coat painted over the tubes to show off the artistic weave pattern of the carbon fiber strips. *Sexy!* I purchased it brand new in March, right after returning home from Marine Corps Hawk Missile training in Fort Bliss, TX. Up to this point I'd only put about 500 miles on her. Enough to break in the drive chain, brake pads, and cables, I presumed, but I was looking forward to tripling that mileage over the next few days as we rolled south together along Highway one.

I grabbed Jezebel's handlebar stem, pulling her away from the wall with my right hand as I opened the main front door with my left. Predictably, the hinges squeaked as it swung, just as it had for the past ten years. Oddly, it only creaked when swinging open, silent as a flying owl when closing. The heavy air of morning followed the swinging door, slowly pushing its way into the now-open entryway. Leaving the door propped against the wall, I rolled Jezebel out into the dark early morning, across the red brick–laden path and down the short driveway over to Mark's blue two-toned 1989 Chevy Camaro.

It was cool outside, and the air was clear and still, a typical pre-dawn October morning in Fremont, California. And it was quiet, so very quiet, Jezebel's clicking freewheel the only sound piercing the neighborhood silence. Not even the birds were chirping yet. I like it like this. It's relaxing, calming, and regenerating.

The sprinklers recently finished their daily rotation of showering the front yard lawn with false rain. Without the heat of the sun to dry them out, tiny beads of water lay suspended on blades of grass, glittering under the golden glow of a nearby streetlamp. The subtle smell of damp grass hung in the air, and several patches of wet concrete ringed the yard's perimeter.

The moon was out, full and brilliant, commanding the full attention of the otherwise dark sky and all things beneath it. Its glow drowned out the shimmering of all but a few of the usually dazzling stars that dared share the same early-morning sky. Floating boldly, it shined as brightly as a white torch in a dark cave, unchallenged, like a lone victor of a hard-fought battle. So bright, as a matter of fact, it cast a faint moonlit shadow of me and Jezebel across the driveway. I always found this phenomenon amusing and still do to this day. My fascination didn't stop there, either. The moon's position in the sky, low on the eastern horizon, backlit the nearby foothills, clearly outlining the rugged ridgeline in dark silhouettes. These hills are part of California's Diablo Mountain Range but, to me, they should simply be called the "hills of memories," considering all the time I spent playing in them over the years.

Matthew Koehler

CHAPTER TWO

M y love for cycling was born in these East Bay hills. They drew me in, always beckoning for companionship. I obliged, and spent an incredible amount of time hanging out in these hills during my teenage years, not only cycling, but hiking and running too. Summitting Mission Peak, the highest point at 2,516 feet, was a rite of passage in my community. Everyone who's anyone in this town had their experience with this adventure, whether they've only done it once, or make a trek to the top a weekly affair. It didn't matter, it was just part of the culture around here. If you shamefully admitted that you hadn't summited the peak and leaned against the "summit pole" for an I-made-it-to-the-top photograph, people looked at you like you just hadn't lived. Mission Peak wasn't all that high compared to other notable peaks in California, but it was "our" peak, and most locals enjoyed having it in our backyard.

The overwhelming majority of visitors made it to the summit by way of hiking, even fewer accomplished the feat on a bike, and only a select part of the population crested the summit running the entire trail. The trail, or trails, I should say, are respectably steep in many places. But most of them aren't very long, about three miles from most trailheads. You could go crazy if you wanted to and take off on an all-day adventure in the backcountry, but most take just a few hours, slap the pole at the summit, come back down, and go to lunch or something.

Depending on recent rainfall, especially in the lower elevations where the soil composition is the consistency of thick clay, the snake-like trail has a tendency to become very slippery. This annoying feature leads to a lot of two-steps-forward-one–step-back type of trekking, and don't even think about getting traction with even the best bicycle tires. Notwithstanding the die-hard mountain bikers and trail runners, this pretty much put a stop to much trail use during the winter months. Good thing too. Extended use of muddy trails degrades their integrity, and the ruts left behind make the trail especially dangerous for your ankles after the longer springtime days dry everything out.

Dangerous or not, it's well known that teenagers hike up there toting heavy, awkward-looking backpacks with the goal of getting lost somewhere "off the trail" to enjoy a few sips of beer, smoke pot, or innocently hang out away from the watchful eyes and condemning stares of what some of these kids see as a repressive society constrained by archaic ideologies. Evidence of these youthful rendezvous—drained alcoholic containers, empty cigarette boxes, and snack wrappers—litter the numerous dry seasonal creek beds at the bottom of the narrow ravines running up and down the mountain.

Fitness enthusiasts, the category many would have put me into, I suppose, used the mountain as a place to test themselves, cocooned within stunning vistas of rolling hills and grassy oak woodlands, all while getting their exercise in for the day. Families even enjoy the beautiful area, making a challenging trip out of it to enjoy the day, or even just a couple of hours. Hiking up to sit in the shade of the oak trees lining the trails, escaping the crazy city life for an afternoon, is an endearing east-bay pastime.

*   *   *

One perfect evening in the late summer of 1992, I decided to take advantage of the long day and head out for a ride up the peak. It was a beautiful late afternoon, sunny and breezy, hardly a cloud in the sky. The hottest part of the day was waning, and the cooler part of the afternoon was settling in, the needle on the thermometer following the slowly sinking sun. I didn't plan to be out long, just a short and fast climb up to the "no mountain bikes beyond this point" sign posted near the final rocky ascent to the summit and down again.

I threw my mountain bike in the back of the Mazda GLC hatchback I was driving at the time and headed off to the trailhead at the south end of Ohlone College. I pulled into one of the parking spaces closest to the pool and adjacent the trailhead, lifted my 1992 Specialized Rockhopper Comp hardtail out of the car, and set her upside down on the pavement, mirroring a procedure I'd performed countless times before.

She was a pretty thing, painted dark green, with purple lettering. Not lightweight by any cycling standards, but made solidly of steel tubes and chromoly forks, all set on top of beefy thirty-two-spoked wheels and fat knobby tires. A few months prior I had installed an aftermarket "Flexstem" suspension system to the handlebars to cushion some of the relentless vibration and hammering my wrists and arms suffered during the rocky descents. By no means was it the best form of suspension on the market, but it was affordable and, after you got used to its awkward sponginess when pedaling out of the saddle, provided an appreciated level of shock alleviation.

I attached the front wheel onto the forks via the quick release skewer, flipped her right side up, and secured the front brake cable. After slamming the hatchback shut, I locked the car, strapped on my helmet, pulled on my fingerless gloves, and slid on my sunglasses. *Show Time.* Straddling the bike, I pushed off, clicked into the pedals, and rolled down the short road to the trailhead, looking forward to enjoying a fast, adrenaline-filled ride to the peak and back.

The previous winter had been a dry one, and the following spring didn't bring much precipitation to speak of either. It was late summer now, and the mountain protected whatever water she held within herself beneath a blanket of dry, cracked dirt. But not all was lost. Nature adapts, and life always finds a way to flourish. The mountain knows what she needs, and she was cautiously generous with her resources, sparing just enough water to let the grasses grow. In thanks, they decorated her dirty skin with wildflowers, providing food for the livestock that would, in turn, fertilize her tender surface, leaving essential nutrients for future growth after the rains returned.

This time of year, these blades of grass boast shiny slender shafts of brown and gold. When viewed from a distance, even from eye level at certain locations, they fool your senses into thinking the entire hillside is covered with grass, growing vibrantly among the relentless, ever-present oak trees. In reality, the wild grasses grew in large dense patches, tall and green under the shade of the trees and shadowy crevasses of countless ravines, bronze and stunted on the sunbaked west-facing hillside.

After a few easy pedal strokes, followed by several yards of coasting, I arrived at the trailhead gate. I dismounted and pushed it open, pulling my bike through by the handlebars with my left hand as I held open the gate with my right. The hinges creaked loudly, more like squealed, really, as the gate swung. After the rear wheel cleared the threshold, I let go and the heavy green-painted iron gate slammed shut behind me, filling the area with a loud vibrating "twang!" It was a sound so distinct that anyone in the vicinity would know iron just struck iron. Like a tuning fork, the sound reverberated for several seconds as the gate shivered to a stop.

I gazed up at the mountain as I straddled my bike and listened to the gate-slamming echo fade into the wilderness. From where I stood, about a half mile of trail was in view. It sharply switch-backed twice up the visible side of the mountain, eventually slipping over a small hill to the south and out of sight. The trail was uncommonly void of people this evening. Surprising, considering the time of year and beautiful weather. Good news for me, though. Nothing better than having the entire mountain to yourself.

I wasted no more time and started the ride pedaling hard up the west-facing slope. *So much for warm-ups.* The lower part of the trail was cut into the rocky hillside and made for secure riding. Good thing, too, because the western edge of the mountain was steep—at least, on this part of the trail. The heat of the day had peaked hours before, but nonetheless, the relentless August sun followed me up the initial part of the trail and my body heated up quickly. The trail ticked precipitously upward right out of the gate, and I gained about two hundred feet in elevation over the first few switchbacks.

A short time later I reached the first plateau on the trail. By then my heart was racing, my breathing already deep and rapid. All my muscles were engaged, and every one of my pores was pushing salty water to the surface of my skin. The predictable afternoon breeze was blowing, thank goodness, and I tried to envision it pushing me up the hill, thinking it might give me a psychological boost with the difficult physical effort. At the very least, the onshore breeze felt cool against my sweat-streaked arms and legs, and I was thankful for that.

The sun was setting, but its position high above the horizon was not making a substantial impact on how hot I was feeling. It might as well have been high noon. No surprise, really. I was riding on the side of the mountain that received the brunt of the afternoon sunshine, after all. Its heat bore down on my back and the right side of my body as I continued my assent. Sweat dripped from every ridge on my face, adding to the climb's difficulty. *It sure would be nice to bitch about this to someone right now,* I thought. But up here, there was no one to complain to. I only had myself to blame. *Dang. And I just got started.*

The onshore winds rushed in as they always did in the early evenings, traversing westward across the Pacific Ocean, climbing, then sinking over the Santa Cruz Mountains, finally skidding over the San Francisco Bay before picking up speed as they banked up the warm mountainside. They blew over and between the resilient grasses on both sides of the trail, the erratic air currents forcing them to dance with each other like teenage ballroom dancers, full of youthful energy and careless craziness. They gyrated and brushed against each other rashly, and I found the graceful unpredictability of it all strangely eloquent. But music is to dance as air is to breathing. And so they swayed; with no orchestra other than the wind itself, they created a music all their own, softly hissing their song into the air for those who chose to listen. If I was standing still and watching them sway in the constantly changing intensity of the wind instead of pedaling by on a mountain bike, it would make me feel as if I were standing in the middle of an ocean full of amber-colored water flowing uphill.

I listened the best I could, slowly pedaling up the mountain, adding to the symphony my own accompaniment of deep rapid breaths and the clicking rhythm of my chain as it circled the gears. If I didn't think too hard about it and accepted the music for what it was, it sounded as if I was being chased by rattlesnakes. I've shared the trail with these reptiles before, and I used the hissing song of the grasses as a gentle reminder that many of these beautiful but dangerous creatures called this mountain home.

After cresting the first of many periodic summits I would encounter on the way to the top, I enjoyed a more leisurely cadence as the trail leveled out for a while. I turned eastward now, into the heart of the mountain range and away from the bay. With the breeze at my back, I welcomed the opportunity to catch my breath and enjoy a change of scenery. Giant oak trees of various varieties, mostly coast live oak, lined the trail here, generously sharing the land with the notoriously drought-resistant chaparral. The oaks tightly gripped the mountainside with thick, deep running roots, granting them the stability to stand strong and broad, daring to be challenged. Their bark, the color of dark chocolate and campfire ash, was encrusted with a mosaic of cracks along its surface, forged by decades and, in some cases, hundreds of years of various rates of growth and exposure to Mother Nature's relentless weather inconsistencies.

Their trunks—dense, contorted, and gnarled—allow one to perceive them as the old wise ones, the protectors of the mountain, older and wiser than they may actually be. Thick patches of tightly packed moss the color of a not-quite-ripe lime fill in the joints where branches break from the trunk, and lightly dust the top side of the tree's bedraggled branches, using the tree's height as an elevator to the light of the sun.

These hardy oaks hold on to their sturdy leaves long into autumn, letting them go, if at all, only after many of the other trees have exhausted all efforts to keep theirs attached. Only then do they stand alone, encased in their evergreen cloaks, each one pontificating as if they alone were the king of the mountain, the true guardian of the realm. Sometimes they don't drop many leaves at all, providing a welcome blanket of protection from winter rains, shielding acorns dropped in seasons gone by. Not only are they beautiful to look at, these magnificent trees, but they're a welcome sight on rides like these. They provide a place of rest or, at the very least, a welcome veil of shade. I pedaled on and recovered quickly among them, riding slowly under a penumbra of fluttering leaves, taking solace in their terraced canopy of densely packed intertwined branches.

The trail continued eastward, and I soon arrived at another gate. This one had a cattle guard attached and consisted of several round metal pipes buried perpendicular to the trail in the dirt beneath the gate. They ran the entire width of the trail, about four feet wide at this juncture and spaced four inches apart. The spacing between the metal tubes was too far apart to cross when riding uphill, so I grudgingly dismounted the bike and clumsily pushed my way through the gate and over the pipes, my bike's chain rattling in protest.

As if transitioning from one movie scene to another, the terrain went from a rocky trail lined with oak trees to rolling hills of fertile grassland where cows grazed openly in its interior. The topsoil was thicker here, supporting lush, grassy pastureland and large boulders, along with a couple cattle-feeding water troughs. The trail, consisting only of hard, dry adobe soil, had been worn smooth over the years by the steady flow of hikers, bikers, and random park service vehicles. However, when wet, it becomes frustratingly slippery and sticky. A few pedal strokes into it, and all the spaces between the knobs on your bike tires become clogged with sticky mud. This causes you to lose all traction and start sliding all over the trail. Frankly, you'd have better traction on a sheet of ice. But I had no worries about my wheels slipping out from under me today. The dirt was dry and smooth, so I continued on.

I stood up and pushed down hard on the pedals, quickly picking up speed under my own power on the slow-winding incline, rolling in and out of lengthening late-afternoon shadows, pitched across the trail by the abutting hills. After traversing a wide right-hand turn, the trail leveled off at the crest of a small hill, separating what appeared to be two different worlds. Dense woodlands to the west, rolling hills of open pasture to the east. Winded and hot from climbing and the gradual increase in speed, and knowing that the trail only became steeper and mostly void of shade from this point on, I decided to take a short break.

I stopped pedaling, coasting to a stop under a blanket of shade on a well-used, but off-trail, path. The unsanctioned path, no wider than a frequently used game trail, led to a nearby oak tree, one of thousands in the vicinity but unique enough to stand out among the masses. It had a trunk so thick and twisted it appeared uncomfortably deformed, like an empty aluminum can with the side walls crushed in a little bit. Its branches flared out in all directions like a giant hand, the ones on the south side growing substantially larger than those in the other quadrants, causing the tree to lean noticeably to the left. These oddly shaped branches had grown so massive over time they drooped heavily toward the ground, twisting, pulling, and gnarling the trunk as they slowly tortured the tree with their quest to touch the earth.

Contemplating its uniqueness for a moment, I allowed my imagination to take over and envisioned there was some type of battle going on between the tree and its mutinous branches. For the time being, the tree appeared to be winning, its fortitude withstanding the constant onslaught of gravity's pull. But time, the ultimate warrior, would be the true victor in this battle, we all know that. It can't be beaten, overpowered, or persuaded. Its resilience makes all things weak, weary, and frail. Surely one day, with its help, the branches will prevail. Then, and only then, their emancipation granted, they will touch the earth they seem to so desperately covet. Time, having broken through the restraints of patience and resoluteness, will finally take its bounty, payment for services rendered, and the branch will rot away to become one with the land, food for the mountain and all its creatures, seeds for the next generation.

One branch in particular had almost succeeded in this endeavor. It hung very low to the ground, sinking almost immediately after emerging from the trunk. It jetted down and swooped up in a wide U-shaped arc, about two feet off the naked dirt beneath it. The tip of it reached for the sky, twisting and splitting into smaller branches as it did. In doing so, its base created a bench-like seat, welcoming and inviting, luring trail visitors to stop by for a visit. People obliged this subtle invitation, frequently taking a few minutes to rest as they walked by, their tired butts having worn the top of the branch smooth over the years. So smooth, in fact, that all the bark on the top of the branch had been rubbed clean, exposing the dark vein-like marbling of the naked hardwood beneath. In addition to the bench, the tree offered a bounty of shade and a beautiful view to boot, a true trifecta of natural indulgence.

I leaned my bike against her trunk, lifted one of two full water bottles from its holder on the frame, and took a seat in the middle of the branch. It sagged under my weight, but held sturdy. Sturdy enough that if others passed by, two or three other people could share the space without any worry of it breaking free. But alas, nobody was here. *Too bad . . . for them, anyway.* I liked being out here alone—it's one of my happy places; a secret treasure of peace and solitude.

As I rested, I took a few moments to savor the view, all the while wiping what seemed to be a never-ending deluge of stinging sweat from my eyes and brow. I spent an unreasonable amount of time swatting away a profusion of nocturnal insects that relentlessly kept landing on my damp skin too. *What gives, man? Leave me alone.* Having recently emerged from their daytime slumber, the tiny carnivorous beasts were all too happy to find fresh meat to feast on so early in the evening. Surely, they looked at me as a welcome source of electrolyte-saturated water, a hard-to-find luxury around here this time of year.

Insects be damned, I took several long swigs of water. Other than the gentle rustling of leaves in the tree branches above me and the chirping of unseen birds communicating with each other, it was quiet and tranquil. Content, I leaned forward, water bottle in hand, and took in my surroundings. Not a cloud to be seen, only blue sky.

Before me, across the trail and through a rusted barbed-wire fence lining the boundary between public and private land, was a seasonal pond, likely dug as a water source for horses and livestock that freely roamed the back hills. The pond was shallow, and fully engulfed in late-afternoon shadows. The sapphire sky reflected brightly off its gently rippling surface, making it stand out among the surrounding dirt like a back-lit mirror.

This late into summer, the pond was hardly a pond at all, more like a mud pit really, having been drained almost dry by the animals and fowl that frequently stopped by for drinks and bathroom breaks. Horseshoe impressions and other animal footprints formed its bank, pressed deeply into mud encircling its constantly shrinking edge. Piles of horse poop and cow patties, mixed with a generous amount of duck and goose excrement, filled in some of the voids. It didn't take a genius to figure out this was the most likely source of the faint smell of shit and decay lingering in the air. During the winter months, when the rains come, the edge of the shallow pond usually ballooned wide enough to reach the fence. When rain was plentiful, its bank broke through the rusty human-planted barrier and flooded this part of the trail, providing the winter trailblazer with a surprise waterlogged challenge.

A few minutes later I leaped from the bench, allowing the branch to spring back to its natural location. Bobbing slightly from the sudden shedding of 175 pounds, the movement rattled the tiny branches above it. It sounded like a couple of kids were playing swords with wooden sticks above my head, and a few leaves fell as convincing evidence that such a battle was taking place. *Oh, Matt, your imagination has run away from you again.* I put the now-empty water bottle back in its cage, straddled the bike, and aimed the front wheel up the trail.

From this point forward the trail narrowed into a sidewinding single track about half the width of the trail I'd been riding on to get here. It followed the eastern boundary of the park and climbed steadily. I was about to enter a world where a plethora of oak trees, shrubbery, and dried grass lay to my right and an old rusty barbed wire fence, severely in need of repair, stood to my left. If I crashed on this part of the trail, I needed to do whatever I could to fall to the right. Taking a tumble in the other direction could, would, cause serious damage to both bike and human. The trail was narrow enough that only one bicycle, or hiker, could traverse it at a time, so keeping your head up and paying attention was important. As a matter of fact, this is standard trail etiquette. As the uphill rider, you needed to yield to downhill trekkers, cyclists, and, more often than you would think, horses.

Just before I pushed off up the trail, the all-too-familiar sound of grinding gears and rubber rolling over dirt broke the silence. A couple seconds later, the first human being I'd seen since I started this ride up the mountain lurched around the corner in the direction from which I'd come. He was out of the saddle, hammering hard on the pedals and yanking his handlebars from side to side, moving quickly over the compacted dirt. When he got a little closer, I waved. He sat back on his saddle, returned the friendly gesture, and coasted to a stop next to me.

"Hey," he huffed with exertion.

Between heavy breaths, he unclipped his shoes from the pedals while lifting his fingerless gloved hands off the handlebar grips. With his feet firmly planted on the ground, he leaned forward, resting his forearms on the inner part of his handlebars. I guessed him to be in his mid to late forties, an old man by my frame of reference. Lean and muscular, his thin frame supported a body that seemed to belong to a retired athlete who couldn't let go of his sport. You could tell from the tan lines on his thighs and upper arms, this guy spends a lot of time on the bike.

"Hi," I replied. "Getting a last-minute ride in on the mountain tonight, huh?"

"Yep," he said, still breathing deeply.

Feeling the need to fill the silence with small talk while he caught his breath, I opened up some conversation.

"Looks like you and me are running the show out here tonight. We seem to be the only ones out on the trail, like we own the place or somethin'."

"Yeah." He reached for his water bottle. "Perfect. I like it that way."

"Me too," I replied.

His breathing slowed a bit, allowing him a sentence between inhales.

"You heading up the mountain or down?" he inquired.

"On the way up. Just stopped to rest on that tree branch over there," I answered, pointing.

"Ah. Yeah. That's a good spot. I've actually taken a nap on that branch before. But the ants get curious after a while, so it wasn't a long one."

"Ha! Yeah, that wouldn't be too hard to do. I could have easily snoozed for a while," I said. "Didn't see any ants this time. Plenty of gnats, though. They kept trying to land on my face."

"Yeah. Those little buggers can be a real pain in the ass, too. Hey, weird question, but did you happen to bring an apple?"

"An apple?" I replied quizzically.

"Yeah. For the horse."

"Horse? What horse?" I asked.

I started looking around for this horse, squinting beyond the fence and inspecting the pond area more closely than before. He followed my gaze as he looked over his shoulder to the stinky pond and shrugged.

"Oh. Well, I guess he's gone in for the night, or he's out wandering around somewhere else on the hill. I don't know what his name is, but he always comes over to the fence when I ride by, nodding his head and neighing at me over the fence. So I started bringing him apples. He loves 'em. Carrots too. See, I have it right here."

His breathing had almost settled into a normal rhythm by now, and he sat up straight on the saddle, taking another drink from his bottle. While doing so, he reached into one of his jersey pockets and pulled out a small green apple.

"Man, if you hold up one of these, he'll come running. Trust me. Maybe I'll see him on the way back down."

He slipped it back into his jersey pocket and scanned the horizon. He was sweating profusely, as much as I was when I arrived at this spot a short while ago, his dark body hair matted together in clumps on his forearms. He wiped away some sweat from the space between his helmet and sunglasses with the palm of his right fingerless glove.

I waited for him to finish taking another long swig from his bottle, then introduced myself.

"I'm Matt, by the way," I said, extending my right hand over my bike frame.

"Oh yeah! Sorry. I got distracted by the whole horse conversation. John," he replied, extending his hand as well. We gave each other a friendly fingerless-gloved handshake. "I don't think I've seen you on this trail before, have I? Do you ride out here much?" he asked.

"Only during the summer, really," I said. "I participate in a lot of other sports that keep me busy most of the school year."

"Oh yeah? Where do you go to school?"

"Irvington High. I'm going to be a senior this year," I said.

"Ah, the final stretch. That's good." He paused. I could see his eyebrows raise, even from behind his sunglasses. "Irvington, huh?" he continued, inquiring through a thin smile.

"Yeah. You know of it?" I asked.

"Sure do. I'm a Kennedy grad."

"Kennedy? Boo!" I joked.

He chuckled as he leaned over to slide his bottle back into the cradle.

"Oh, the days of high school rivalries. Those were always a whole lot of fun. If only those friendly contests were the limits of what we needed to stress out about, even after leaving high school." He nodded his head as if recalling some old memories. "Things get real complicated, real fast out there in the real world, if you're not careful," he said sternly.

"That's what my dad tells me . . . all the time," I said, rolling my eyes even though they were hidden behind my sunglasses at the moment.

"Well, he's a wise man then. But don't worry about all that crazy stuff yet. Enjoy your senior year and this bike ride. Speaking of that, I need to get moving before my muscles cramp up. Not as young as you, you know," he said, smiling. "I can't just sit around and rest too long and then get back on the bike." He jabbed a thumb at his chest. "At this age, my muscles like to call it quits before my mind does."

"Well, it doesn't look like you're doing all that bad for yourself. Look at those tan lines, man! You either spend a whole lot of time at the beach wearing your cycling clothes, or you're on that bike all the time," I said, laughing.

"I try," he said, chuckling. He clicked into his pedals. "Yeah, I do spend a lot of time on the bike. It's a great release for me."

"I get it. I feel the same way."

"Well, hey, it was great to meet you, Matt. Happy riding. I'm off."

"Yep, I'm taking off too. I need to get going while I still have some light left."

"See you at the top then," he said as he made a quick adjustment to his helmet strap and pushed off up the mountain.

I clicked in and pushed off right after him. *I'm going to follow this guy and see if I can beat him to the top*, I thought to myself. *It shouldn't be too hard. This guy is older than my dad!*

I took off, putting full power into the pedals, and followed about five or so bike lengths behind him. We both pedaled out of the saddle, back and forth along the single-track, hopping over tree roots and swerving around the iceberg-like tips of deeply imbedded trail-bound boulders. I kept pace with him as our tires seesawed across the winding trail, climbing and descending, ducking under low-hanging tree branches and dodging fence posts until we broke free from the cover of the trees.

As if exiting a tunnel, we followed the trail, now wider than the single-track we'd just traversed, into hilly grassland. We pedaled quickly up a short and steep pathway, arriving at another gate and cattle guard a short time later. A little frustrated by the interruption, we dismounted and awkwardly maneuvered our bikes through the gate, allowing it to slam shut behind us. *"Twang!"*

From this point forward the trail was well-groomed, maintained in part by local park rangers and trail maintenance volunteers. It was generously lined with gravel and small rocks, and about as wide as a single-lane road. Looking up toward the summit from here, you could see most of the lower trail snaking up the mountain in wide, sweeping loops, bending around small hills covered in brown grass.

John took off first again, setting the pace high from the get-go, and I followed. I lagged behind, *intentionally, of course*, pedaling faster than before but sticking to the same five-bike-length distance I maintained on the lower trail. The smoothness of the well-groomed dirt encouraged a quicker cadence, and our powerful pedal strokes kicked up dust behind our tires. When John swerved left, I swerved right, trying to avoid breathing in some of the arid dust he was kicking into the air. Through my heavy breathing I heard the gravel grumble under our weight, rocks and gravel crunching together as we pushed closer to the summit . . . and the unforgiving sun. Its heat beat down on us relentlessly. We hadn't been climbing in the full sun for five minutes and I was already trying to wish into existence the generous amount of shade afforded us on the lower trail. That, my friend, is just a memory now. *Why is it so hot this late in the day? Or, maybe a better question: Why are you being such a bitch, Matt? Just ride, man.*

We continued, out of the saddle and pedaling hard, John maintaining a consistently challenging pace that forced me to work much harder than I thought I would need to just to keep up. Sweat leaked from every pore with each pedal stroke, and streaks of it dripped down the interior of my sunglass lenses, drying almost instantaneously into hard, salty veins.

Soon, we were halfway up the mountain. My head begged for shade, and my body screamed for ice water, neither of which were within reach. My legs ached from the effort, and my lungs burned from the heavy breathing of hot afternoon air. The lining of my nose felt fragile, like it was ready to break open and bleed as dry as it was, and I could hear the pounding of my heart in my ears.

Dang, this guy is no joke, I admitted to myself as my subconscious mind started contemplating a retreat strategy. He was a lot faster than I thought he would be, ya know, being so old and all. I was holding my own, but I had my limit; and he found it. I was able to follow him for about a mile, a mile and a half at best. After that, I broke. I didn't have much of a choice, so I swallowed my pride and let him go at it alone. Well, I didn't "let" him go anywhere. He just kept pedaling, and I couldn't keep pace. I sat my tired ass back on the saddle, downshifted, and settled into a smoother, more comfortable rhythm. I took solace in the fact that there was nobody around to witness my failure. But hey, all I wanted was a good workout, right? Well, I was definitely getting my money's worth of that.

I rounded the following turn feeling defeated. John was nowhere in sight. He was already around the next turn, speeding his way to the summit, leaving only a momentary cloud of dust in the air as evidence of his prior existence. Lucky for me, this part of the trail was lined with another grove of oak trees growing up out of a steep ravine adjacent to the trail. Their branches stretched out wide across the trail, providing the welcome shade I'd been wishing for over the past mile. Other vibrant plant life flourished here too, fed with the measly but constant trickle of water from an underground stream, a small gift of life from the famished mountain. I slowed my pace to a crawl and took it all in, catching my breath as I pedaled through the fluttering shadows. An onshore breeze, also welcome, was still blowing softly and erratically, rustling the leaves above me.

Physically spent from my efforts, I continued up the rest of the trail at a more reasonable but respectable pace, nodding my head to a few hikers stomping their way down the mountain. Back and forth I continued up the trail, pedaling hard out of the saddle on the steep parts and sitting down for the easier ones.

The last quarter mile or so of the trail was steep and less maintained than the portion I just emerged from. My pace slowed as I zig-zagged across the width of the trail in my lowest gear, maneuvering through rain-hardened trail depressions, dried footprints, rodent holes, and protruding stones.

Another twenty minutes of riding finally brought me to the base of the final ascent. I arrived fatigued and disappointed with my inability to keep pace with John. But all that quickly passed, and I allowed the humbling experience to dwindle into memory. Here, the terrain was bare of vegetation, and the soil took on a polished appearance, rubbed smooth by decades of pounding feet, rolling tires, and rainwater runoff. It reminded me of the smooth, almost unrecognizable surface of my grandfather's Saint Christopher pocket token he carried with him everywhere he went, worn almost featureless after years of praying with it clasped between his thumb and index finger.

*   *   *

Several of the lower mountain trails converged at a small plateau in front of the beginning of the rocky ascent to the summit. There was a resting area here with long wooden benches scattered about. A place to recover, relax, and take in the 280-degree view of the San Francisco bay, the foothills to the west, and the continuation of the mountain range to the east. Looking up from here, you could also see the spire marking the summit. But if you wanted to reach it, you had to hike the rest of the way. Cyclists were not allowed beyond the benches. Mountain bikers needed to decide whether to turn around and coast back down the mountain, or leave their bike and hike to the top. I guess you could shoulder your bike and carry it to the top if you were so inclined; many do just that. But that would be in violation of the sign, and I'm sure the rangers would love to ticket you should they catch you.

That aside, it wouldn't be very smart to do that, anyway. The last quarter mile to the summit is rocky and steep, with gaps between the stones just wide enough to trap shoes and mountain bike tires. You need at least one hand available to maneuver over, around, and between exposed boulders and mini crevices. There is also a respectable sloping drop-off that shouldn't be ignored on the east side of the ascent. If you slip and tumble down that, it's guaranteed to leave a mark or two.

Famished, I pulled up to the benches. John was there, of course, sitting on one of the benches next to the "No bikes beyond this point" sign, looking rested and relaxed. *How long has he been here?*

"Hey there," he said as I coasted to a stop. He shot me a wave. "You made it!"

John was chilling out with his back toward the peak, chowing down on some kind of a snack, his water bottle standing upright and open on the bench next to him. His bike was lying on the ground at his feet, helmet dangling from the end of the handlebars. He had pushed his sunglasses up to rest in a bed of dark curls on the top of his head, exposing deep-set brown eyes and a lean narrow face. Prominent folds in the skin of his forehead showed more of his true age, and I had an easier time believing that he was every bit as old as I thought he was.

"Hey," I answered shyly, shaking my head in disbelief. "Man, you're pretty fast . . ."

He cut me off.

"For an old guy?" he said, finishing my sentence.

"No, you're just fast. Either that, or you're average. And if that's true, then that would make me slow. I don't think my ego can handle that," I said, now laughing. "So I would rather think of you as fast. That way, after swallowing a bit of pride, I can consider myself average. That, I can accept. Not well, but I can deal with it," I said, my laughing face transitioning to a sulking one.

He laughed. "Ha ha! That's a good way to look at it, man. Just remember, there are a lot of cyclist out there faster than me!"

I leaned my head to the side, started to unclip the chinstrap of my helmet, and sighed. "Is that supposed to make me feel better?"

"Hey, don't beat yourself up, man. I've been riding these trails for years. You get faster after a while, don't worry. Just keep riding. Pretty soon, you'll be saying the same thing to somebody else." He took another bite of his snack and a long swig from his water bottle.

I gently dropped my bike, pulled out my second water bottle, and took a seat on a bench on the other side of the trail from John. Resting my helmet on the bench next to me, I continued to talk about the ascent.

"I was trying to keep you reeled in man, at least within striking distance, ya know? But I just couldn't catch you. You set a pace I couldn't keep up with."

"Well, thanks. You know how to make an old man feel good."

"How old are you, anyway?" I asked. I had to know.

With a mouth full of energy bar, John smiled. "Just turned fifty-two last week."

"What? No way! Fifty-two?" I said, cracking a smile across my parched lips.

"Yeah." He shrugged nonchalantly. "But I've been riding since I was your age. What are you, eighteen or so?"

"Seventeen," I said.

"Seventeen! Well, there you go. Let's turn the tables, shall we? You rode pretty well for being such a young guy."

John chuckled, and I tried to get comfortable on the bench while stealing a glance at the peak. Just a few people were meandering among the boulders.

"Well, thanks," I replied.

"Hey, you would have left me in the dust if I was seventeen and we were riding together. I didn't even get my first bike until I was about your age."

"Really?" I said.

"Yeah. Grew up in Montana. I was riding horses at seventeen, not bikes, like you'd expect from someone living in that state, I suppose. Raised on a ranch in the foothills of Mount Sentinel, along the Blackfoot River."

"Is that near Missoula?" I inquired.

"Yeah, pretty close."

"I love Missoula. A couple years ago I went there on a church youth group trip. We stayed in the freshman dorms at the university. Beautiful place."

John nodded in agreement. "That it is. Sometimes I miss its allure. It's a charming piece of country. Were you just there for a visit?"

"Kinda. We helped clean trash out of the Blackfoot River. Part of a community service project. Amazing the amount of stuff we pulled out of the water. Rusted car frames, old farm equipment, lots of beer bottles. No bikes, though."

"Huh," he grumbled. "I'm not surprised. Nobody rode bikes in Montana, at least back then they didn't. Shoot, not many people lived in Montana when I was a teenager. And those that did didn't do much more than work. It's too freaking cold, man. There was a blanket of snow on the ground at least six months out of the year. It's not a place for the faint of heart. It's a land for ranchers, men as tough as nails and women who don't complain. Everyone had to work back then, there were no easy days. Montana had two seasons, winter and getting-ready-for-winter. It never sat well with me. I didn't like the fact that we always had to be preparing for something."

"Doesn't sound all that fun of a place when you put it that way. I had a pretty good time when I was there, though."

"You were there in the summer, I presume?"

"Yep. July I think."

"Yeah, the summers are nice. I'll give it that much. And I do have to say, horrible winters aside, it's God's country, that's for sure. I do miss it sometimes. Not the cold, just the open beauty of it all. You can't help but reserve a special place in your heart for the place you were born. There is nothing like a Montana sunset, let me tell you. I don't care what season it is."

"Better than watching the sunset over the ocean? It can't be better than that," I countered. "That's one of the most beautiful things ever."

"Well, that is a tough one, I'll agree. It's just different, I guess. They're both great, but there's something about watching the sun go down high up in the mountains in pure silence that makes it special. Sometimes, if conditions are perfect and the sun is setting at just the right angle, it looks like it's setting both in the west and the east. That, my friend, only happens in the mountains, and it's pretty amazing to watch."

"Woah, cool. I haven't experienced any of that, but it sounds cool. Seems like a wonderful place to ride a bike. But riding in really cold weather? No, thanks. I don't like the cold much. Especially exercising in it. Burns my lungs," I said.

"Yep. I feel ya. I'm not a fan of cold weather either. The winters there were miserable. That's the main reason why I moved to California. I came out here to attend college and never went back. I left my mom and dad there to fend for themselves." He snickered. "Sometimes I feel guilty about it, but they don't seem to mind all that much. At least that's what my dad tells me. I don't know if I believe all of it, though. They surely aren't getting any younger. But I try not to worry. My brother lives just up the road from them if they need any help." John paused and looked around for a few seconds, taking in a deep breath as he did. He seemed lost in some memories. "I do love it here in California, though." He stretched his arms out like he was waiting for a hug but instead just twisted around at the waist in a half circle. "The weather. Man. You just can't beat it."

"Tell me about it. The weather is pretty nice here. I mean, just look at this evening. Amazing, huh?"

John dropped his arms and let his hands slap against his thighs. "Yep. A perfect evening for riding."

I took another long drink from my bottle.

"So, where did you go to school?" I asked.

"Started at Stanford, then UCSF. Spent way too much time in both places. Made me soft," he said, shooting a glace across the bay toward his undergraduate alma mater.

"Soft?" I answered quizzically. "What do you mean, made you soft?"

"I suffered through four confusing years at Stanford, somehow managing to earn a degree. Then, because I felt like I needed to torture myself even more, grinded out eight years of medical school at UCSF. Didn't do a damn bit of exercise during all of those years." He paused for a second. "I gained forty pounds in twelve years," he said.

"Are you serious? So, are you a doctor?" I asked, intrigued.

"I was. Well, I guess I still am. I maintain my medical license. I just don't practice medicine anymore. I spent twenty years working as an emergency room doctor. Just retired last year."

"Huh. Why did you retire so young?"

"I didn't like it anymore. I got tired of the crazy hours. And the stress. Man, the job just stressed me out. It felt like all I did was work. It became my only identity."

"So, you started riding after you retired?" I probed.

"Oh no. I started riding back in my thirties. Once I started working as a doctor, I actually had time for myself, believe it or not, even though it felt like I was working all the time."

"Okay," I said, puzzled.

"I know, that sounds confusing. But it was just how I felt at the time."

"It's cool. I get it. I think."

"I got really into it once I started, addicted might be the best way to put it. I had so much free time, as a matter of fact, that I started making my own bicycle parts. Attempting to help out with a little 'problem' I was experiencing on longer rides, I designed a bicycle seat that prevents penile numbness. Believe it or not, my design actually helped, surprisingly good I might add, and I told a few friends about it. They were, of course, fellow doctors I was working with at the time, and they blabbed their mouths to their friends about what I was doing. That ended up attracting the attention of a couple bicycle seat manufacturers. And the rest is, well, history, as they say." He raised his hands up and extended them out to his sides again. "And that's what I do for a living now. I design bicycle seats," he said with a laugh, his demeanor dripping with prideful astonishment. He seemed to anticipate my interest and dropped his hands back down onto his lap.

"What? Really?" I couldn't stop a snicker from leaving my lips. "You design bicycle seats that prevent penis numbness?"

"Yep! See that? I'm riding with one of them right now."

He pointed over to his bicycle. I took off my salt-stained sunglasses and stared at his saddle.

"It has a hole in it!" I said.

"Yeah, that's the point," he said, raising his eyebrows. This caused the lines on his forehead to squish together. He leaned forward and rested his elbows on his thighs. "Taking pressure off the pudendal nerve is essential to prevent this numbness from occurring." He traced the hole in his saddle with his right index finger. "By cutting a hole out of the middle of the saddle it drastically reduces the pressure on your perineum." He dropped his hand and let it hang between his knees. "That way you don't get as much numbness in your nether regions when sitting on a saddle of this design, especially on long rides," he said, his tone switching to "doctor mode" as he talked.

"That seems crazy. Do they really work?

"Well, the jury's still out, but I've had some positive results, or should I say fewer negative ones. I don't think the perfect saddle's been designed yet, but I'm working on it."

"You've got to be kidding. That's the reason why you don't practice medicine anymore?" I asked. Now I was pointing at his saddle.

He shrugged. "Well, let's see, if you had the opportunity to design bike seats for a living and then get to test them out by riding on them all day, and get paid for it, would you work in a windowless office and be stressed out all the time?"

John placed his hands on his knees and pushed himself back up to an upright seated position, still smiling. No, he wasn't smiling. He was smirking, apparently quite entertained by our talk.

"I guess not. Sounds like a pretty good plan to me," I said, enthusiastically agreeing. "But what about all that medical education and experience? You must miss it. No?"

"Sometimes I do," he said, bobbing his head and looking amused, taking the final bite of his snack. "But it's not like I'm letting my skills go to waste. In order to make these seats work properly, you need to have an intricate understanding of the human body and how it works. My medical experience provides me that."

"Huh. Okay. That makes sense. I'm just used to doctors, well, only being doctors," I said. "I guess I have a little to learn."

"We all do. That's how life works. The older you get, the more you'll understand."

I looked up and around, still amused by the conversation, and noticed the sun was very low in the sky now, its ever-softening light throwing shadows far off into the east and slowly transforming the harsh whiteness of the western horizon to a warm crimson hue. It was making me a little nervous. The onshore breeze, following the sun's declining intensity, had calmed down a bit and was now only blowing in gentle gusts. The temperature seemed to be dropping too, a welcome development as there was no shade at the top of the mountain.

It was a fine evening, nonetheless. The south end of San Francisco Bay, clearly visible from where I stood on this fogless early evening, appeared beneath the horizon as a rippling pool of lava bathing under the striking red and yellow glow of the setting sun.

I followed the land with my eyes, tracing the topography from the muddy shoreline of the bay, across the flatlands of the city of Fremont, and up the rapid incline of the mountain on which I now sat, perched on a small plateau near the summit. Ohlone College, my starting point, was smaller than the thickness of my thumbnail when I stuck it out in front of my face. But even then, I could make out the vibrantly blue water in the pool, contrasting jarringly against the browns and tans of the draping mountainside.

I took a long drink from my water bottle, almost draining it dry. Standing up from the bench, I reached down and pulled my bike up off the ground by the handlebars, straddling the frame in the same motion. I picked up my helmet from its resting place on the bench and strapped it on.

"John, I've got to get down this mountain. Thanks for the . . . interesting conversation," I said as I maneuvered my bike around, facing it downhill.

He grinned. "It was nice to meet you, Matt. I'm going to hang out here a while longer. Have a nice ride down. See ya next time."

"Sure thing. Take care. And good luck with the bike seat designs," I said and waved goodbye.

"Thanks," he said, waving me off.

The pedals clicked as I pushed my cleats down on top of them, making me one with the bike, and I let gravity take me back the way I'd come. Quickly picking up speed as I accelerated into the decent, I narrowed my concentration to the trail, and only the trail, hopping over small boulders and swerving around larger ones. This was not the time for sightseeing. That's a luxury reserved for the climb. The increase in speed and elevated level of danger lit a fire in my brain. *No more daydreaming, Matt. Time to pay attention.* This was the best part, the downhill. It's the reason for all the suffering to get to the top.

I've always felt that you need to "earn the downhill." Is that a metaphor for life? Maybe. But relishing in the ecstasy of the descent after pushing myself to the summit, or, in this case, almost to the summit, was a feeling like no other. Pure joy. It might be unfair, but that's what I always thought was odd about people who only ride the downhill, especially on the ski runs after the snow has melted. Really? You use the ski lift to bring you to the top of the mountain? Ehh. It's immensely practical, I'll admit that, but there seems to be a certain element of cheating going on there, or at least a lack of respect for the mountain. Whatever. There are those who will disagree, and that's fine. No skin off my back. It's just the way I see it.

The downhill shenanigans had begun, and my Flexstem vibrated wildly as I bounced over the rough boot-packed and mountain-bike-tire-compressed dirt, the suspension bottoming out completely as my front tire repeatedly slammed into shallow rain-carved depressions. When managing this type of terrain, I rise out of the saddle and push most of my weight over the rear end of the bike—avoiding damage or an over-the-handlebar tumble—and gain better control over my steering. My Rockhopper was a hardtail, which means there was no rear suspension to cushion the blows as the back tire bounced along the terrain. So, after getting up to speed, I stood up on the pedals, riding with my ass floating over the back end of the bike.

I slid the rear tire out around the turns to maintain my speed and keep the bike safely near the middle of the trail, spraying rocks and dust over the trail embankment. I kept my speed in check, not looking to get myself into a situation I would regret. Humans and animals alike frequently use this trail, and you could experience an unfriendly get-together should you neglect to scan ahead for other visitors, or blindly go into a turn at high speeds. Best to avoid a hospital visit if you could. So far, so good. And I was all by myself at the moment . . . exactly the way I liked it.

*   *   *

Growing up, my parents drilled into me the dangers and life-altering effects of drugs and alcohol. It was made abundantly clear if I was ever caught engaging in such behavior, things wouldn't go very well for me. Fearful of these unknown repercussions, I heeded their warnings and stayed away from it all during my teenage years. Otherwise, the ramifications of my deceitfulness would surely come home to roost at some point. As such, I didn't know the feeling of being high on drugs, but I did know what it felt like to be high on life. At that stage of my young life, boundless freedom was plentiful. My youth shielded me from the reality of its exorbitant cost, allowing me to experience the outside world through a veil of immature adolescent clarity. Mountain biking was my drug of choice, my release, my escape from everything else. It rejuvenated me, forced me into a window of concentration that contained my all-to-frequent lack of focus. Screaming down a sidewinding trail of dirt and rock after suffering through a challenging ascent, basking in the euphoric endorphin-rich fog of my "earning the downhill" mantra, was the pinnacle of the whole experience, and I welcomed the immersion of it all when I saddled the bike.

I continued the descent, skidding my rear tire around the turns and pedaling way too fast for my own good on the straightaways, yelling with innocent adolescent excitement and sheer joy. I heard nothing but the wind in my ears, the grinding of dirt and gravel under my tires, and the rattling of my bike chain against the chain stay as the rear wheel bounced wildly from one compacted dirt mound to another. *Heaven is real,* I thought, and I was in riding right through the middle of it.

Another couple minutes of riding, and I was already halfway down the mountain. It leveled off a bit, and I stopped underneath the first grove of oak trees I saw. On the way up the mountain, these same trees gave protection from the sun. Now, with the sun almost set on the other side of the mountain, they provided me an opportune place to pull over, adjust my gear, and give my hands a much-needed break. The muscles in my forearms were swollen with blood, starving for oxygen and burning like fire, a consequence of holding on to the handlebars tightly during the decent. This short break also gave me a chance to adjust my helmet and sunglasses and finish off the contents of my water bottle. I thought about putting my sunglasses away, but they were the only eye protection I had at the moment, so I left them on. It wasn't that dark yet.

I spent a minute pushing back on my fingers to stretch out my tight forearm muscles and then shake my hands wildly in the open air to force blood into the area. I took a deep breath, clicked in, and pushed off for the final descent. I didn't have much time to waste and needed to get back to the car before sunset. The fading sunlight illuminated only the tips of the back-country hills now, and while the sun continued to sink, the growing shadows quickly swallowed the valleys. This gave me all the evidence I needed that evening had settled in.

I continued my speedy descent down the back side of the mountain, sliding around each of the snake-like turns and leaving small clouds of dust in my wake. I took notice of cows grazing casually in the dry grass along a nearby hillside. Livestock roamed freely in these backcountry hills, mostly in the lower elevations, as grass was plentiful most of the year. I didn't concern myself too much with their meanderings as they mostly kept to the grassy areas and off the main trail.

But today was a different story for one of these cows. Apparently, one of them lost a bet with another cow and was required to stand unmoving in the middle of the trail and do nothing outside of chewing its cud. As I rounded one of the wide-banked turns at breakneck speed, I abruptly came face-to-face with this "adventurous" rebel.

She was standing right in the middle of my projected path when I first caught a glimpse of her, facing down the mountain, her large broadside spanning most of the width of the trail. My eyes widened with fear at the sight of her and the first two fingers of both hands instinctually lifted off the handlebars and reached forward for my only salvation. Almost immediately, my vision narrowed to tunnel-like proportions as the rest of the world fell into blurry irrelevance. The scene was surreal, unbelievable really, and even though I sensed I was screaming, I couldn't hear a thing in the eerie quiet of the moment.

Panicking, I pulled back on both brake levers with death-grip strength, immediately freezing both wheels and putting me in an uncontrolled slide toward the outside of the turn, kicking clouds of dust into the air and spreading dirt and gravel all over the trail. The Flexstem compressed completely with the rapid deceleration, and my body lurched forward in response. To save myself from flying over the handlebars, I threw as much of my ass off the back end of the saddle as I could manage, trying desperately to regain some kind of control and bring my bike to a stop. That helped me stay upright and balanced for the time-being, but I wasn't slowing down fast enough. I just didn't have enough traction, or distance. *Thanks a lot, Isaac Newton!*

My sudden appearance caused her to jerk forward a step, further into my path—just my luck—at the same time turning her head toward me to see what was going on. Her eyes as wide as silver dollars, her body unflinching, she held her ground and stared at me as I slid uncontrollably in her direction, willing myself to stop through clinched teeth, or at the very least, skid past her to tumble into the grass. I unclicked my left foot from its pedal and dragged it behind me in the dirt as a third brake. At the same time, I threw as much of my weight and momentum into my right pedal as I could, digging my tires deep into the loose gravel and begging for traction, but getting little.

Everything happened incredibly fast, so fast that all my actions materialized by instinct, not thought. My hearing came back online as fast as it had vanished a moment ago, and I found myself screaming at the top of my lungs, apparently trying to scare the cow into moving out of the way. "Ahhhhhh!" was all I could muster, a natural reaction in this situation, but it didn't work. Nothing worked. I couldn't figure out a way to stop soon enough, and she refused to move. Before I could think of anything else to avoid the collision, the moment was upon me. Nothing could stop the inevitable now.

*   *   *

The front wheel hit first, slamming hard into her right hind leg. The rest of the bike followed in the blink of an eye, then came to an abrupt stop against her massive backside. My upper body joined the party a split second later, and I was thrust from the bike, right into her hindquarters. The force detached me from the bike and I tumbled helplessly over her big ass, flying through the air for what seemed like forever. Hands and arms outstretched in an effort to cushion the inevitable blow, I landed hard on my chest in the dirt. An uncontrollable "ommff" sound escaped me when I landed, the impact knocking the air out of my lungs. My body rolled like a rag doll, first onto my left shoulder, then head over heels, and finally sliding to a stop on my belly a couple yards away. I was still on the trail, but just barely. *Oh, lucky me.*

I leaped from the ground immediately, staggering away from the edge of the trail. I paused, placed my hands on my hips, and sucked in several deep breaths. Shaking from adrenaline and incredibly pissed off, I turned my gaze uphill toward the cow. *Damnit!* Anger brewed in my chest and suddenly came out in a flurry of expletives.

"Shit! What the fuck?" I screamed at her, waving my fists in the air in front of my face. "You dumb, stupid animal!"

Filled with rage, I tore off my helmet and threw it in her general direction. It missed and bounced off the ground, skidding to a stop in the grass on the side of the trail. She was undeterred and refused to move. *Stubborn bitch,* I thought. She just stood there, comfortably content, completely unfazed, chewing her cud and staring at me with unblinking eyes. The screaming continued.

"Damn it! I can't believe this is happening!" I screamed, lowering my face into my hands.

Trying to rationalize with her, I guess, I yelled at her again. "Why the fuck are you standing in the middle of the trail!? Ahhhh!" What I was really trying to get out of this exchange, I'll never know. I'll just chalk it up to aggravation and frustration. Ms. Cow and her friends up the hill were the only living things around, at the moment anyway. They were the only ones to yell at. None of them cared what was happening to me. She didn't give a shit about what I was saying, and none of them even flinched more than their tails at my screaming. That was probably done only to swat at a fly, something they surely found more irritating than the tantrum I was throwing.

Fueled by frustration and budding aggravation, I began running up the hill toward her, but a sharp pain in my left knee stopped me before I even got started. What was I going to do to her anyway? Beat her up? The pain forced me to look, and under the fading light of day everything I did not want to see was revealed to me in horrible clarity: a dirty oozing mess of mangled skin and blood hanging off my knee in all directions.

"Ah, man."

I spoke in surprised astonishment. The words came out in a gasp, the kind of involuntary tone you use when you know things are going to be really screwed up for a while. All the anger and frustration I was about to unleash on this cow evaporated. My voice dropped to a whisper, and I became more concerned about myself than little Ms. Cow over yonder. "Just what I needed," was all that came out. I began to inspect the rest of my body, assessing the extent of the damage. It was a good thing I decided to wear gloves that day. The thick cushioned pads on the palms of my fingerless gloves were scraped completely through to the skin, and the palms of my hands were bleeding from a gaggle of tiny scrapes, as were several of my fingertips. Not much more like a bad raspberry, though. Kinda like what you get when you slip and fall on the sidewalk and catch yourself with your hands and knees. My jersey and biker shorts were torn open in several places, and a few shallow cuts on my chest and left shoulder revealed themselves through the ripped fabric. *Okay. I think the rest of me is alright. But my knee! Shit!* The thought directed my attention back to my knee and lower leg. Blood had already reached my sock, a growing pool of it staining the white threads a dark red. I bent over for a closer inspection and noticed dirt and small rocks imbedded deep underneath small flaps of skin, swimming in the thick stain of slowly oozing blood.

My quiet concern snapped back to frustrated anger, and I felt the need to let the entire world know about it in one more loud yell. I stood up, placed my hands behind my head and screamed loudly into the empty twilight sky.

"I can't believe this!" was all that came out.

My body still shaking from shock, I dropped my hands back down to my sides, leaned over, and tried to brush some of the gravel out of the wound. But the effort only made the situation worse, smearing blood all over the place and grinding debris further into the wound. I grimaced in pain while attempting this field-style first aid and finally concluded I was probably doing more harm than good. That, and considering the lack of remaining daylight, it would be better to leave it alone and deal with it when I got back home anyway.

Attempting to calm myself down, I stood silently for a moment, head bowed, the quiet concern from earlier settling back in. I tried to breathe deeply for a minute or so while my knee throbbed in unison with the pounding of my heart. With the exception of my breathing, there wasn't a sound to be heard. Silence.

After what turned out to be only seconds of reflection and thought—amazing what can go through your mind in such a short period of time—I raised my head up to see that Ms. cow was still staring me down, still chewing her cud with a look in her eyes that said, "Thanks for the back rub, dude." Then, like nothing had even happened, she turned away and slowly lumbered off the trail. Off to "greener pastures," I guess. Too bad she couldn't have made her way over to those greener grasses before, or after, I passed by.

After lumbering her fat ass down the hill, the mangled heap of steel and rubber that used to be my bike came into view, lying unnaturally on its side. It was obvious, even from where I was standing, that it wasn't in very good shape. Even in the dimming light of day, the prognosis didn't look promising. Basically, it looked like it had been run over by a tractor.

I limped painfully up the incline, hoping it was still in good enough condition to get me down the mountain. *That's all I need. Just get me back to the trailhead. Please.* The closer I got, however, the dimmer my hopes became. I stopped a foot or so away from the front wheel and, with a heavy sigh and drooping head, looked it over. As expected, it wasn't in good shape, at all. After another heavy sigh, I bent over at the waist, grabbed the handlebars with my bloody hands, and pulled it to an upright position.

Even before my initial inspection was complete, it was obvious that no matter what I did, there was no possible way I was going to be able to ride this bike down the rest of the mountain. But I was still going to give it a try. It's not like I had many options available anyway. I finagled the chain back onto the front and rear sprockets and tried to spin the back wheel using the cranks. I didn't notice right away that the rear derailleur was bent, but that became quite clear after I pushed down on the crank and the chain immediately slipped off the rear sprocket again. I pulled on the derailleur, bending it away from the rear wheel and doing my best to get it back to a workable position. My efforts weren't perfect, but I was able to straighten it out enough to give it another try. This time the chain stayed on and the wheel spun while the derailleur fidgeted back and forth from misalignment. The wheel wobbled back and forth like a fish caught at the end of a line, but it was spinning, and that meant maybe, just maybe, I had a tiny shred of hope. "Not great, but I think it can make it," I said in a whisper.

So I allowed myself to bathe in a sliver of hope, but the soaking didn't last long, shattering like glass as soon as I began to inspect the front wheel. So badly bent in the collision, several spokes snapped under the pressure and the wheel scraped against the forks when I gave it a spin. The forks were also bent, jetting far out in front of the bike like it was reaching for something.

In a last-ditch effort to see if there was any possibility it could make it down the mountain, at any speed, I straightened out the crooked saddle and gingerly straddled the bike. Surprisingly, both tires were still inflated. *How is that possible?* I slowly sat down to see if it could take my weight. It could, but supporting my weight and rolling downhill were two completely different things. It didn't take but a moment to realize this was a no-go.

Regardless of the bike's condition, I pushed it forward, slowly. Every time the bent portion of the front rim rubbed against the forks, the bike would skid to a stop. I would have to be moving pretty fast to overcome this friction or push through the rubbing with every revolution, neither of which was a viable option. The wheel seemed to move as far sideways as it did forward. Reality set in. The bike was a paperweight. So, through a grunt and a frustrated sigh, I dismounted and started working on a better plan.

The sun was noticeably further down the horizon now, making me very nervous. Its descent had released its grasp on the inland peaks, gracefully bathing all the land in sight under the pale shade of summer twilight. Any other time I would have found this beautiful. Unfortunately, my current situation tarnished its appeal and, instead, I found it frustrating, stressful, and nerve-racking. It gets very dark on the eastern side of the mountain after sunset. You're basically at the mercy of the moon after sundown, and she was nowhere in sight. I also noticed, for the first time since the crash, that I didn't have my sunglasses on.

They must have fallen off in the crash, I said to myself, frustrated. *Where the hell are they?* I gave a cursory look around and when they didn't immediately reveal themselves, I quit looking. "Ah, fuck it!" I said out loud. "I'm not looking for those now." My helmet, on the other hand, was up the trail a couple yards away, resting against the hillside in the grass. I laid my bike down gently, unnecessary under the circumstances—habits die hard, right?—and limped the few yards uphill to retrieve it.

I looked down at my helmet and noticed something sticking out of one of the air vents. With bloody fingers, I picked up my helmet and yanked free a three-inch-long rock that had lodged itself in there during the crash. *Woah.*

That could have been bad. The realization quickly settled in that if I didn't have that brain bucket on my head, *this* rock would have been embedded in *my* head. Humbling to say the least. Thank goodness I'd fallen into the habit of wearing a helmet whenever I ventured out on my mountain bike. After staring at the rock for a moment, suppressing the thought of what I really wanted to do with it, I dropped it back onto the trail.

Helmet in hand, I continued my slow and purposeful slog to my resting bike, being careful not to slip or slide on the loose gravel. Sidestepping down the hill, I soon realized that I was walking right next to the groove I'd carved into the trail attempting to come to a stop. It was longer than I would have guessed. *I must have been screaming down this trail,* I thought. *God, everything happened so fast.* So fast, in fact, that at that moment, it almost seemed like it didn't happen. Well, all it took was one look at my bike and my bleeding body to realize it was all too real.

I soon came to grips with the fact that there was no other choice but to walk the rest of the way down the mountain. It really was my only option. So, after finally arriving at my bike a few moments later, I picked her up by the handlebars and started limping down the trail into the shadow-filled valleys below, feeling defeated but trying to make the best of the situation with the remaining daylight.

I wasn't planning on riding after dark, so I didn't bring any lights with me. The stark contrast between now and pedaling up the mountain earlier in the evening became unpleasantly apparent with every lumbering and painful step. Less than an hour ago I rode past this area in the opposite direction, tired, sweating profusely, and begging the sun to set sooner rather than later. Now in a very different state of mind, I prayed the sun would take its sweet time before handing over my part of the world to the night. I was injured, my bike was trashed, the sun was setting, and my sweat-soaked Lycra cycling gear was torn to shreds. For the first time all day, I was starting to feel the chill in the air.

I continued gingerly down the mountain, bike in tow off to my left side. With every revolution, the mangled front wheel rubbed against the bent forks like a wounded soldier. It squeaked as it rubbed, in sync with the aching in my knee with every step.

A few yards down the trail, I stepped on something and heard a subtle crunch. Lifting my foot and cocking my head to the side to get a better look, I found the icing for the cake. *Well, would you look at that?* I said to myself, my lips stretching out into an irritated grin. *That's fucking terrific.* I bent over and picked up my crushed, and now completely worthless, pair of sunglasses. Shaking my head in disgust, I threw them down the hill in the general direction of my archnemesis, Ms. Cow. They must have flown off my face while I was flying through the air, landing just out of view of the crash site.

*   *   *

I heard him speeding down the trail from the higher elevations before I saw him. The fluttering of gravel and dirt echoing off the surrounding hills became louder with every bend in the trail. He was approaching fast, and he was close. How fast and close I wasn't completely sure, but with every passing second the grumbling of his tires and the click of rocks disturbed by his tires became louder and more pronounced. Before he made it to my location, I moved over to the innermost part of the trail, hugging the mountainside. With a little bit of luck, maybe he wouldn't mistake me for a cow as he rounded the corner, ending up in a similar situation as I had been in. I jest somewhat, but I don't think I could have taken a hit like the one the cow took a short while ago in the condition I was in, then just walk off the mountainside like nothing happened. His brakes squealed as he rounded the corner just up the hill from me, his back tire kicking a large cloud of dust and rocks into the purple sky.

I'm sure I gave the impression that I needed some help. I mean, who limps down the hill, pushing a bike, wearing bicycle shoes, at twilight, with his helmet draped over the handlebars? I tried not to concentrate on him and kept walking, minding my own business and keeping my eyes focused on the ground in front of me. The grinding of the rocks beneath his tires slowed as he pulled up alongside me and the familiar sound of a cycling shoe disengaging from a pedal filled the air. He stopped just ahead of my front tire. To him I must have looked like hammered dog shit, even from the rear. I stopped too, even though I wasn't really in the mood for conversation.

"Hey, man?" he asked, with a respectful level of apprehension. "You okay?" He was breathing hard and taking shallow breaths between each word.

The dimming light hid some of his identifying features in the shadows, but I recognized his voice immediately.

"I've been better, but yeah, I'm alright. Just took a spill."

He recognized my voice as well.

"Matt?" he said commandingly. "Woah. What happened, man? You sure you're alright?" he asked again, this time his voice sounding uneasy and slightly alarmed.

He disengaged his other cleat from its pedal and started duck-walking his bike in my direction, straddling the frame. I looked up. Sure enough, it was John. We were the only cyclists chilling out on the benches at the top of the mountain after all. I mean, who else could it have been? In the twilight I wasn't surprised that it took him a little bit of time to recognize me. Once he did, though, and with a genuine look of concern on his face, he continued to probe.

"You slide out on one of the turns?" he asked.

"You could say that. That's definitely *part* of what happened." I paused for a moment, then continued. "Make sure you watch out for the cows on your way down," I said sarcastically. "They seem to be having a lovely time hanging out on the trail tonight."

He seemed to take notice that I was in good spirits—well, giving it a good shot anyway—and I sensed him becoming more amused about my pending story than concerned about my well-being. That was okay. I didn't want anyone to worry about me. With an aura of disbelief surrounding him, a thin smile stretched across his face. Without saying a word, he leaned his head back in such a way that, without saying a word, begged the question: "Are you fucking with me?"

"What?" he asked incredulously. "A cow knocked you off your bike?"

Now he was snickering through unmoving lips, and I looked away and down the hill, a little embarrassed. Regaining my composure, I gave him a quick rundown of the situation. We weren't too much further down the trail from where the incident happened, so I was able to point out all of the events.

"Kinda. I came barreling around a couple turns up the hill over there. That cow, that one right over there . . ."—I let go of the handlebar with my right hand and pointed her out—". . . was standing right in the middle of the trail." I arced my arm to the right and pointed to the impact site above the now-grazing cow. John's gaze followed my pointing finger. "I did everything I could to avoid the crash, but I just couldn't stop in time. I slammed right into her, right into her big fat ass, flew right over her back and landed right there. See that body-shaped skid-line?" Still pointing, I directed my finger to my landing zone.

"Oh snap," he added, sounding a little out of place with the phrase, being fifty-two and all. "No way!" he continued and started laughing. I didn't blame him. I would have laughed too. Quickly coming to terms with the fact that I was injured, he kept it to a minimum and stopped as soon as he could recover. "Ah, man." He snickered again and reached for his water bottle. "Sorry, Matt. I don't mean to laugh, but that's a little funny."

He shot a long stream of water into his mouth, helping him sober up a little bit from the laughing. It worked, and he started showing a little more concern.

"You sure you're okay?" he asked as he pushed down the stopper on his water bottle and slid it back into its carriage.

"Yeah. I'll be fine. My knee's a little beat up, though,"

Now that I made it the center of attention just by bringing it up, I looked down at it. It had stopped bleeding, for the most part, and I could see that the blood was starting to dry and scab over a little, turning the front of my lower leg into a dirty façade full of clumpy streams of mangled hair and dried blood.

John put on his doctor hat for a moment and bent over to have a closer look.

"Ouch. That looks nasty, Matt. But luckily, it only appears to be superficial. Clean it out really good when you get home, and you should be fine. You have any water left in your bottles?"

"Na. I'm all out," I replied.

"Here, let me rinse that out for you."

"No. It's okay, John. Don't waste your water on me."

"Really, it's fine. I'll be home in no time."

John laid his bike down and squatted to get a better angle on my knee. He sprayed several streams of water in and around the wound. Each time the water touched raw, exposed skin I wanted to scream, but held back to protect my pride. Only a few deep breaths and a couple grunts hinted at my level of pain.

"How bad is it really, do you think?"

"Well, you'll need to dig those tiny pebbles out. That won't be comfortable," John said. "I've seen worse, though. I can tell you that. How 'bout the rest of you?"

"I'm scraped up in a few places, but the knee is the worst of it," I said, glancing around at a few of the other obvious injury sites and showing him the palm of my right hand.

"Yowzers. Man, you took quite a spill."

"Yeah, tell me about it," I agreed.

"I just did!" he said, trying to lighten the mood.

"Ha," I replied, unimpressed.

"Sorry. That was bad," he admitted and cleared his throat. "Your bike looks pretty messed up, though. You sure you can make it down the rest of the way? I can help you out if you need it," John said. "No problem."

"I can't ride it, that's for sure. The front wheel is warped pretty bad and the forks are bent. Even if I could, I'm still a little shaken up. I can walk it back to my car, though. It's fine."

"Are you sure?" John asked. "There aren't too many other people out here that can give you a hand at the moment. And it's going to be dark soon."

"Yeah, I know. Really, I'll be okay. Thank you for stopping. It's only a mile and a half or so back to the parking lot. I'll be fine."

"Okay. Well, shoot, take care of yourself. I'm sorry that happened to you. Tell you what, if I see a Ranger, I'll let him know what's going on and maybe he can drive one of the trucks up here and give you a lift the rest of the way down."

"Okay. If you find one of them, that would be great. Thanks."

"Sure, man. Well, I hope to see you up here again," John said, with a sorrowful, almost apologetic, grimace on his face.

"Me too. Thanks again for stopping. See ya around."

John patted me reassuringly on the shoulder and took off down the trail. I continued my slog down the mountain after him, again following in his wake just as I did on my way up here, limping with every step and wishing with all my might that one of the regional park rangers would drive by so I could hitch a ride to the Ohlone College parking lot. *God, I hope John runs into one of those guys.*

As was the way wishes usually worked out, this one didn't come true, and I was forced to walk all the way down the mountain to my car. *Put wishes in one hand and shit in the other, Matt. See which one fills up first. Yeah, thanks, Grandpa Koehler. I know, I know.* I passed the time swatting at mosquitoes buzzing around my ears and landing on my skin. I wasn't surprised by their relentless pursuit, but I was sure irritated by it. Not that I was ever in the mood to be eaten by mosquitoes, but damnit, they were doing a darn good job of pissing me off. *I'm really not in the mood, you stupid miniature vampires!* The condition I was in provided easy access to fresh blood. All they had to do was land and lick, or suck, or whatever they do to get at it. I really didn't give a shit what technique they used. I found it annoying, and I killed as many of them as I could.

When I finally arrived at my car, it was almost dark. The sun had officially set a while ago and only a sliver of its golden light was still hanging out above the western horizon. The first stars of the evening dotted the summer sky in the east, peeking out from above the mountain ridgeline. The darkness had put the city to rest and allowed the nighttime lights around the college the opportunity to illuminate the campus walkways. Even the pool deck glowed gold under bright sulfur bulbs.

The streetlights were on as well, casting soft glowing amber spotlights beneath them onto the pavement, helping me easily locate my car. These weren't really necessary as the parking lot had mostly cleared out by the time I got back to it. I wasted no time popping open the hatchback and throwing the remnants of my bike into the back compartment. I took off my now-destroyed bike shoes and threw them in with the bike as well. Slamming the hatchback closed, I took a deep breath, sealing up not only the trunk of the car, but also the most eventful bike ride of my young life.

I opened the driver side door and slowly, painfully lowered myself into the seat. My left knee ached, and it started bleeding again as I twisted around to face the steering wheel. Several spots on my back began to sting as I leaned against the seat. Apparently, there were a couple of abrasions back there too. I could do nothing about them at the moment, so I leaned forward, fired up the engine, and started driving slowly out of the parking lot. It was a short drive home, but every time I pushed in on the clutch to shift the manual transmission, the pain in my knee made the drive feel like an eternity. I usually enjoyed driving stick shift cars, but right then I desperately wished my car was an automatic. *There you go, Matt, wishing again, huh?*

*   *   *

I could think of a hundred different ways to spend the evening other than nursing my injuries, but I really didn't have much of a choice. Best to get on it as soon as possible though. I arrived home after dark and parked the car in the street next to the mailbox. I shut off the engine but stayed seated, relishing the last few moments of silence I would experience for the foreseeable future. I turned my head toward the house and surveyed the scene, intentionally delaying my exit from the car. Warm light from two large lamps in the living room beaconed out from the two front windows of the house, welcoming me inside. *Time to face the music, Matt.*

Getting out of the car was as much of a painful endeavor as I anticipated it would be, but I was prepared for that and dealt with it in stride. I sucked in a deep breath, managed to wrangle myself out of the car without further injury, and hobbled like an Ewok up to the front door. I turned the handle and pushed it open, sounding the alarm that I was home with its perpetual squeak. *I wonder if Dad purposely never fixed that. Kinda hard to sneak out of the house, at least by the front door. It's like a built-in alarm.* My mom, as always, heard the noise and came out from the dining room.

"Hi, Matt, how was the ride? You were out for quite a while."

"Yeah. I had a little . . ."

"Oh!"

Mom came to an abrupt stop in the middle of the hallway, and her left hand instinctually came up to her face and covered her mouth. This started the trial of the evening I'd been expecting after starting my hike down the mountain. I shut the door behind me and for the next several minutes traversed through the inevitable "Oh my God, what happened?" conversation with my mom the best way a seventeen-year-old boy could. I kept repeating, "I'm okay, Mom. I'm okay," and, "It's not as bad as it looks. Really, Mom. Please stop freaking out."

Like all moms when they hear such statements from their children, no matter how old they get, she didn't believe a word of it. My dad, appearing in the hallway a short time later, looked on with concern but smartly stayed out of the conversation, at least for a little while. I was still breathing, talking, and walking—well, it was more like gasping, wincing, and limping, but whatever—so all was good in his eyes. He'd seen this type of thing countless times before. Mom, however, never quite got used to all the blood, bruises, and broken bones that came along with raising three crazy balls-to-the-wall kind of boys. We were always damaging ourselves in one way or another, and there seemed to be a constant cycle of first aid that needed to be administered in our house.

Opting not to sit down—shit, it was hard enough getting out of the car—I summarized the entire thing to my parents standing up. I kept it brief as I needed to jump in the shower and get cleaned up. Mom wanted details and tried to convince me to take a seat on the couch. *Sorry, Mom, that needs to wait.*

"I need to get these clothes off and jump in the shower," I said apologetically, "Then we can dive in and see what I need to do." I sighed. "Hopefully I can get most of the dirt out."

"Alright," Mom said quietly, bowing her head and crossing her arms across her chest. It looked like she was about to start crying. She wanted to, I could tell, but she found a way to hold it in. Mom has a gentle soul, but time spent raising us boys had hardened her soft exterior. Raising our sister kept her heart soft, though, and that's what makes her special.

"I'll be out in a few minutes."

I slowly limped down the hallway to the bathroom. After rounding the corner, Mom continued, "Let us know if you need any help. And when you're finished, we'll get that cleaned up and take you to the doctor."

"Mom, I don't need to go to the doctor. I didn't even break anything," I answered grumpily, my frustration brewing again.

"But it looks really bad. There's so much blood. What if you need stitches?" she said, her voice quivering now. Again, the tears almost came, but she held them back. Her face seemed to harden right in front of me.

"I know, Mom, but it really isn't that bad. I mean, it hurts, but a lot of the blood is going to wash off in the shower and you will see it's only coming from the scrape on my knee."

That was a lie. A white one, but a lie nonetheless. My injuries, especially my knee injury, were far beyond a mere scrape. Forcing myself to keep that frame of mind helped me think it wasn't all that bad, even if it was. She didn't say anything else after that, turning away and walking into the kitchen. My eyes followed her as she did, passing right by my dad leaning against the wall under the archway between the kitchen and the hallway.

"Hey, Dad?" I said.

"Yeah?" he answered, unclasping his hands and slipping them into his pockets.

"Could you get my bike out of the car? Or what's left of it, anyway."

"Sure."

"It's pretty beat up, so you can just throw it on the porch."

"Alright," he said and started walking down the hallway toward the front door. Passing by me on the way out, he pulled his left hand out of his pocket and laid it on my shoulder. "Glad you're okay, Matt, for the most part."

"Yeah, I'm fine. But when this knee scabs over it's going to hurt like crazy for a while." I grumbled at the thought of it. "That's going to suck," I said, leaning my head back, looking up at the ceiling fan, spinning slowly and silently.

"Well." He paused. "It could have been worse, Matt," he said, trying to sound encouraging as he continued walking down the hall.

I closed the door to the bathroom and proceeded to get undressed. I didn't anticipate getting naked would be such a difficult problem, even considering the condition I was in, but it turned out to be quite an awkward and uncomfortable experience. Thankfully, it wasn't much of a painful one. My jersey slipped off easy, only a few moments of discomfort when the fabric rubbed against the abrasions on my back as I lifted it over my head. I wasn't worried too much about the jersey removal, though. If anything was going to give me trouble, it was going to be the shorts. They were going to be the real challenge. *I sure hope I don't have to cut these damn things off.* It hurt to bend over, and I was going to need to figure out a way to pull the Lycra shorts out far enough away from my leg while at the same time pulling them down over my wounded knee. This would all need to happen in one motion, too.

Attempting this feat with raw fingertips was going to be painful, at the least. *Dang it,* I said to myself as I contemplated the best strategy. I decided I would take care of it like I seemed to take care of everything else in life, fast and without putting too much thought into it. *Don't worry, Matt, it will be just like ripping off a Band-Aid, over in a hurry, with hell to pay on the back end.* Yeah, sure. That should work out just fine, right? Well, much to my amazement, it did work out just fine, all things considered. I was able to pull my shorts down without further injuring myself. *Nice work dude.*

I stood up and tossed my ruined clothes into the corner next to the bathtub. I turned around to find myself staring back from inside the mirror. *What a mess,* I thought. I gazed intensely at my beat-up self for several seconds, and for the first time since the crash, I was able to evaluate the full extent of the damage. I dipped my head toward the sink and, using the main mirror in conjunction with the mirror on the side wall medicine cabinet, briefly looked over both of my shoulders, inspecting my back. Not as bad as I was expecting, really. Just a few abrasions on my left shoulder blade and another in the small of my back. Turning back around, I noticed two raw spots on my lower chest below my slightly protruding lower ribs.

There was a soft knock at the door, and I knew immediately it was Mom. There was a limit to her patience. I was already testing that limit, and I hadn't even gotten into the shower yet.

"You okay, Matt?" she said from the other side of the closed door.

"Yeah, Mom, I'm good. Almost ready to get in the shower. Be out in a few minutes."

"Okay."

I stopped with the body-gawking and mentally prepared myself for what would most likely be one of the most painful showers of my young life. I shuffled over to the bathtub-shower, slid the door open, and adjusted the water temperature to lukewarm, cooler than I usually liked it. I knew once the water hit the raw exposed flesh of my knee, fingertips, and other abrasions, the dull, throbbing pain would instantly transform into an intense stinging one.

I stepped softly into the tub and stood hesitantly under the falling water. True to my assessment, I instantly became aware of every spot on my body missing the top layer of flesh. I grit my teeth at the sudden onslaught of pain. It felt like someone was pressing the lit end of burning cigarettes into my left knee, fingertips, left palm, low back, lower ribs, and left shoulder blade, all at the same time. I hung my head and held my breath, letting my chin rest on my sternum as the water rinsed me from head to toe. After several seconds, seconds that felt like minutes, I exhaled and took in another lungful of air through clinched teeth. A painful groan followed. Through streams of water dripping from the tips of my hair, I watched the dirt from the mountain and blood from my injuries mix together near the drain in red and brown spirals. Concentrating on this mesmerizing drain-dance provided a small, but welcome, diversion from the pain, and was oddly satisfying to watch.

The initial shock of pain subsided after the tender exposed skin adjusted to the water and I carefully washed my body down with a generous amount of soap, cleaning out my knee the best I could without rubbing it. All of this took a while, longer than my typical five-minute shower, anyway, but I finished up soon enough, dried off, and wrapped the towel around my waist. I limped into the living room, my right arm swinging widely out to the right, keeping my out-of-balance frame upright as I moved, my silent screams masquerading as grimaces with every footfall. The shower not only washed away much of the dirt and blood, but also the remaining adrenaline that, up to this point, had been keeping the pain at bay.

Mom was ready for me, having already found the family's frequently used first aid box, and had it sitting on the dining table when I entered the room. I lumbered over to the couch and positioned myself carefully next to the right side. Mom rushed over to help as soon as she saw me start to sit down. I raised my hand in a stop motion.

"I got it, Mom. I'm good."

"You sure? Here, let me help."

"Nope," I said sharply. "It's okay. I got this. Just a second."

Mom waited for me to either plop my butt down on the couch or injure myself even further in the attempt. From experience I can tell you the chance that either of these would end up happening was 48 percent, with a 2 percent chance that I would succeed at both. I lowered my hand onto the armrest for support and groaned as I slowly lowered myself onto the cushion in a single-leg squat, keeping my left leg as straight as possible. Success, no extra injuries.

The second my butt hit the couch, Mom pulled over a chair, first aid kit already in hand. She laid it down on the cushion next to me, sat down, and, almost instinctually, opened the kit and pulled out the hydrogen peroxide bottle, aka the "brown bottle of death."

"Hold on, Mom. There are some small pebbles underneath the skin in my knee. Those need to come out first."

"You need to clean that before we go digging around in there. Now sit back," she said forcefully.

It was usually a bad idea to ignore Mom's commands, especially when Dad was around, but I did anyway and leaned so far forward that I was only inches from my wounded knee.

"Do we have any tweezers, Mom? What about a small pair of scissors? I'm going to need to cut some of this skin off too."

Frustrated, she fumbled around in the first-aid box but could only find a pair of tweezers.

"I'll be right back," she said. "I have a pair of small scissors in our bathroom."

She shot up from the chair and walked out of the kitchen and down the dark hallway toward her bedroom.

"Don't touch it until I get back," she said as she disappeared into the darkness, her voice fading in intensity the closer she got to her room. "You could get an infection if you get it dirty."

Dirty. Shit, it's been filled with dirt and grime for hours now. Keeping true to my rebellious nature, however, I squinted to get a better look at my knee as soon as she rounded the corner. I pulled back on a piece of skin, allowing a small trickle of fresh blood the opportunity to escape from the wound and dribble down the back side of my calf. The skin pull-back exposed several tiny pebbles, still buried beneath the folds of skin, along with some stubborn dirt the shower was unable to wash away.

"Dang it," I whispered.

"Heck of a crash, Matt," my dad said, walking back in the room after retrieving my bike from the car. "I took a look at it while you were in the shower." He sighed. "You're right. Bike's pretty messed up. Look at the bright side though. At least you didn't break another bone."

My parents were used to broken bones. I was only seventeen and had already snapped seven of them. Mark added several to the family tally over the years as well. So many bones were broken between the two of us that if my parents had had the forethought to invest in plaster, say in 1980, they might have been pretty wealthy by now. My sister and youngest brother Shaun, however, still to this day, have never added to this terrible tally. Their skeletons are unbroken. Mark and I, apparently, the only ones willing to participate in this "contest."

"Yeah, that's the worst part," I said. "Don't know if I'm going to be able get it fixed. It looks too trashed to repair."

I let out a sigh and shook my head.

"It's too dark to see if the frame is cracked or dented, but if it is, it's as good as junk," Dad said.

"Well, I know the forks are bent. I'll have to take a look at it tomorrow to see how bad."

I leaned back into the couch, grimacing. My dad continued.

"It might not even be worth spending the money to fix it if the forks are bent. That probably means part of the frame is too."

"Yep, probably so," I replied sadly. A sudden spike of pain hit my knee, forcing me to suck in a breath of air through thinly pursed lips. "Man, it's starting to hurt quite a lot now. Tomorrow is not going to be a good day, at all."

"Probably not. But it could have been worse. You want something to drink?"

I gently pounded the armrest and let out another sigh.

"Dang it," I said, frustrated. "No. Thanks, Dad. I just want to get this stupid knee cleaned out."

Almost on cue, I heard Mom's quick footsteps coming back toward the kitchen, getting louder with every stride. She appeared in the living room carrying a small pair of manicure scissors, a towel over her shoulder, and a book of matches.

"These should work," she said.

Mom slowly let out a sigh as she sat back down in the chair and got herself situated, shooting me an all-to-familiar "I can't believe you got yourself into this kind of mess again" look. She grabbed the tweezers and laid them down next to the scissors on her lap. After tearing one of the matches from the book, she lit it, then ran the flame up and down the cutting edges of the scissors. The steel turned black with soot, and when the flame died down, she shook the match out with a quick whip of her hand and dropped it on the linoleum floor. Out of the corner of my eye I could see Dad wasn't thrilled about that, but he—very intelligently mind you—kept his mouth shut. *Not the right time, Dad. Not the right time.* Mom was not in the mood to be challenged at the moment. She reached over, grabbed a piece of gauze from the first aid box, and carefully wiped the scissors clean.

"Lay out a piece of gauze on the couch," she said, matter-of-factly.

I laid out a piece of gauze and she placed the sterilized pair of scissors on top of it. She tore another match from the book, lit it, and repeated the sterilization procedure with the tweezers, afterward dropping the spent match next to the other one on the floor. After wiping the tweezers clean, she laid them next to the scissors and wiped her hands on the towel.

"I can take care of it, Mom," I offered, leaning forward and reaching for the newly sterilized tools. Mom wasn't having any of it. She tossed the towel back over her shoulder.

"Don't touch it," she said aggressively, then sucked in a calming breath, centering herself. Mom sure hated doing this "body repair" dance. All she ever wanted was for all of us kids to have fun, but not get injured. It stressed her out and filled her with worry. I knew it, my siblings knew it, we all knew it. But it seemed we just couldn't help ourselves. It all came with the territory, I guess. We had to do something to keep busy. Dad would only let us watch so much TV, and he limited our Nintendo time to what we considered ridiculously low levels. The rest of our leisure time needed to be "productive." This could take many forms: learning a new skill, reading a book, building something, or simply playing outside. We typically engaged in the latter, and that came with consequences.

"Just sit back. I'll need to cut some of that loose skin away first to get at the rocks. Give me the scissors," she said.

I leaned over quickly, reaching for them.

"And don't touch the blades."

"I won't, Mom. I got it."

I picked them up by the handles and handed them over. She grabbed them with her right hand, being careful not to touch the blades either.

"All right. Now relax," she said.

"Please be careful, Mom. It's sensitive and it hurts," I whined. A wave of embarrassment washed over me at how wimpish I sounded. But it did hurt, and I knew this wasn't going to make it feel any better.

Scissors in hand, she scooted a few inches closer, the feet of the chair grinding on the linoleum as it skidded across the floor. She yanked the towel from her left shoulder and held it behind my knee with her left hand.

"I know, but this has to be done. Now grab the bottle of hydrogen peroxide and pour some of it over your knee."

I let out a sigh.

"Can you do it, Mom?" I asked pathetically. "I don't want to."

"Fine. Here, take the scissors."

I took them and leaned back, holding the handles against my leg with my right hand, the blades sticking straight up in the air. She picked up the "brown bottle of hellfire and pain," (That's not what it's called, obviously, but it should be.) pointing the top of the bottle in my direction.

"Open it," she said.

I twisted off the cap and laid it next to me on the couch. I closed my eyes and prepared for the inevitable. Without any level of restraint or warning, she poured the innocent-looking liquid all over the raw, exposed flesh of my knee. So much for the "don't apply this to deep, open wounds" warning printed on the side of the bottle, huh? Too late for that conversation. Sometimes you just can't stem the ingrained traditions of your mother.

The wound sizzled and bubbled furiously, emitting an odor of burning flesh and sterilization. The smell reminded me of the countless visits I'd made to the hospital over the years. And the agony. Oh my God, the torture! The pain was so intense that it made me think that my mother, my dear, sweet mother, had released an entire hive of hornets loose on my knee, and they were all stinging me at the same time. *Ahem. Hey, Matt? I don't know if you realize this, but you're falling into a hole full of melodrama bullshit, buddy. Why don't we climb out of there, huh? Yeah, that would be great. Toughen up, buttercup.*

"Agghh! Gawd, that stings so bad," I groaned as my head flew back, thumping gently against the wall behind the couch. Grunting through clinched teeth, I instinctually placed my lower thigh in a death grip with my left hand, just above the knee. My raw fingertips burned from the pressure and friction. But at least it distracted me from the pain in my knee.

The initial shock subsided after a few, very long, seconds. Trying to pull myself together and out of the hole of melodrama, I loosened the death grip I had on my leg, allowing the white spots left by my fingertips to return to their natural hue. I pushed back against the urge to grimace and groan, distracting myself watching the pink foaming mix of blood and hydrogen peroxide run down my leg and collect in the towel Mom still had cradled behind my knee.

The pink liquid quickly saturated the towel and started dripping onto the floor. The bubbles died down a few seconds later and Mom poured another waterfall of fire out of the "brown bottle of bullshit." *Man, I have all sorts of names for this stuff, don't I?* This round of pain wasn't as intense, and my reaction less dramatic, but the wound continued its sizzle-and-bubble performance, sounding as if Mom was cooking my knee in a frying pan. The absorption threshold of the towel now at capacity, all of the residue from the washing rapidly started pooling on the floor, soaking the spent, charred matches beneath it. Without saying another word, my mom dropped the wet towel right in the middle of the growing pink puddle, placed the bottle of hydrogen peroxide on the floor, then stuck her hand out.

"Give me the scissors."

I did, without comment.

"Grab that piece of skin and pull it back," she said, pointing at the largest flap of skin near the outside of my knee with the tip of the scissors.

"Okay," I said.

I leaned forward, figured out a way to grab hold of the wet flap of skin with shaky fingers, and gently pulled the skin out and away from my knee, exposing a dark line of embedded dirt and several tiny pieces of small rocks.

"Now hold it there and don't let go," she commanded.

"Okay. Be careful."

"Just don't move."

"I won't. Just be careful."

"Will you just . . . "

Mom stopped mid-sentence and glared at me. That was her way of saying "Shut the hell up" without having to say it. So I did. She was the only one holding the sharp, pointy scissors, after all.

I held my breath and watched her slowly cut away the largest piece of loose skin, slicing it off as close to the knee as she possibly could. She was deliberate in her movements, but gentle. Having three injury-prone boys, this wasn't her first rodeo and she didn't even flinch as she performed the little in-home surgery.

She finished cutting through the largest flap of skin, and I dropped it on top of the mounting pile of spent matches and blood-soaked towels. She continued with the process, removing progressively smaller flaps of skin and exposing a plethora of dirt and tiny rocks in the previously covered crevice, and I continued to add them to the mounting pile of biohazard waste on the floor. She didn't say a word as she worked. She didn't shake. She didn't freak out. She just did what she does best: take care of me. There must be a little bit of doctor in every mother's DNA.

"Okay. I think that's enough. Give me the peroxide," she commanded, handing over the scissors.

"Again? Really, Mom?"

"Hey, don't get mad at me. This isn't my fault. I'm just trying to help you out and get this cleaned. Do you want it to get infected?"

"No."

In her concentration, she must have forgotten that she had placed the bottle on the floor. I leaned over, picked it up, and, reluctantly, handed it over. As we exchanged the bottle, she looked over at Dad, sitting at the dining room table.

"Glenn, can you get me another clean towel and a bowl of water?"

Without saying a word, he got up and trotted off to the kitchen.

I took in a deep breath and held it as Mom took the "brown bottle of hellfire" from me. She rinsed the wound again with yet another large gush of the innocent-looking liquid, washing away most of the, now exposed, dirt. She returned the bottle to the floor. I was surprised, and relieved, that this rinsing was not nearly as painful as the first couple. I exhaled just as quickly as the hydrogen peroxide bubbles faded from the deep corners of the wound.

"Tweezers," she said.

I handed them over. She began picking out the stubborn pieces of gravel still buried in the deep, tender crevices of raw flesh. Each time she plunged the tip of the tweezers into my skin to reach another buried piece of debris, it felt like she was shooting lightning bolts into the wound. And every time she removed a piece of the mountain, it bled a little more. The bleeding hid the few remaining targets from her, and she couldn't continue without rinsing some of it away. She paused and turned her head toward the kitchen.

"Glenn, I need that towel and water. You coming?" she yelled, her voice dripping with recessed frustration.

"I'm coming," he said hurriedly. "Almost there."

Dad was fumbling around for a bowl in the Tupperware cabinet deep in the bowels of the kitchen, the one room in the house where he was a legitimate foreigner. For my dad, finding a bowl in the kitchen, or anything else for that matter, is like asking my mother to locate the 9/16-inch wrench in the garage. Both of these tasks are going to take a while. He managed to succeed, though. A moment later I watched as he filled up a plastic bowl in the kitchen sink. When he finished, he pulled a clean dishtowel out of the towel drawer, walked both items over, and set the bowl on the floor next to the biohazard pile.

Mom grabbed the towel out of his hand and placed it in the cool water. "Thank you."

Dad silently shuffled back to his seat as Mom rung out the towel and gently placed it over the wound. It's coolness, pleasant and soothing, took some of the sting away. Unfortunately, this only provided temporary relief.

A short time later, she started wiping away some of the blood, using the towel to gently, yet deliberately, scrape dirt out of the hard-to-reach areas. Most of the remaining gunk washed out with minimal pain, at least compared to the piercing lightning bolts delivered by the tweezers, courtesy of Zeus himself no doubt. But, after few more minutes of motherly care, the wound was pretty well cleaned out.

"Looking pretty good now," she said, leaning back in her chair to admire her work. She shook her head from side to side, still in disbelief, or shock. Maybe both. It was hard to tell sometimes. It was impossible for me to believe that anything surprised her anymore. She let out a long sigh as she looked up from the knee and into my eyes. "You need to let this air out for a while. We can put some Neosporin and a dressing on it later, before you go to bed."

"Thanks, Mom," I said.

"You'll be the death of me yet, I tell you."

The look on her face morphed into one of worry and relief, a look only a parent knows how to make. She'd been through a lot with us three boys, and I think she was just happy that we didn't need to spend the night in the hospital . . . again.

"You did great, Mom. Nice and clean. Thank you."

*   *   *

Until recently I'd only ridden mountain bikes. I had the idea that road biking was for the older, less adventurous types. I loved the excitement and element of danger that came with mountain biking and enjoyed not having to worry much about traffic, potholes, police officers, stupid people, and rules. On the mountain trails I was in control, in charge of my own destiny. Well, at least most of the time I was. Every so often, Mother Nature reminded me that I didn't have as much control over my environment as I thought I did, even to the point of putting a cow in the middle of the trail to remind me who's boss. It's every man for himself out there on the trail.

So, a couple of days after the crash, I took the crippled remains of my mountain bike down to the local bike shop; "my" bike shop as it were. Everyone has "their" bike shop, don't they? Well, I did, anyway. I needed to see if it could be repaired, or at least be told by a professional that it couldn't. My hopes weren't high, but it couldn't hurt to ask.

I propped open the front door of the shop and dragged the carcass inside. My knee still limited my range of motion, so I moved around like a wounded animal. The door chime alerted the staff that I had entered, and Steven trotted out from the service area.

"Yo, Matt. What's up?"

Steven was my go-to guy at the bike shop. He was tall, standing about a head taller than me. This doesn't really mean all that much as I only stood five-foot-eight, *in the morning*, but I had to look up when I talked to him. So, to me, that made him tall. He was in his mid-twenties, a handsome man with soft features and shoulder-length blond hair who sported the lean body of an avid cyclist. *Popular with the ladies, I'm sure.* He fit the part of the stereotypical cyclist to a T, complete with sunglass tan lines and exposed veins on his fatless, hairless calf muscles.

"Hey, Steven," I said sorrowfully. "I got something for you. Check this out."

He continued his carefree strut across the sales floor in short, erratic strides, weaving in and out of bike racks and merchandise displays.

"Whatcha got?" He stopped in his tracks when the bike came into view. "Oh shit, man! Woah!"

"Yeah, tell me about it."

"Dude, what happened? You get hit by a car?"

"No. Not a car."

As tradition dictates, the entire "fish story" needed to be told. Cyclist are very much like fishermen in that regard. So I obliged and let Steven in on the whole fiasco. There was plenty of laughter at my expense and a lot of "Oh damns!" and "No ways!" thrown around. Surely by the time I came back to the shop again, the entire community, or at least everyone who worked there, would know what had happened to me, with a bit of embellishment thrown in for good measure, no doubt.

"Woah, man. That sucks, big time." Steven spoke these words slowly, under raised eyebrows and a sorrowful head-nod, with genuine regret and bewilderment, all the while shaking his head in disbelief.

"Sure does. So . . . what do you think? Is she dead, or can she be fixed?"

Steven had been exchanging glances between me and my bike during the entire story, so I'm sure he already had an opinion about what could be, or couldn't be, done.

"Well, shoot man, I hate to say it, but it doesn't look good from here." He grimaced. "But, hey, let's take it back to the service area and take a closer look anyway."

"Okay."

I leaned over to grab the handlebars, but Steven jumped in.

"I got it, man." He chuckled. "You've been through enough."

Steven picked up the bike and carried it over to the service area and threw it on one of the empty bike stands.

After bestowing upon me his heartfelt condolences for the condition of my bicycle, the same bicycle he'd sold me a year earlier, he gave my bike a once-over inspection. It didn't take long for him to inform me, as I expected, that the bike was way beyond repair. The inspection revealed the obvious: the forks were bent, which could be easily remedied with the purchase of a new pair. But the frame was bent too. That was the nail in the coffin for my two-wheeled companion. No easy remedy for that. *Well, bummer.*

With that downer of a conversation out of the way, Steven and I started talking about what kind of mountain bikes were available as replacements. Not long into our conversation, as we walked past the shiny new road bikes on our way over to racks of mountain bikes, the topic switched to road cycling. Well, at least Steven started talking about it. I just listened. Kinda.

Steven was a member of the local road cycling club, a club I didn't even know existed before this conversation, and felt the need to tell me all about it. There was a gaggle of them, about twenty hardcore "roadies," that partnered up for long rides every weekend when the weather was nice. I was told none of them owned mountain bikes, but I found that hard to believe. I mean, what kind of person owns a road bike but not a mountain bike? Anyway, he gushed about how fast they could ride on these skinny-tire bikes and how much fun it was to ride over the mountain roads and into Livermore on Highway 84. He even told me about a seven-day trip he took, on his road bike, by himself, through the Sierra Nevada Mountains. *Crazy weirdo,* I thought.

I had to give it to him, he had a passion for it. A passion I really didn't understand, mind you, but he sure knew how to sell the whole road bike thing. That kind of dedication, and his likable personality, makes it easy, I guess. The conversation was intriguing, I'll admit that. I'll also admit that it got me a little curious too. But it was going to take a lot more convincing to get me to jump to the other side. He did plant seeds of doubt, or should I say, seeds of thought, in my mind though. The more he talked about it, the more I allowed myself to imagine road cycling might actually be something I could get into.

Over the next several weeks, while my body recuperated from the crash, I visited the bike shop several more times, continuing my conversations with Steven about a replacement bike. After my knee healed up enough that it could make it around a pedal rotation without the scabs cracking and bleeding, I walked in looking to "kick some tires," for real this time. Still mostly set on getting another mountain bike, I took several models out for a spin around the neighborhood. I was in that shop so often I didn't even need to leave collateral for test rides, no keys or driver's license. My word was enough. But every time I brought one of the mountain bikes back after a test ride, Steven would try and persuade me to try out some of the road bikes. That was his price of admission. He was wearing me out about it, to tell you the truth. So, partly out of curiosity, and in an attempt to shut him up about it already, I agreed to test ride a few of the road bikes as well.

I didn't want to get hooked, but it didn't take long for me to take the bait hook, line, and sinker. At the very least, the test rides sparked some genuine feelings of freedom and a remedy for my consistent "need for speed." Steven was right. You can ride so much faster on those road bikes than you can on mountain bikes. With their skinny high-pressure tires and large gear ratios, the only limit to your speed was your physical strength and endurance. Contrary to my initial reservations, and much to my amusement, after taking a few of these speed demons out for a spin or two, I was putty in his hands. I made the decision right there, not giving myself the chance to talk myself out of it over the next few days. Because I would, if given the chance. I have a habit of doing that to myself. I bought it. Merry early Christmas to me!

Steven only smiled. "I told you, Matt. You're going to love it, I promise," Stephen said. "I assure you, this is not a mistake. You'll be a road addict in no time."

"I'm a little nervous, Steven. I'll tell you that. This will be quite a change for me. But I'm excited too."

I took a bewildering look at my new road bike leaning against the sales counter.

"Pretty, isn't she?"

"Yeah. She sure is," I agreed. "I can't believe I let you talk me into this."

"Oh, come on. You won't regret it."

"I hope not."

"Tell you what, when you get some miles under your belt, come talk to me. I'll see if some of the other guys will let you tag along on one of our shorter weekly rides."

"Ha. I don't think I'll be at your level for quite a while, bro."

"Hmmph. Well, let me tell you somethin', bro," Steven said sarcastically. "I think you might be over-estimating the abilities of some of the guys I ride with. Let's just put it this way. I'm twenty-six, and I'm the youngest guy in the group, by at least ten years."

"Well, maybe." I smiled. *He obviously doesn't have my Mission Peak companion John in his roadie group. That guy's fifty-two and could probably keep up just fine, might even give Steven here a "ride for his money," if you get my drift.*

"Deal. Congratulation on your new bike. And I'm glad you're all healed up from your crash. You look good."

Stephen stuck his hand out and we had a good shake.

"Thanks, Stephen. Wish me luck."

"I wish you all the luck in the world, man. Have fun out there, and let me know when you are ready to join us for one of the rides."

"I will. Thanks."

Jezebel and I were officially teammates now, she a brand new—fresh off the factory floor—road bike, and me, a brand new—nervous and apprehensive—"roadie." At the time it felt like an odd matchup, but I also felt it wouldn't take long for us to gel. She looked fast, built for speed. And that opened up a whole new world of adventures.

CHAPTER THREE

I turned the key, and the trunk of the Camaro popped open with a "clunk," then slowly raised to its fully open position, the hatchback struts hissing as it rose. I laid down the rear seats so Jezebel would completely fit inside after the hatch was closed. Even with the seats down, Jezebel wouldn't fit fully assembled, so I loosened the quick release skewer and removed the front wheel. I laid her down flat on the black-carpeted upholstery, then tucked the front wheel between the rear of the front passenger seat and the back seat headrest and made my way back inside the house to gather up the rest of my things.

Over the past several days, I'd packed two panniers full of all the essential gear I would need for the three-day ride, and several emergency items I hoped I wouldn't need at all. The essential items were: two pairs of cycling shorts, two cycling jerseys, one pair of cycling leg warmers, one pair of cycling arm warmers, four pairs of cycling socks, one pair of gel-filled fingerless cycling gloves, one pair of full-fingered gloves, one helmet, one pair of Oakley Razor Blade sunglasses, one lightweight windbreaker jacket, one pair of slip-on toe warmers, laminated maps of my pre-planned route, one $10 roll of quarters for phone calls, one bottle of sunscreen, one canister of Carmex, a one-gallon plastic bag full of Cytomax energy drink mix, ten power bars, ten quick energy Gu packets, $200 in cash, and one single-use camera with thirty-six exposures. *Only the essentials, of course.*

The emergency items consisted of one lightweight sleeping bag, two spare tubes, one tube repair kit, one foldable spare tire, one set of three plastic tire changing levers, one spoke tensioner tool, two large plastic garbage bags, and one set of appropriately sized allen wrenches. I also carried an under-the-frame hand pump, snuggly attached under Jezebel's top tube.

I planned to stay for two weeks after arriving at UC Irvine, shacking up in Mo's university apartment, so I shipped down a large box of my regular clothing and other personal items a couple days prior to leaving so they would be there when I arrived. The less weight on the bike, the better.

I carried the packed panniers out to the car, laid them down in the back with Jezebel, and took a final inventory of my gear before closing the trunk. Everything looked in order. I was ready to go, so I shut the trunk and went back inside the house again. This time to get Mark. As I walked up the driveway to the front door, the motion-sensor-activated porch light clicked on, illuminating my mom standing in the open doorway, arms crossed, hair frazzled. She was wearing a teal-colored robe over loose-fitting pajamas.

"Hey, Mom," I whispered.

"Hi," she replied in a tired voice. "You want me to make you some breakfast? Do you need any food for the trip?"

I tried to be quiet enough not wake anyone, but should have known Mom would be up to see me off anyhow. There was no way I was getting out of Dodge without her knowing about it and seeing me off. I could have floated out of the house as silent as a ghost and she would have still woken up. I guess her light sleeping is partially my fault anyway, so it's kinda stupid for me to criticize her about it. After I sneaked out of the house in the middle of the night more than once during my high school years, it was impossible for her to sleep soundly through the night anymore. But putting all of the blame on myself wouldn't be fair. Mark probably woke her up, innocently enough, when he flushed the toilet. Yeah, that sounds reasonable. I'm going to go with that.

"Na. I think I'm good, Mom. Thanks. I drank a glass of milk and ate some granola already. I'm okay for now."

"There's eggs. And I have lots of snacks."

"Really, Mom. I'm good. I don't want any extra weight on the bike anyway. I'll eat as I go."

"Okay. You sure?"

"Yes. I'm fine, Mom. Thanks."

Mark suddenly appeared behind her.

"You ready, man?" he asked drowsily, gazing at me over Mom's right shoulder through tired eyes, buried deep under the bill of a baseball hat.

"I think so. Shall we?"

"Yeah. Come on. I want to get there and then come get back into bed," he said, grunting tiredly.

"Dude, you're going to be wide awake in like twenty minutes."

"Maybe. But right now, I'm tired."

"Okay. Let's go." I smiled.

"Please be careful," Mom said, her voice filled with concern and worry.

Mark scooted by her sideways and walked right by me, sinking his hands deep into his Irvington High School sweatshirt pocket. He walked slowly out to his Camaro and fired it up. The engine roared to life, and he let it warm up at idle. I looked over my shoulder and watched him make his way to the back of the car and gaze in through the rear window at my stuff, most likely checking to see if I left any grease marks on the carpet. No immediate complaints, so I must have done an acceptable job. Lucky for him, I kept my bike as clean and maintained as he kept his car. Both tuned to perfection and clean as a whistle.

I turned back to Mom.

"Don't worry, Mom. I'm going to be okay, really. I got through Marine Corps training. This should be a breeze, and I'm expecting it to be a whole lot of fun."

I smiled reassuringly.

"I know. I know. I'm just worried. Will you call me along the way?"

"Yes, Mom. I'll call, every night. I promise. I have a whole roll of quarters just for that purpose."

"Here, take this." She reached into the pocket of her robe and pulled out a $20 bill. "Now you'll have plenty of money for phone calls." She smiled.

"That's okay, Mom. I have plenty of cash for the trip," I said.

"Just take it," she said.

"Shoot, if you don't want it, I'll take it. I could use it to fill up the car," Mark said from behind me. "Come on, man. Let's go."

I took the twenty and put it in my pocket.

"Thanks, Mom."

She reached out and gave me a big hug.

"Say hi to Mo for me when you get there. And please call me. Be careful."

"I will, Mom. Love you."

"I love you, too," she said, her voice cracking. No tears this time, though. That was good. *She's getting better at that.* Nothing rips your heart apart more than when your mother sheds tears because of something you did, or for something you are about to do. I don't care how much of a man you think you are. She'd already shed enough of them on my account when I left for the Marines. But this was different. She was worried, and legitimately so. I think most mothers would be. Highway 1 isn't the safest of roads, especially for cyclists. I knew it, and she did too.

We parted, and I walked around to the passenger side of Mark's car, got in, and buckled up. I pulled on the handle and the door shut with a solid "thump." I took one final look behind me at all my gear in the back seat. *Everything looks good to go man.*

Mark didn't waste any time at all getting out of the neighborhood. He threw the car in reverse and we were out of the driveway and into the middle of the street in a matter of seconds. As we took off down the street, I waved back at Mom through the passenger window. Following a long-time family tradition, she returned my goodbye wave from the edge of the porch, refusing to go back inside until we were out of sight.

CHAPTER FOUR

It was hard to contain my enthusiasm now that we were on the road. I was way more awake than I should have been and couldn't wait to get in the saddle and start pedaling.

"Well, shit, man. I guess I'm really doing this, huh?" I said eagerly, bouncing in the passenger seat from nervous excitement as we merged onto I-880 South toward San Jose.

"Yeah. Looks like it. Hope you have a good time," Mark replied, not sounding nearly as tired as he did when we left the house.

"I hope so. I don't see why I wouldn't. Weather should be nice for the next few days too, so that'll help."

Full of excitement and anticipation, I clicked on the radio. Guns N' Roses' "Welcome to the Jungle" was well under way and came blasting through the speakers.

"Dude! Too early. Too loud," Mark said through a frown, his voice barely audible over the music.

He reached over and turned the music down about halfway. Mark might have been tired and not in the mood for loud music this early in the morning, but he was always in the mood for speed. He pushed the Camaro's accelerator all the way to the floor, opening up all six cylinders and hitting the speed limit well before exiting the on ramp. The back of my head slammed into the headrest as we merged onto the freeway.

"Car's pretty fast, man, for a six-cylinder. Still can't believe Dad lets you

133

park it in the driveway." I smiled and let out a chuckle.

"Hey, this six-cylinder's taking you where you need to go, so I'd watch it, buddy," he responded sharply. "And Dad's a softy for cars, you know that. Yeah, he put on his little Fords-are-the-best-muscle-cars-in-the-world show when I brought this home. But he respects all muscle cars, and it didn't take him long to reconsider. His Mustangs get the royal treatment in the garage, though."

"Yeah, I don't see your Camaro ever getting a parking spot in there," I said.

"Nope. Not even going to ask," he agreed.

We cruised a little faster than the posted speed limit for a couple miles, still traveling south on I-880. It was the calmest time of day to be driving around here. Shoot, the pre-dawn hours on a Saturday were the calmest time of the week to be driving. Traffic so light it was virtually non-existent. The emptiness was eerie and felt like we weren't even supposed to be there, like there was a curfew in place or something. In 1994, this basically meant there was hardly a soul out on the road. Not surprising really, as most of this area, now known as Silicon Valley, was farmland and open space at the time, dotted with the occasional office building and small business. The most significant attractions were Great America and the yearly air shows at Moffit Field.

When I was a pre-driving teenager, my mom would drop me and my friends off at Great America and we would get the most out of the long summer days riding the fastest roller coasters in the Bay Area, scamming on girls, and eating food only teenagers could enjoy. We got the most out of our season passes, that's for sure. Ah, fun times!

Once a year my dad would take the whole family to the summer air shows at Moffit Field to watch the Blue Angels fly and check out all of the aircraft. I remember squinting into the sky during the show, always having trouble finding where the jets were. I could hear the booming of the engines moving across the sky, but the jets never seemed to be where the sound of their engines indicated they should be. I found that frustrating, and fascinating. My dad, always looking for an excuse to rain down a little scientific knowledge on us, used it as an opportunity to give me my first lesson on the physics of atmospheric sound travel and the Doppler Effect. There was always a lesson to be learned.

We soon merged onto CA-17 S toward Santa Cruz. Time to head over the mountains. We passed through the city of Los Gatos and immediately started climbing the eastern side of the Santa Cruz Mountains, and didn't stop until we hit the summit. It was a calm morning, and the drive was pleasant and peaceful, but not pleasant enough to forget about the dangers of this road. The need to pay attention when driving Highway 17 over the Santa Cruz Mountains cannot be overstated. Deceptively safe, its danger lies in its most favorable attribute, the beauty of the drive itself. The mountain pass is breathtakingly alluring, but you should enjoy it from the passenger seat. The beautiful trees and eye-popping vistas pluck your gaze away from the highway any chance they get, pulling them into a roadside forest of oak and redwood. It's hard not to get sucked in, trust me.

Highway 17 is a narrow and curvy four-lane highway with two lanes in each direction separated by a beefy concrete center divide. It snakes up, around and over the woody mountain range for about twenty miles. Tall redwood trees, densely packed together like an overcrowded high school gymnasium, stand strong in groves along both sides of the highway, sharing the mountain with various species of California Native Oaks. Together they saturate the steep slopes, hardly leaving enough open space for anything other than small shrubbery and grass to take root. If you happen to roll your windows down, the sweet smell of pine and damp forest duff fills your vehicle. Only those with the greatest willpower can resist the urge to breathe deeply. When you do, you think you've just driven through the gates of heaven. But be careful, dear traveler; its beauty is dangerous and comes with a price. Those who don't show enough respect may actually end up there.

California highways are notorious for weaving their way around mountains. Very rarely does one go through a mountain or attempt an aggressive climb over one. Highway 17 is no different. There's hardly a straight length of road longer than a quarter of a mile over the entire mountain. The highway sweeps right and then immediately cuts left, wreaking havoc on people suffering from bouts of motion sickness. While maneuvering your way through one turn, the next twist in the road is almost always in sight, but you can't see too far into it as the densely packed trees along the side of the highway obstruct your view. On a constant trajectory up or down, the road follows the same trajectory as a Wall Street stock-market graph: lots of peaks and valleys on the way to the top, or the bottom.

If you approach the summit from the east, you're likely driving headstrong into ground-hugging fog. In the youthful part of the day, before the sun's had a chance to bake away the encroaching marine layer, fingers of pale grey fog spill over the mountain ridgelines like cold honey, slowly tumbling down the inland slopes and drainages towards the valley floor, drowning the tall coastal pines in an ocean of mist along the way.

In the evening, when the fog is thin and the sun creeps ever more closely to the horizon, its radiant amber glow becomes amplified by the water in the air. Like an irregularly flashing strobe, the sunlight blinks wildly between the trees as you drive past. This phenomenon can create a situation of limited visibility, which could drop your field of view to dangerous levels in a matter of a few hundred feet.

We arrived at the foot of the mountain about 5:30 a.m. It was still dark out, but a glimmer of dawn's first light was starting to break. Notwithstanding the intrinsic dangers of the highway, Mark navigated over the mountain in light traffic with no issues. The lack of cars and absence of fog made for an uneventful jaunt.

We shared small talk along the way, chatting mostly about our high school years, reminiscing about football games and old friends. I shared some of my Marine Corps training stories too, finding the ones relating to drill instructor/recruit interaction the most entertaining. Infinitely entertaining for sure, but they—usually—related to important lessons, for Marines and civilians alike.

*　　　*　　　*

One of the most popular lessons I learned in Marine Corps Boot Camp was about unity, and looking out for my fellow man. The experience took place on the illustrious hump to the summit of Mt. Motherfucker, a real bitch of a climb located in the backcountry of the Camp Pendleton, a West Coast Marine Base. The climb is a rite of passage for the brave—some say crazy— souls that choose the Marine Corps as their branch of service. Every recruit needs to reach the summit during their quest to earn the prized Eagle, Globe, and Anchor. Many rumors surrounding the trek's allure are true. The ascent is a long, gradually slog of a hike, with several steep inclines sprinkled in for good measure. As if the length and steep inclines weren't enough to make it a real pain in the ass, someone, Satan most likely, thought it would be a good idea to scatter sand in some of the not-so-steep areas. And I'm not talking just a sprinkle of it, either. I'm talking about sand deep enough that your boots sink an inch or two with every step, making traction difficult. I'm not sure of this, but I wouldn't be surprised if they flew a helicopter over the trail and dropped piles of that shit all over the place just to screw with us. No easy steps, not on this mountain, not in this challenge.

Rumor has it the mountain got its informal name from the most common word used to describe the piece of dirt while one of the poor bastards was climbing it. When viewed from afar it doesn't look all that difficult of an ascent. It actually appears quite manageable, as most things do from a distance. Once your boots hit the dirt though, and you start putting one foot in front of the other, fully loaded down with battle gear and a rifle, the previously tight formation begins to fracture. It's inevitable, really. No matter how loudly the drill instructors yell to keep the formation tight, the ranks inevitably break under the relentless hardship. Guaranteed. Every time. The drill instructors know this, but it's their job to make you realize there is strength in numbers and getting separated from your team can get you and your teammates killed. It's an important lesson, one of many to be learned.

The fit recruits can, and frequently do, reach the summit significantly faster than the not so fit or less mentally strong. It gives your ego a little pat on the back. And that's all good for the individual, but not so much for the drill instructor meeting you at the top of the mountain. See, the problem is, the Marine Corps isn't about the individual. When you're alone, you're weak, and that makes you vulnerable. True strength resides in your ability to work as a team to accomplish the mission, usually a very dangerous one. The drill instructors will make sure you understand that. One way or another. I found one version of that understanding when I reached the summit . . . alone.

*   *   *

"Well, well. Lookie here. If it isn't Captain fuckin' America!" The drill instructor snarled at me through a sadistic grin as I pushed through the last few painful steps to the summit plateau. "Good for you, maggot! You made it to the top, all by yourself. I'll make sure to tell your mama that you were one of the first to make it up here. Oh, and the first to get killed too! Maybe she'll even bake you a pie for your efforts. Wouldn't that be wonderful?" I didn't respond, just stood at attention like a good little recruit, swaying with exhaustion. "Look around, dummy. You see anyone else up here?" The drill instructor invited me to survey the area with a sweep of his right arm. "No? Oh, okay. Sweet. Let's hang out then, shall we? Pull up a chair, mate. Come on, don't be shy. There's a show to watch. Can I offer you a pina colada? Oh! Wait a minute, you're a beer man, aren't ya? How 'bout a massage while you wait for everyone else to get the fuck up here? Then maybe we can all sit down together for dinner. Wouldn't that be nice?"

The drill instructor stopped his sarcastic rant and pressed his lips together tightly beneath his perfectly creased cover, his dark eyes never deviating from mine. Streaks of sweat ran down his cheeks on their way to the collar of his perfectly tailored camouflaged blouse, pausing momentarily only when encountering one of the protruding veins on his dirty neck.

"No, sir!" I was breathing so hard I had to separate each word into its own breath.

"Well, ain't that perfect." This would have been a question in the civilian world, but the drill instructor worked his magic and turned it into a statement. "Now you're just a pretty little target for some sniper across the valley to take aim at! What a waste of all that effort to get up here first." He paused. "Where's your support, shit-for-brains?"

Dang it. I'd messed up. I knew it now.

"Down the mountain, sir." I replied.

"Holy shit!" The drill instructor jumped back in an exaggerated display of keystone cop astonishment. "Look at you! All the sudden the clouds have parted and you've turned into a damn genius. I think I'm going to recommend you for promotion to the CIA. How 'bout that? Albert Einstein's got nothing on you, huh?"

I wished he hadn't added "huh?" to the back end of that sentence. Without it, it was but a humble statement, easy to reply with an equally humble "no sir," or better yet, no response at all. With it, it was a question. *Why do they always do that? Sometimes I just don't know if they want an answer or not.* And now I had to answer it. The drill instructor paused, raised his hands from his waist and crossed his thick arms below his massive barrel chest. I said nothing. But my silence didn't make it disappear. The question hung in the air like an apple dangling from a branch just out of reach. Both "Yes, sir" and "No, sir" would be the wrong answer.

"Sir . . . This recruit doesn't . . ."

The drill instructor cut me off with a yell, lurching toward me.

"Hey! Hey!" He dragged the words out so long he needed to fill his lungs with air before continuing. "Shut your pie hole Koehler!" He bent over at the waist to add emphasis to his unending rant. "Shit, you're a squad leader for Christ's sake. Well, at least you were before this stunt. You're fired!" He paused for another deep breath. "Your team is down the mountain and you're standing up here all by your fucking self? Do you want a cookie? Chocolate chip? Snickerdoodle? How 'bout a glass of milk? Would you like that? Well, I don't give cookies to dead men! Now hike back down that fucking mountain and help the rest of your crew. You will keep moving until all of your teammates are up here! Do you understand me, you stupid cock-sucker?"

"Yes, sir."

Before I could turn around, the drill instructor took another step forward and butted the edge of his cover with the edge of my helmet. *Oh God, please don't let his cover fall to the ground. If it does, you'd better catch it before it hits the ground, Matt.* He glowered at me, his eyes peering through me like I wasn't even there. I didn't dare look at them. I stared straight ahead, breathing heavily, but only through my nose to avoid breathing on him. His tightly clinched teeth were mere inches from my eyes. They appeared bright white behind his dark skin. I could smell his breath and dripping sweat, neither of them appealing. His mouth moved only enough to make himself heard.

"I didn't hear you. Did you say something? Here, let me spell it out for you . . . do-I-make-my-self-clear?" he growled.

His spittle splattered on my face and mixed with the sweat dripping from every one of my pores.

"Yes, sir!"

"Yes, sir, what?"

"This recruit heard you clear, sir!"

His growl now morphed into a full yell.

"Ahhhhh! If even one of them doesn't make it, I will hold you accountable, and you will pay. Do you understand?"

At the top of my lungs, I screamed. "Yes, sir!"

"Then why the fuck are you still here? Get down that mountain and bring your brothers to the top. And tell Richardson he's been promoted to Squad Leader. Go. Now!"

"Aye aye, sir!"

And with that, the ass-reaming was over. I did exactly as I was told, several other quickly ascending recruits following suit. They had the advantage of overhearing the ass-chewing and—very intelligently—turned around immediately upon reaching the summit.

The entire platoon made it, a few leaving the contents of their breakfast as a sacrifice to the mountain, but we all made it, nonetheless. An important lesson was learned that day, and the drill instructor at the top of the hill never said another word about it. He made his point, and he knew it. Marines are conditioned from the start to be the best, so getting to the top in the first group, or as a lone wolf, is noted by your drill instructors. They like seeing that kind of self-dedication and self-motivation in their future Marines. However, what is truly important, the pinnacle of all Marine Corps training, is that it's not about "the self," it's about the notion that no Marine will ever be left behind, that you will suffer for your brother-in-arms. If you're fit enough to reach the top while some of your future Marine brothers were still struggling with the mountain, you had better be marching your ass back down to help them, or die trying.

*   *   *

After cresting the summit, we started our descent toward the ocean. The closer we got to the sea, the more drastically the terrain began to change. The progressive transition from dense forest to the more open terrain of the lower sandhills happened quickly. Ponderosa pines, native coastal shrubs, and wildflowers dotted the lower elevations, intermingling with the growing density of houses, businesses, and side roads that branched off the highway like veins on the top of a hand. Even the smell in the air changed. The subtle onshore breeze, carrying with it the salty, organic scent of the Pacific Ocean, pushed the earthy smell of the forest up the mountainside and away from the coast.

We exited CA-17 at the base of the mountain and headed south on Highway 1, following the western edge of the continent. Shoot, with the state of mind I was in, it might as well have been the edge of the world, a world I had made simple for the immediate future. There was only one goal: get to UC Irvine in three days. That was it. Nothing else mattered.

Ah, the famous Pacific Coast Highway. Over the next three days I was going to become intimately familiar with this treasured shoreline and the highway that follows it. The Pacific coastline, traversing the jagged western edge of North America, is known by many to be one of the most beautiful coastlines in the world. Dangerously harsh, the rocky terrain protects most of the Northern California coastline, stretching all the way from the southern end of Monterey Bay to the northern border of Santa Barbara. From there, all the way south to Mexico, everything changes. It's like the continent had a change of heart and actually wanted people to come and enjoy what the ocean has to offer. The ocean warms with every mile traveled south, inviting everyone to the western edge of America with promises of wide sandy beaches and so much sunshine that every so often you catch yourself wishing for a passing cloud.

*   *   *

I settled on Capitola as my push off point. This quaint beachfront town lies just south of Santa Cruz, a few miles past Twin Lakes and Pleasure Point. It's a laid-back town, home to retirees, surfers, and coastal vagabonds. The social contrast is stark at times, but taken together they all add something unique to the town's charm and allure. I was quite familiar with the area, having spent countless memorable days over the past several years chilling out with my best friends on its beaches. We burned the salty daylight hours bodysurfing its gentle breaks, gliding into shore riding the whitewater on "borrowed" Taco Bell serving trays. *I say "borrowed," but I don't think we ever really asked. Don't hate me for it, please.* They were the perfect size and shape to use as rudders; we couldn't help ourselves. When the surfing bug bit us, which happened quite often, we headed north to Santa Cruz and tried to work our way into the lineup at Steamers Lane, attempting to catch one of these famous rides into shore while trying our best not to get our faces bashed in by local surfers who accused us of stealing "their" wave.

No matter the activity, our days were full and, inevitably, they soon gave way to night. When we didn't feel like taking the long drive home, we would slip into our sweats and hoodies and spend the night camped out under the stars on the beach, curled up in blankets and telling jokes and stories around a burning log in the sand. At some point late into the night we would eventually, and illegally, drift off to sleep on top of the cool sand, our bodies wedged precariously against the ice plant–laden sandstone cliffs. The soft hissing of the nearby surf gliding gently across the sand would ultimately sing us into slumber. As we drifted off, our small beach fire would slowly burn down to ash, relinquishing ownership of the darkness to the moon and stars.

I couldn't think of a more appropriate location to start the trip, an homage to my history there. Santa Cruz would have worked too. The land between these two towns, this small stretch of coastline where Maureen and I spent some of our final moments of the previous summer, was a summertime fantasyland for us, a coastline playground of shining memories that define some of the best days of my life. Really, it was the perfect place to begin this journey.

On one of these memorable days before Mo went back down to school to start her senior year at UC Irvine, both of us, and my best friend, Matt, drove to Santa Cruz to enjoy the day. As usual, surfing or boogie boarding was on the agenda. We didn't bring our surfboards this time, so the decision was made for us. We parked near a rocky beach just south of Steamers Lane, where the tail end of some of the best waves on the west coast finished their journey. The weather was perfect, the kind of day you hope for when thinking about spending the day at the beach. The sun was out, the day was warm, and the onshore breeze pushed the cool, salty air of the great Pacific gently across our skin. Seriously, a perfect day. We walked out to a cliff overlooking the famous Steamers Lane to check out the surfing conditions. The waves were decent but not scary enough to frighten away a bunch of amateurs like ourselves. We were boogie boarding anyway, and the conditions were ideal for that.

"Looks good, man," I said, glancing at Matt for his consensus on the matter, my arms outstretched toward the ocean like I was offering up the whole thing to him as a gift. He didn't immediately say anything, but the smile on his face told me everything I needed to know.

Matt was standing on my right with his hands in his pockets, lost in a moment, his oversized T-shirt fluttering gently between his forearms in the light breeze. He always got like this when he looked out towards the edge of the world. His world, my world, our world. I'd never seen anyone so entranced by the sea. It seemed to consume him, turn him into the person he was born to be. He would drop anything to go. And not just to go surfing. It didn't matter what it was. Surfing, body surfing, boogie boarding, fishing, or just hanging out. If you could come up with an excuse to go, he was there. The ocean was like a magnet. It pulled on him, drew him in. On many occasions he dragged me to Santa Cruz when I really wasn't feeling the urge to go. Truthfully, it's not that I didn't want to be there. I just didn't want to drive there sometimes, especially in the evening. Never, not even once, did I regret being dragged along, though. He was, and is, always willing to share his love of the beach, and of life, with anyone that is willing to let him. Thank goodness for his persuasive tendencies. Outside of my life with Maureen, Matt has been the cornerstone of many happy memories.

I turned to Mo, who was standing on my left, eyebrows raised in anticipation.

"Looks nice," she said, beaming.

"Darn right it does!" answered Matt suddenly. He pulled his hands from his pockets and stretched his arms out wide, mirroring mine. He took in a deep breath through his nose, breathing in the ocean air like he was sniffing a bouquet of roses. "Smells like I need to get in the water. Come on, Haole Boy! Let's move."

Mo laughed at Matt's playful outburst and grabbed hold of my arm.

"Shall we?" I asked her.

"Hell yeah!" she said.

We took off running back to Matt's old, beat-up Vanagon and rummaged around inside for our wetsuits. We stripped down to our underwear and pulled our wetsuits on, right there in front of God and everyone. We didn't care. Shit, people walked around practically naked in this town and nobody even gave them a second look, so what did we really need to worry about? Matt danced around in the parking lot in his boxers for a fleeting moment, singing some kind of Pearl Jam tune, while Mo and I struggled with our wetsuits, attracting the attention of a few onlookers and making everyone laugh. He laughed too. He could care less, and so did we, and that's exactly how it needed to be.

My buddy Matt was always the life of the party. I've never met a man who knew how to enjoy life more than him. After squeezing into our wetsuits, we snatched our boogie boards out from behind the rear seat, walked down the heavily used stairway behind the iconic surfer sculpture at West Cliff Drive, and made our way down to the shallow rocky beach. Matt was the first one in the water. The three of us followed and spent the next couple hours enjoying the cold Pacific Ocean and the gentle waves she shared with us. And we did not get punched in the face. That helped to make it a good day, a very good day.

The memories surrounding this place are fruitful. Not so much because of the place itself, but the people I spent time with when I was there. They reflect countless moments of unbridled happiness and long-lost adolescent innocence. What a gifted opportunity I had sharing these experiences with Mo before springboarding full-speed into my 20's. To bring her into the fold and build on the memories of this cherished place felt so natural it was hard to believe it all wasn't meant to be.

To the thoughtful type, riding down the coast to reunite with Mo in Southern California, connecting two places that will eventually define so much of our young life together, might be interpreted as destiny. I guess there's some merit to that, but personally, I wouldn't raise the experience to that level of introspection. I'm not one that holds too much stock in fate, believing much of what you want in life comes less from happenstance or luck and more from purpose and fortitude. But, sometimes, things line up in such a way that explanations fall short.

Matthew Koehler

CHAPTER FIVE

The start of my journey didn't need to be dramatic. It wasn't the start of a race or a benefit fundraising event or something like that. It wasn't even the result of a schoolhouse dare or a macho Marine Corps bet. It was just something I wanted to do, a personal challenge. One that carried with it a certain element of difficulty and at the same time harbored a risk of failure. And failure, above all else, especially as a nineteen-year-old Marine, wasn't an option. Unacceptable. "No Fear Koehler." I mean, that's what I was known as in high school. I even had it embroidered on the back of my letterman's jacket. *Don't even think about backing out, Koehler. Just do it man.*

But I wanted to begin the journey at a memorable place, a place that meant something to me and Mo. So I asked Mark to drop me off at a well-known overlook parking lot located on a seaside cliff just north of the Soquel Creek Lagoon Bridge. This particular bridge, which led you into the downtown shopping area of Capitola, would be a unique and memorable push-off point. One that would, at some point down the road—like if I should decide to write a book about the experience someday—bring to the surface fond memories of my past while at the same time creating new ones. Crazy thought, I know.

Mark exited the main highway and maneuvered his Camaro through the narrow streets of the quiet beach town. Both sides of the two-lane street were usually packed with cars parked bumper to bumper, allowing just enough space in the middle of the road for two passing cars to squeeze by each other. Luckily, we didn't have to perform this delicate dance as we were the only vehicle on the road this early in the morning. At the end of the road he pulled into one of several public parking spaces lining the overlook where we were treated to an expansive view of the ocean and much of the town. *Well, would you look at that. We're finally here.*

Although small in comparison to other piers along the California coast, Capitola's wharf sticks out into the shallow bay just far enough to let everyone know they're important. Every coastal town worth its salt has a pier, right? Built with locally harvested timber in 1858, the short and narrow wharf has been repaired and extended multiple times since then, but its quaintness has managed to remain intact, attracting year-round tourists and local fishermen alike. It was a great choice. Even looking at it from behind the windshield inside a climate-controlled car, I knew I'd chosen the perfect, most picturesque spot to kick this whole thing off.

Mark killed the engine and we stepped out of the car. I slid my hands into my jean pockets and adjusted to the change in temperature with a single shiver. The sky was brightening, but it still harbored more of the night than the day. A few resilient stars fought back against the encroaching daylight and shone like lonely fireflies high over the wharf in a clear sky. I took in several deep breaths of the salty air and, with it, memories of days gone by. The air was cool and heavy with humidity, and carried with it the taste of the sea; unique, alive, and energizing. The only sounds greeting us were the lapping of waves on the nearby sand and the muffled hum of passing cars on Highway 1 behind me.

After taking a brief mental survey of the area, I looked around beneath the dim scattered light of nearby streetlamps. A few early risers mingled about. One person sifted around in a trash can on the beach, looking for tossed-away treasures. Another quietly walked down the sidewalk toward the ocean, carrying a surfboard under his arm with his wetsuit pulled up only to his waist, the stiff upper half of it dangling out in front of him and bouncing forward off his knees with every step. It was around 6:30 a.m., and with every passing minute the yet-to-be-seen rising sun was slowly transforming the eastern skyline above the Santa Cruz Mountains from a dreary gunmetal-gray to a welcoming, mood-lifting array of gold, orange, and purple, gradually bringing the day into focus.

Mark broke the silence.

"Man, it's chilly out here," he said as he slipped into his jacket and quickly zipped it all the way up to his chin. "No fog or wind either. That's kinda weird." Mark made his way to the front of the car as he made his weather observations. He stood next to me and put his hands in his jacket pockets. I was already leaning against the wind-beaten wooden railing when he walked up. It creaked against my weight, giving way slightly but holding sturdy. Good thing, too; it was the only thing keeping me from falling fifty feet straight down to the rocky beach.

"Yeah. I figured the marine layer would have moved in already. But there it is." I pointed above the ocean at what looked like a great wall of clouds, ominously parked offshore, threatening to move inland with the rising sun.

Mark looked out over the horizon and shrugged, bumping the jacket higher onto his shoulders. "How long you going to wait until you take off?"

"I think I should get started now," I said. "No time like the present, I guess. If I get as far as I want to today, then I have a lot of tough miles ahead of me."

"Humph. Shouldn't be that bad," Mark replied.

"Maybe not. Weather's cooperating, so that'll help. But I need to get through Big Sur today, and that means I have a lot of climbing to tackle. Definitely not my forte, know what I mean?"

"Yeah, I guess."

I turned away from the beach and faced the car. "Can you pop the trunk?"

"Sure."

We walked to the rear of the car together, and Mark opened the back hatch. I reached in and removed both panniers, setting them down on the sidewalk next to the front bumper, then carefully lifted Jezebel out, placed her upside down on the pavement and attached her front wheel. Once secured, I installed the panniers. These settled in easily with hooks that clicked into place on the rack I installed over the real wheel.

Each pannier was as carefully balanced as possible so there wasn't a drastically unequal distribution of weight over the bike. If you absolutely must put more weight on one side versus the other, put it on the left. This will balance out the weight of the chain and sprocket on the right side. *Okay, Jezebel's ready. My turn.*

I kicked off my shoes, pulled off my sweatshirt, and stepped out of my jeans, then threw everything in the back of the Camaro. Underneath my clothing, I already had on my cycling shorts, socks, and jersey. But it was chilly and I was going to need a little more protection from the cold for a few hours, so I sat down on the curb and pulled on my compression leg warmers before sliding into my cycling shoes. These were essential for cold weather, at least for me. Having no hair on my legs—yes, as Mo and her friends knew very well, I shaved them—they would otherwise get bitterly cold in the chilly early morning air.

"Would you mind taking those home?" I asked.

"Sure," Mark responded.

"Thanks, man. It's finally starting to get light out. I think I'll be abl—"

Mark cut me off.

"Hey, check it out," he said in what came out as an urgent whisper.

I looked up to see him pointing toward the ocean. I turned around and followed his extended finger but didn't immediately see anything extraordinary.

"What am I looking at?"

He wiggled his finger and continued pointing.

"Look straight out and to the left, in the water, past the pier," he said earnestly. He lowered his hand and slid it back into his jacket pocket for warmth.

"I don't see anything," I said, squinting out into the sea.

"Just wait a minute," he insisted.

Before I could say anything else, I received an elbow jab to my upper arm as his voice boomed.

"There!"

Mark's hand whipped out of his pocket and pointed into the ocean again. This time I saw what he was waiting for, clear as day. The sun had risen enough now that I could see all the way out to the stalled marine layer. Under the dim light of early morning I watched the hump of a whale crest the ocean surface. This slowly rising mountain of ocean mammal was close enough to shore, and it was quiet enough outside that I could hear it exhale what sounded like all the air in his lungs, spraying a cloud of mist high over the ocean's glassy surface. It loudly sucked in another breath, and I watched it disappear under the surface again. It left only a ripple in its wake, a temporary imprint of its presence. I couldn't identify what kind of whale it was. All I knew was that it was not a dolphin, and that it was heading south. Maybe it would follow me all the way to Orange County, or I him.

"Well, check that out! That's awesome, man. Looks like I might have me some company on the way down the coast."

"Maybe so," Mark said. After another minute or so of looking out for the whale to resurface, he lost interest and turned back towards the car. By now I was mostly ready to go. I was standing up, leg warmers pulled up to the base of my shorts, cycling shoes on. As I was sliding my hands into fingerless gel-padded gloves, he asked, "You need anything else out of here?" placing his left hand on the hatch and pointing inside the car with his right.

"Still need my helmet and sunglasses. They're on the floor behind the driver's seat."

He let go of the hatch and gathered up the rest of my gear. On his way back, he slammed the hatch shut, then handed over the last of my equipment.

"Thanks," I said.

I slipped the helmet on, clicked it securely under my chin, then tucked the sunglasses into the center of three pockets sewn into the back of my jersey. It was too dark to wear them at the moment, but I knew I would need them soon enough.

"Well, I guess I'm out. Thanks for driving me down, man."

"No problem, bro. Be safe out there, and call if you can."

"Sure thing, brother."

I took a few awkward clip-clop steps in his direction and embraced him tightly.

"Now go home and take a nap," I said.

"Na. I'm too awake now."

"I told you!" I said, smiling.

And that was that. I straddled Jezebel's freshly cleaned frame, clicked into the pedals, and rolled south on Cliff Drive. As I slowly pedaled over the Soquel Creek Lagoon Bridge, I looked back and threw up a wave. He didn't see me, though. He was already walking around to the driver's side of the car, preparing to leave town.

Matthew Koehler

PART THREE

Highway One, My Lonely Friend

Capitola ⟶ San Simeon

CHAPTER ONE

I turned right on Capitola Avenue and slowly rolled through the center of town. Capitola's a sleepy town in October. Most vacationers had gone home for the season, and children were back in school. This seasonal shift in population hands the area back to the locals this time of year, allowing the community a chance to breathe and the land an opportunity to recover from summer's ephemeral injection of mischief and revelry. The busy season takes its toll, and now the slow season was settling in to balance everything out.

On the avenue's west side, brightly colored buildings fashioned in the style of the Italian Riviera, complete with fresco-painted stucco walls and street-level windows, contrasted sharply against the soft neutral tones of sand, driftwood, and sea. They stood out against the landscape just as dramatically this time of year as they did during the summer months, but the colorful contrast aroused less of a draw now that the tourist season was scaling back for the year.

Summer may have passed, but the slowdown in tourism didn't hamper the trendy entrepreneurial spirit of the town. Upscale shops sporting coastal motifs lined the streets nearest the beach, their small sales floors bursting at the seams with seaside-themed merchandise, sometimes even spilling out onto the surrounding sidewalks. Common items for sale include beach-suitable clothing, surfboards, artwork, and fancy ice cream. Yes, even in the cooler months of the year, you can get ice cream here. Several real estate offices dotted the downtown's perimeter, their street-facing windows lined with posters of local properties for sale. Wood-sided houses stuck out from the surrounding hillsides like thumbs. In contrast to the garish nature of the brightly colored riviera-esque beachfront hotels and restaurants, the owners of the hillside homes worked hard to camouflage themselves into the surrounding environment: Hiding among the local foliage seemed to be a popular tactic, consisting of indigenous trees of all sorts and several species of non-indigenous ones, the most popular being the eucalyptus and palm trees.

It was a quiet pre-dawn morning, and most of the town was still sleeping. At least that's the vibe I got as I rolled through. The only sounds I heard were the clicking of Jezebel's freewheel; the shallow rippling of gentle waves on the nearby beach, breaking softly against the sand; and the splashing of seagulls taking a bath in the lagoon. I waved at the lone employee setting up the coffee station at my favorite restaurant in town, Zelda's by the Beach, and coasted past the benches lining the breaker wall at the south end of the beach. Only one person was sleeping on them this morning, a rare event when it's not raining or foggy. *I wonder if the waves ever reach this wall?* Leaving the center of town behind, the sound of a lone sidewalk cleaner spraying water onto concrete echoed off the nearby buildings and through the empty streets, cheering me on my way. *Goodbye, Capitola. See you later.*

I turned left onto Monterey Avenue and took a long, sweeping left-hand turn onto Bay Avenue, pedaling slowly up the road toward the Highway 1 onramp. A quarter mile up the road, on the right-hand side, I passed by the Capitola Dairy Queen, which I'd frequently visited with my buddy Matt during our seaside adventures over the years. I smiled and suddenly had a craving for an ice cream cone.

*   *   *

Matt and I visited this Dairy Queen so often that we got to know the Korean owner, let's just say, a little too well for her liking. I'm pretty sure she would have been much happier without us poking around all the time and causing her grief, unintentional though it was. I think she actually thought we were pretty cool guys, she just couldn't bring herself to show it. She was middle-aged, probably in her mid-fifties, and didn't open the shop until 10 a.m. sharp. But she would arrive sometime in the early morning to get the restaurant ready for the day, and we knew it.

We usually strolled up around 9 a.m., craving a chocolate-dipped soft serve ice cream cone. Slowly pulling our car up to the drive-thru around back, we would sit there and wait for her to come to the window. My buddy Matt would get out of the car, usually from the driver's seat, and knock gently on the window, staring inside through cupped hands. She would recognize him immediately after rounding the corner from the back-kitchen area. The second she saw Matt smiling at her she would throw her hands in the air, then immediately drop them to her hips in exasperation. That's when the performance would begin. She leaned forward and started squawking from behind the glass. I swear, it happened like this every time. She just couldn't bring herself to disappear into the back of the shop and ignore us. She had to stand and fight.

"No! No! We closed! You know already!"

Her voice was muffled by the thick glass of the drive-thru window, but we could still hear every word she was saying.

Matt attempted to bargain and spoke loudly so she could hear him through the glass. He would un-cup his hands from the window and press them together in a praying pose, pleading with a pitiful grin and beseeching eyes.

"I know, I know. But please. We really want some ice cream. Please?"

The woman stood her ground in the middle of the dimly lit restaurant. She refused to give an inch.

"No! It 9 o'clock. Too early. I tell you every time! We closed! Come back 10 o'clock," she would say, frustrated.

Matt persisted. He wasn't a quitter.

"What if we paid double?"

"No! We open 10 o'clock. No ice cream right now. Come back 10 o'clock!" she scowled.

"We can't come back at 10 o'clock. We'll be surfing by then. Please?"

Again Matt pleaded, this time with a pathetic puppy-dog smile that stretched ear to ear, shaking his still-clasped hands forward and back between his chest and the window. No joy. She yelled again, crossing her arms over her chest, her head still leaning heavily to the right.

"Not my problem! You come back when open. Ten o'clock!"

Undeterred by the push-back, he persisted. Matt knew he was going to make this all work out, he always did. He turned around, bent over, and leaned in through the open driver side window. I was still sitting in the passenger seat, staying out of it. He figured he'd reached the breaking point in the conversation.

"I think she's cracking. Almost there! I know what'll get her. Watch this," he said.

She must have thought Matt had finally gone away because in the few seconds it took Matt to tuck his head back in the car to talk to me, she was gone, back to her business. But Matt refused to take no for an answer. The art of charm has always been a shining quality of his. He could convince a mother to give up her child if he wanted to. He was that good. Besides, this wasn't the first time we'd tried to score some ice cream from this lady before 10 O'clock. He walked to the front of the car and, using one hand as a pivot, leaped over the walkway railing adjacent to the drive-thru window and started singing and dancing in front of the restaurant's main entry door without a care in the world.

"You are my sunshine, my only sunshine. You make me happy when skies are gray!"

What a sight. He swayed back and forth, singing at the top of his lungs, not a care in the world and without an ounce of embarrassment, his arms outstretched like he was dancing with someone, twirling round and round. He leaned over the railing and shot me a thumbs-up, then continued.

"You'll never know, dear, how much I love you, please don't take my ICE CREAM away."

I scooted over into the driver's seat and leaned out the open window. I pushed up on the car door frame and stretched my neck to look over the drive-thru tray and through the closed drive-thru window. I couldn't make out any movement in the back room of the Dairy Queen, but there was no way she couldn't hear him singing. Not one to be ignored, Matt continued, this time with a Biz Markie Song, shaking his ass and tapping on the glass entrance door to the rhythm of the song. He was determined to get her attention. Persistence, with a generous side of annoyance, was the recipe he needed to let simmer.

"Oh baby you, you got what I need. But you say he's just a friend, but you say he's just a friend. Oh baby you, you got what I need, I need ICE CREAM, I need ICE CREAM! Oh please please please!"

She couldn't help herself. I watched through the drive-thru window as she came stomping out of the back room and over to the entrance door. Matt threw his arms up in jubilation. He didn't care at all that she was clearly miffed at our inability to leave her alone. She stormed over to him, stopped, and stared at him through the windowed door. Matt extended his arms out wide like he was ready to give her a big old hug. He had her, and he poured on the charm.

"I love you! We love you! You're our favorite ice cream lady! Will you let us have some ice cream for breakfast? Pleasssssssse!" He wasn't on his knees yet, but he was getting ready to do that. His ego had no bounds.

I never saw it, and she would never admit it if you asked her about it, but Matt swears he saw the crack of a smile across her face.

She crossed her arms and stared. Her wall was crumbling under the consistent bombardment of charm, smiles, song, dance, and relentless perseverance. Matt knew it, I knew it, and she knew it. A few seconds later, she uncrossed her arms and pointed at him through the door with her right finger.

"Go sit in car. I come to window."

Matt let out a scream of jubilation and jumped in the air.

"Woo hoo!"

I was all smiles as I watched him single hop back over the railing and run the wrong way up the one-way drive-thru and back to the car, laughing all the way. He knew her soft spot. All it took was a little resilience to break her down. I scooted back over to the passenger seat, and he squished himself back into the car.

"That was amazing, bro. You are definitely a pro," I said.

"At what, getting ice cream at 9:30 in the morning?" He laughed.

"Exactly," I said. "I'll never know how you do that."

"Amazing what you can do when you really want some ice cream," he said, rubbing his hands together in excitement as he shuffled in the seat. "Yeah, baby!"

A couple minutes later, the drive-thru windows slapped open and she leaned out of the window with two slightly dripping chocolate-dipped vanilla soft-serve cones. Matt reached up out of the car window, meeting her halfway. He giggled as he grabbed the dripping cones and handed them over to me. I held them steady as he pulled money out of the center console.

"The ice cream not fully frozen yet. That why it dripping. You guys get going. I don't want others to see. Go. Go. Get away," she said, annoyed. Her hands now free after handing over the ice cream cones, she used them to shoo us down the driveway and out of her parking lot.

"Thank you so much! You're the best ice cream lady ever!" Matt said, handing over a five-dollar bill.

She refused to take the money.

"No. Pay later. I can't open cash drawer yet." She pulled her arms back inside and stood leaning against the counter, a stoic look never leaving her face.

"Well, then this is your tip," Matt said.

"No. Pay later. Now go. Come back after 10 o'clock," she fired back. She leaned back from the counter and reached for the window levers.

"Okay, we'll be back for lunch, or maybe dinner. But this is yours no matter what."

She still refused to take it and started to shut the window.

"Goodbye. Go surfing," she said, glancing out into the street to see if our little "performance" had attracted any unwanted attention.

Matt tossed the bill through the closing window and I watched it flutter past the window latch and into the restaurant, coming to rest on the counter.

"Keep it! We love you! Best ice cream lady ever!"

She slammed the window shut and continued shooing us from behind the glass as we drove away. We waved back out of the car windows and exited the drive-thru ramp. We enjoyed every bite of those dripping ice cream cones. Who cared if it was 9:30 in the morning? Breakfast of champions, right? Or, at the very least, amateur teenage surfers.

CHAPTER TWO

I swear, almost every street around here spawns a memory or two. Truth-be-told, most of the good ones have to do with a little mischief. The Dairy Queen story is only one of many. What can I say? We were teenagers.

There was the time when Matt and I were driving home from Santa Cruz after a long weekend of surfing. While cruising over the mountain summit, the tip of Matt's surfboard suddenly disappeared from view out the front windshield. We watched through the car mirrors in horror, and a tad bit of amusement, as the wind flung it from the top of his car. It tumbled through the air and shattered into what looked like a hundred pieces all over the fast lane. Cars swerved out of its way and braked quickly to a stop. We thought about pulling over, but what was the use? We weren't going to run all over the freeway picking up the pieces. Luckily, as far as we know, no damage was done. Except maybe to one guy. I think we must have hurt his feelings, or something. Several miles down the road, after we had had a good laugh about the whole ordeal, a car pulled up next to us on the driver side and started honking. We looked over to see this guy screaming at us from the driver's seat and pretending to reach into his glove compartment for a gun. *What the fuck, man? Chill the hell out.* He kept making the gun sign with his right thumb and forefinger, insinuating that he was looking to cause us harm. He didn't, and finally went on his way. *Geeze. Relax, man! We should be the angry ones. We lost a nice surfboard.* Remember how I said the greatest danger on Highway 17 was the "other driver"? Yeah, that wasn't a joke.

There were other interesting times as well. Teenagers hanging out in Santa Cruz get tied up in a little mischief from time-to-time, especially when bored; all of it innocent, I assure you. *Wink, wink.* Believe it or not there were moments—just a few, no big deal—when we didn't feel like getting in the water. These were the times when we would buy a few potato latkes from a street vendor, drive around in circles, and, how should I say this . . . "communicate" with the locals. I would usually drive, and Matt would hang his head out the window, point behind a sidewalk pedestrian, and, very convincingly, inform them they'd "dropped their pocket." Almost everyone looked back so see what he was pointing at, and some even walked back a few paces to check it out. If we were really looking for a laugh, we might have told them they "dropped their penis." Even the girls fell for this from time to time. There were those that didn't bite, though, women for the most part, and they usually answered our PSA (public service announcement) with their middle finger. Regardless of the response, we roared with laughter.

*   *   *

Oh man, such good times. So many fertile seeds planted in the garden of memories over the years. How exciting that after traveling a few miles further down the road, I would be entering unfamiliar territory, this very same garden of memories growing even bigger with every pedal stroke.

I continued east on Bay Avenue. Before turning right onto Highway 1, a few pedal strokes from the onramp, Mark drove by and shot me a friendly honk and a wave on his way back to Fremont. Even though he owed me a wave, having left me hanging when I crossed the bridge a little while ago, I raised my left hand and returned the gesture. Then I turned right and merged onto the shoulder of the highway, heading south.

The highway was mostly empty and open this early in the morning. It was a pleasant way to start the day, I'll tell you that. Only an occasional vehicle sped by me at the start. I hugged the right side of the white line with my wheels, a good technique for avoiding most of the debris scattered about on the side of the road.

Highway shoulders, and most any well-traveled road for that matter, are full of sharp debris just waiting to slice open or punch a hole into your skinny, high-pressure bicycle tires. Nails, glass, gravel, crumpled remains of car bumpers left over after a collision, you name it. Other not-so-sharp items find their way onto the shoulders as well, lying in wait for you to slam into them and pinch your tire flat or break one of your wheel spokes. These usually take the form of intact glass and plastic bottles, planks of wood, tools, pieces of furniture, the remains of blown-out truck tires, clothing, and short pieces of rope or wire just long enough to find their way in between one of your wheel spokes and cause havoc. Get one of these puppies caught between a couple spokes and, before you even realize what's going on, your bike instantly comes to a stop, most likely snapping a few of them in the process as you're sent flying over the handlebars while your bike crashes to the ground. What's the lesson to be learned here? Take your eye off the road, even for a second, and you are almost guaranteed to hit something.

"Riding the line" is a pretty good way to prevent coming in contact with most of this debris. It's safer for the cyclist in other ways too, especially on curvy roads, putting you in line of sight with drivers earlier on right-hand turns. If a driver finds himself hugging the line as well, which happens more frequently than you might imagine, they will see you sooner and, ideally, adjust their trajectory to prevent what would eventually be a very bad day, especially for the cyclist. Occasionally, this technique results in a few middle fingers being thrown your way after they pass you and maybe even a few cuss words as a bonus. Because, hey, roads were made only for cars and trucks, right? Screw the tax-paying cyclist, right? Unfortunately, that is the viewpoint of some. But at least their ranting means they saw you before joining them as an uninvited, and unwanted, guest in the front seat of their vehicle, via their windshield.

For now, I wasn't dealing with any of these issues. The weather was mild, and with the road lightly traveled and the shoulder mostly clear of debris, the ride started off smoothly. I didn't anticipate many challenging road conditions until I started climbing the mountains of Big Sur, and hoped it would stay this way until then. I only expected the change in elevation, if anything, to cause me trouble. Right now, I didn't need to worry about such things. Nothing could be as difficult as Mount Motherfucker, right? Right. So, pushing that thought aside, I warmed up my legs with an easy cadence, pedaling rhythmically along the level well-paved highway under a clear and slowly brightening autumn sky.

Waking up before dawn gives one an opportunity to witness some interesting natural events. Today was no different. The birth of day set the stage for the rising sun and the setting moon to fight for dominance in the early light of dawn. The fight was a draw at the moment, but the moon's luminous strength, so prominent just a few hours earlier, was fading. Soon, the sun would break the horizon and the moon would have no choice but to throw in the towel.

Far beneath this silent celestial battle, I pedaled on. I was creating my own wind as I sliced through the heavy, humid air, and it pushed tears from the corner of my unprotected eyes and back toward the top of my ears. It still wasn't bright enough for sunglasses, so I had to deal with the wind in my eyes for a little while.

My plan for the first day of riding was to make it to San Simeon, another quiet coastal town resting snugly against the base of the foothills along the eastern side of the Highway, a couple miles south of the entrance to the famous Hearst Castle. If I wanted to arrive before nightfall I would have to push through the flat coastal farmlands of Watsonville and Castroville, and the city of Monterey, all nestled in between the crescent-shaped coastline of Monterey Bay and the Santa Lucia Mountains. Beyond that I would need to safely maneuver the notoriously dangerous road hugging the rugged Pacific coastline, a forty-mile stretch of highway starting just past the city of Carmel-by-the-Sea and continuing all the way to the famous Big Sur Mountains. Then, and only then, could I make my attempt at summiting the mighty Big Sur. Should I succeed in accomplishing that feat, having "earned the downhill," I would be treated to the privilege of enjoying a graceful snake-like descent all the way back to the coast, connecting the tiny town of Gorda with Rugged Point. From there it should be a relatively smooth ride the rest of the way to San Simeon.

Pretty easy plan for day one. Piece of cake, right? *I wish.*

CHAPTER THREE

I t didn't take but a few miles for the highway to break out into flat, seemingly unending, farmland. The first small farming towns I came to were Watsonville and Castroville. They tended to blend into each other in such a way that distinguishing one from the other could be difficult if you didn't know what to look for. Part of the difficulty lies in the fact that they are connected by hundreds of small farms filling up most of the fertile ground between the ocean and the mountains.

To the north, closer to Watsonville, tens of thousands of acres of strawberry fields line the highway. The California Strawberry Commission— yes, that's a thing—boast that California produces about 88 percent of strawberries grown in the United States. And almost all of them are grown along the California coast on approximately 38,000 acres of land. *Dang. That's a lot of strawberries!* Peering out over these perpendicular lines of green and red as I rode by was mesmerizing, to say the least. What appeared to be mile-long rows of raised earth were covered end-to-end in bright red strawberries and shiny green leaves. I would hesitate to call bullshit on someone if they told me these rows of plants stretched all the way to the ocean. Evenly spaced apart, they rhythmically ticked past in time with my pedal cadence, making the experience oddly hypnotic.

Looking further down the road and into the fields as countless rows of plants fluttered by, I spotted scores of farm workers fanning out from what appeared to be a command center of sorts, complete with a tent, porta-potties, and numerous green trucks with open trailers. Scattered among raised rows of green, they walked in the shallow dirt valleys between, slowly progressing to the heart of the field. Some were engaged in conversation while others walked quietly alone, staring at the ground and kicking up weeds out of the soil. I presumed they were preparing to start a long day working in the fields.

I continued down the road, passing by a strawberry "U-pick" center on my right. These are common enough attractions in these parts, and during the strawberry harvest you could immerse yourself in the "farm worker experience" by paying money to be taken out into the field to work for your own haul. You would be given a basket and were free to pick your own strawberries for an hour or so and keep your basket of bounty. I've done it and it's a lot of fun, for that hour. My paternal grandfather and all eight of his brothers did this kind of work as children prior to losing their farm during the Great Depression, so that propensity for hard work flows in my veins. But, even with this farmworker pedigree, if I had to break my back in the fields under the hot sun for another eleven hours, I wouldn't think it was so much fun anymore.

Further down the road, several weatherworn fruit stands, constructed of wood siding and hastily protected with flaking white paint, dotted the highway. All of them were closed this early in the morning but still advertised "Strawberries: $10 per flat" on hand-painted green signs hanging from the outside rafters. A few early-rising tourists driving through the area got curious and slowly began pulling over, flashing their brake lights at every stand, hoping one of them would be open. I tried to telepathically inform them their efforts were unrealistic. *Sorry, folks, 7 a.m. is a little early for fruit stands to be open. Come back at 10 o'clock!* I smiled into the peaceful morning as the thought of my favorite Dairy Queen lady came to mind.

I wanted to scowl at them but didn't. I just kept quiet and went along with my business, keeping an eye on their bumpers and a finger on the brake lever. Riding but a few inches away from such erratic driving also reminded me that I needed to be an advocate for my own safety out here on the pavement, even here in the flatlands between sea and mountain where roads are well-paved, saddled by wide shoulders, and not usually congested with commuter traffic. There are no official driveways for these makeshift farm stands, though, and drivers pulled over wherever they wanted along the gravel shoulders. Keeping an eye out for a cyclist is the last thing on their minds while they fumble around in the car for their AAA maps while also trying to find an open fruit stand to fill their empty bellies.

Shortly thereafter, I left Watsonville behind and rode into Castroville, along the way passing over the westernmost part of the Elkhorn Slough via the Moss Landing Bridge. The Elkhorn Slough, a natural watershed barrier separating the two farming communities, contains the largest tidal salt marsh in California outside of the San Francisco Bay. Comprised primarily of soft slippery mud, the marsh soil is too soft to walk through without knee-high rubber waders. Even with those on, you might still get some rotten mud in your boots. The aroma in the air is pungent and uniquely coastal, smelling of decaying plant life, dead fish, and salty brine. This smell is partly due to the largest concentration of sea otters in California, which frequent this Slough, eating the fish and shellfish that flourish in the shallow tidal-infused estuary.

Set back away from the shoreline, the Slough opens up into a 1700-acre wetland habitat and wildlife reserve, where hundreds of species of animals and waterfowl reside. Near the foothills, at the eastern end of the Slough, pools of brackish water lined with cattails and tall grasses host irresistible breeding grounds for migrating birds. Some of these pools dry up during the hotter months of the year, leaving behind a thin, and deceptively sturdy-looking, crusty salt cap. If you try to walk across, before you know it you'll be unsticking your foot from the soft foot-sucking mud beneath the not-so-solid surface. Many boots have been lost in such adventures. So stick to the trails, people.

After passing over the mouth of the Slough, the highway turned away from the ocean as it led me into Castroville. To the right, nearest the beach, was Moss Landing Harbor, a small community of coastal restaurants, day cruise launch points, and, if you want to learn a little more about the surrounding Slough, the Elkhorn Slough Safari is there too. Private small-craft boat docks fill in the open space in the middle of the channel, the boats moored in line along two-sided piers.

Monterey Bay Aquarium Research Institute also calls this place home and is constantly using the Slough for research and working to restore, preserve, and protect the native plants and animals of the area.

But not all interesting things in this area have to do with the surrounding coastal preserve. The Moss Landing power plant came into view just beyond the south end of the bridge, across the highway from the harbor. It stuck out like a sore thumb against the surrounding natural landscape, its two massive stacks stabbing at the cloudless sky. Oddly out of place as they were, it was interesting to peer up at them as I rolled by, even if they were as unbecoming as a mosquito swimming in one's soup.

Several hundred feet down the road, with the Slough and power plant behind me and now out of view, the land opened up into massive fields of pale-green plants, looking like something straight out of a sci-fi movie. Protruding widely from the center of each one were long pointy leaves, lots of them, with edges like that of a serrated kitchen knife. All planted in nice, tidy rows, they stood like obedient soldiers, similar to the strawberries on the north side of the Slough in the Watsonville fields.

It became abundantly clear that I had crossed over into the land of artichokes, or, to show respect to what the Castrovillians like to call it, the "artichoke capital of the world." It was October, so the plants were young—and therefore small and unimpressive—but the proud people of this town had evidence to back up their claim of artichoke supremacy, regardless. Come summer, these artichoke fields would be in full bloom, their spiny leaves intermingling with the ones next to them. Tall stocks of edible meaty flowers will protrude from the heart of each plant and turn the entire field into a seasonal forest of silvery-green west-coast vegan delicacy. And to think Midwesterners used to call these things "pig food." Crazy. *Just to be clear, I'm talking about the artichokes, not the vegans . . . but I digress. Please forgive me.* They're far from pig food, in my opinion. Steam these suckers up or roast them in the oven for a while to soften their sturdy fibrous exterior, dip the ends of the leaves in a little garlic aioli, and voilà, you have a delicious side dish to your meal.

I continued down the highway, passing several more currently closed fruit stands along the way. Instead of signs advertising strawberries, however, these small shacks had green-painted signs nailed to the highway-facing walls sporting slogans like "Best artichokes in the world" and "You don't know what an artichoke tastes like until you've had one grown in Castroville!"

"Castrovillians" are very proud of their artichoke heritage. Italian immigrants planted the first artichokes in Castroville in the early 1920s, and they have been raised there as the primary crop ever since. They even have a festival once a year, sponsored by the local artichoke farmers of course, to commemorate and promote the consumption of this perennial delicacy.

Before reaching the outskirts of town, I turned right at the junction of Highway 1 and CA-183, continuing my journey south on Highway 1. The turn put the early rising sun to my back, aiming Jezebel southwest and back toward the ocean. But you wouldn't know it by the endless fields of artichokes and other random vegetables around me. The ocean felt oddly distant, like I had ridden into another world for a while and was lost in a maze of green lines. I was used to vegetables of all types being grown in California's Central Valley, but seeing so many crops growing so close to the ocean was relatively new to me. I always knew produce was grown here, but now that I was actually in the middle of it all I was surprised that it was such a large operation and there was so much more here than just strawberries.

A consequence of pedaling with my back to the sun was my shadow got pushed far out ahead of me, so absurdly in the early morning sunlight that it appeared as a solid black monster against the perpetually gray pavement. I was amused at how the circular motion of my pedal strokes exaggerated my two-dimensional likeness, making it appear as if I was clumsily running down the street. The air, however, was not so two-dimensional, harboring a multitude of complex aromas; fertile dirt, green plants, and the unmistakable scent of the sea.

Akin to when I passed through the strawberry fields in Watsonville, I rode past another pop tent on my way out of Castroville. Unlike the first one I rode by, here a group of about ten or so men were congregating around a makeshift kitchen about a hundred feet off the road in a cleared-out section of the field, holding steaming cups of what I presumed to be coffee in one hand and breakfast in the other. They were mumbling amongst themselves, talking about this and that. I was too far away to hear what they were saying, but after I entered their field of view and attracted their attention, they all turned and stared at me as I rode by. Their loud mumbling conversations toned down to a hum, and everything became eerily quiet as their gaze followed me down the road. I don't know if they were curious or what, but they watched me for such a long time that I started to feel a little uncomfortable until I was out of sight.

It didn't take much longer to reach the beach again. The sun was up, now fully awake, predictably victorious over the moon. But don't shed any tears for the moon, it'll be back. The morning light brought the coast out of its slumber and illuminated everything with liveliness and warmth. Warmth. Heat. Yes, it was warming up, quickly too. It wouldn't be too much longer until the rising heat would get me sweating. *Okay, time to get this cold weather gear off.*

I rolled into Monterey State Beach a short time later and decided this was a good time to take a break and remedy the rising heat situation. I pulled off the highway for the first time since leaving Capitola and coasted to a stop at a place where the pavement ended. I disembarked and leaned Jezebel up against a concrete barrier at the end of Tioga Road.

I sat down on a nearby concrete cube, the kind used to prevent vehicles from traveling any further, forming a junction where the road and the sandy beach came together. Notwithstanding the concrete cubes, there was no distinguishing line between sand and road. Years of shifting sands had blurred the border, and the very end of the road appeared swallowed up by the beach. Of course, if you left it alone long enough, the beach would take it all, concrete cubes included. *Nature always wins. All it needs is time.*

I took in my surroundings as I began the removal of my cold-weather clothing. On the beach, several early risers were hanging about, standing quiet and still with their bare feet buried in the cool morning sand, staring out over the ocean and perfectly content in their bubbles of solitude. My gaze wandered and I watched one man running up the beach from Monterey all by himself and a woman running in the opposite direction, her dog in tow at the end of a long leash. Laughter soon won my attention and I turned to my right to see a group of three guys in the final stages of putting on their wetsuits, standing next to their upside-down surfboards lying flat in the sand.

I stripped off my leg and arm warmers and put them away in the right-side pannier. No time to waste—I had to keep rolling. I straightened Jezebel up from her leaning-tower-of-Pisa pose against the stone cube, straddled the frame, kicked the sand off my shoes against the pedal cranks, and clicked in. Finally, now that the sun was up and all was bright, I pulled my Oakley Razor Blade sunglasses out of the center rear pocket of my cycling jersey and slid them on. *Showtime!* I was off again, quickly rejoining Highway 1 and continuing south.

This stretch of highway hugged the top of the beach. You couldn't walk any further west without stepping into sand. Shoot, you could easily argue that the highway cut right through the beach. So much sand had blown to the eastern side of the highway over the years that in some places it looked like a new beach was growing there among large patches of ice plant. Ice plant, almost as synonymous with the Pacific Northwest as the beaches themselves, grew unencumbered along the coast, taking root in the shallow soil and frequently bleeding over the border between pavement and sand. Their glistening strings of French fry–like appendages creeped onto the highway wherever cracks in the pavement appeared. As I toed the line between beach and highway, Jezebel's tires sliced through them easily, making faint crunching and grinding sounds.

It's inevitable that you'll need to deal with sand in some capacity when riding your bike along the California coast, but it's not my favorite thing to do when riding on top of such skinny tires. Sand gets everywhere: in your socks, bike chain, hair, and ears, just to name a few. And it can be dangerous to ride through. Thick patches slow you down quickly and could easily make you lose control. Fine coverings of sand, like what I was dealing with here, can make the pavement slippery, even when dry, leading to one, or both, of your wheels sliding out from under you.

Fortunate for me, the pavement here was level and that made it easier to pass through the multitude of sand patches scattered along the shoulder. If I was pedaling uphill, there might be some slippage of the rear tire to deal with. But none of that here. I just coasted through the sandy patches and applied power to the pedals when no sand was around.

Another mile or so down the road, the highway veered away from the beach. I was forced to follow, and, consequently, the beach slowly slipped from view. Sand no longer lined the shoulder, only sidewalks, plants, and dirt, with an occasional tree thrown in for good measure. From here, Highway 1 continued due south as the coastline abruptly shot westward, blocking out a chunk of extremely valuable land for the luxury coastal cities of Monterey, Pacific Grove, and Carmel-by-the-Sea, as well as the famous Pebble Beach golf course.

I would have loved to hang out for a while in downtown Carmel. I love that little town. It's so . . . romantic. And not just because of the town itself. The surrounding mountains and white sand beaches form the boundaries of this town, confining you within a subtle embrace of rock and ocean. My parents spent their honeymoon there in 1971, in December. Brrr! But hey, they probably hardly ever left the hotel room anyway, right? Okay . . . enough of that thought. I still had a long day ahead of me, so let's move on, shall we?

Unfortunately, it was necessary for me to ride by Carmel without stopping, skipping all the perfectly clean streets, quaint little restaurants, and aggregate stone sidewalks lined with fancy shops. It would have been nice to take a short jaunt off the highway and hang out on Carmel's white sand beach for a while, shielding myself from the gusty onshore breezes so typical of this area under wind-wacked juniper trees, but I had no time. I continued south, on the fast track, catching only fleeting glimpses of Italian-style gardens of terra-cotta pots and unique, one-of-a-kind architecture as it flitted by.

Once out of town I started the climb up to the Carmel Highlands, past Point Lobos Natural State Preserve. The Carmel Highlands is a place like no other, at least no other place I've ever seen. One cannot simply pass by without stopping at least once to take it all in. Pardon the cliché, but the views are truly breathtaking. If I wasn't standing there looking at it with my own eyes, I would think the stories of its serenity were the stuff of legends, a place that becomes more dramatic with every telling of its story. Alas, the stories are true. There is such a place. A tiny piece of paradise the ocean carved out of the mountainside eons ago before leaving Mother Nature in charge to make it a heavenly place.

This spot, this little piece of paradise, is a place to visit if you need to clear a cluttered mind, take a rest in the middle of a journey, or just relax. Gaze out into the ocean long enough from one of the many vista point pull-outs, and you'll soon develop an urge to pinch yourself, just to make sure that you're not dreaming, or that you haven't been transformed into a character in a giant painting. The only other place I've ever seen with vistas as stunning as those from the Carmel Highlands is the Italian Riviera.

I pulled over at one of these vista pull-outs. I had to. It would be a shame if I didn't. This particular one, stationed atop one of the high points of several rolling hills along the cliffs, was a popular one—and for good reason. The view from here was blissful, enchanting almost. I coasted to a stop and hopped off Jezebel, the clips on the bottom of my shoes crunching into the pine-needle-blanketed dirt. I leaned her against the stone wall

169

outlining the perimeter of the pull-out. To my left, on the eastern side of the highway, custom-built homes were scattered along the cliffs, each one chiseled securely into the rocky face and taller than they were wide. Massive windows of thick glass covered their ocean-facing facades, providing minimally encumbered panoramic views of the coastline. *Gotta get your money's worth.*

To my right was the Pacific Ocean in all its glory, blue and massive. I pulled a water bottle out of its cradle and blindly reached into the outermost pocket of my left-side pannier for my first snack of the day. I happened to grab hold of a chocolate flavored PowerBar. Not my first choice, but it would do. I walked over to the cool stone barricade, water bottle and PowerBar in hand, and sat down. I carefully swung my legs over the edge, gazed out over the ocean, and while breathing in the salty air through deep breaths, took it all in: the sights, the sounds, the smells, and all the feels.

The view of the ocean was sliced vertically by trunks of tall, oddly straight trees growing out of the slanted earth several yards down the cliff from where I perched myself. Squinting through the multitude of thin trunks and then to my right, I was able to make out the outline of the Pebble Beach fairways in the distance, strikingly green against the light-brown cliff face. Small wind-blown waves lapped rhythmically against the rocks beneath them. Directly in front of me, through the trees and over the high shrubs, more of these gentle waves, tuned to the same tempo, rolled onto a small sandy beach. I was too high up and too far away to hear the hissing of the whitewater as it mixed with the sand, but I could imagine the music it was making, having listened to it sing me to sleep countless times before.

Just as fast as the wind pushed the waves onto the beach, the mighty ocean, the true conductor of this natural symphony, pulled them right back into her with a rhythm all her own. This pattern has endured, and will likely continue to endure, for eternity, water and wind gradually, relentlessly turning mountains into boulders and boulders into sand. Large forests of dark green kelp rooted themselves in the shallow waters just off shore, and I watched as the large green mass moved in sync with this natural rhythm. Back and forth, in and out.

To the south my view was unobstructed, bearing witness to the mountainous shoreline reluctantly nosediving into the ocean, its foundations crumbling into the surf. Among the fragmented remains of a millennia of lost battles, pillars of tall lonesome rocks stood bravely out in front of the mountains among the pounding waves. Like soldiers protecting their general, they absorbed the initial hits from the ocean relentlessly fighting to reclaim her lost territory. For now, the pillars stand tall and strong, beating back the punches, the pounding of the ocean waves glancing off their rocky shields.

Their efforts are valiant by any measure, I'll give them that, but futile nonetheless. The ocean will never tire, but the pillars' strength will wane. In time, the towering skyscrapers of stone will fall, and the ocean will swallow them up. All she needs is time, and she has plenty.

I continued munching on my PowerBar and drinking from my bottle of Cytomax-infused water, replenishing the morning's burnt calories. I let my feet hang limply off the edge of the wall, taking note of how weightless they felt swaying in the breeze. The plastic heels of my dangling cycling shoes tapped lightly against the stone with each gust of wind. But none of this deterred me from the experience. Immersed in the beauty, my mind wandered, as it frequently does, and I wished that Mo was there with me to share in the grandeur.

A cool gust of wind blew off the ocean and into my face. The chill of it forced goosebumps to form on the surface of my exposed arms and legs, already damp with sweat. I remained still, despite the chill, and yearned for Mo to come walking up behind me and wrap her arms around my neck, something else that would have surely given me goosebumps.

My imagination tends to run rapid when thoughts like these come to mind. This time was no different. In my silly little daydream, she would be wearing high-waisted denim shorts and a one-size-too-large UC Irvine sweatshirt, collar cut out, hands tucked inside the sleeves. She would walk over and take a seat next to me and lean into my shoulder for warmth and companionship, goosebumps covering the lower half of her thighs, same as my own. With my arm draped around her, I would pretend the cold was no bother to me. She would battle with her auburn hair, half pulled back into a tight ponytail, the other half whipping me in the face as it frolicked in all directions amidst the gusty breezes, finally tucking it into the cut-off collar of her sweatshirt.

What a shame I only had Jezebel to share this view with, and about ten cars full of camera-toting tourists, most having already come and gone from this spot over the past fifteen minutes. But hey, maybe it's not all that bad. Some would have me believe Jezebel is the perfect woman for me, anyway, and I shouldn't complain. She's quiet, pretty, and only does what I tell her to do. And she lets me ride her whenever I want. The rest of the time she is just waiting around for me to tell her to do something else. Ha! Yeah, that may be true, and for some men that might be ideal, but the reality is, Jezebel's cold, and made of metal, carbon fiber, and rubber. Not my idea of an ideal woman. *Don't tell her that, though, at least not until the end of the trip.* Right now, I need her, but she's not what I want.

Maureen, on the other hand, now there's a woman with everything I want; one with a heart as warm as a campfire on a cold mountain night. She speaks loudly and sings exuberantly but whispers all the right words when the time is right, giving me goosebumps without the assistance of the biting coastal breeze. When we embrace, it's a perfect fit. And when she kisses me? Ah, man! Everything around me slips away and she makes me feel as if we're the only ones around. Yeah, let me tell you. That's the kind of woman I want. And that woman is waiting for me several hundred miles down the road. *Shit, quit daydreaming stupid. You better get going. What the hell are you waiting for?*

Good advice. Feeling rested and highly motivated, I took one more look at paradise while finishing up the last of my snack and bottle of Cytomax. Afterwards, I threw my feet over the wall and walked duck-footed on my heels over the sand-covered dirt to Jezebel. "All right, Jezebel, let's do this. It only gets harder from here," I whispered as I hopped on to her saddle, clicked into the pedals, and got back on the road.

The ride from the summit of the Carmel Highlands to Andrew Molera State Park felt longer to me than it actually was. Partly because, for my own personal safety, I was forced to concentrate intensely on the road and my surroundings, so my progress was not as fast as I initially planned. *Ride like you're invisible, Matt. Safety first. Remember, it doesn't matter if you hit them or they hit you. YOU lose.* Not only were the shoulders narrow on this stretch of highway—except for the turnouts, of which there were many—but the cliffs were steep, and vehicles constantly drove past me at speeds that felt way too fast. The closeness of the passing cars made me the most nervous. There just wasn't enough room on the shoulder to make any adjustments. Sometimes you just need to put some trust in the other people around you, including drivers.

Trying not to think about all the horrible things that could happen, I concentrated on riding the white line, keeping my elbows tucked in close to my body, and following all the rules of the road. I prayed they did too.

CHAPTER FOUR

It was late morning and turning out to be such a beautifully clear day that it felt like I'd been cast in a scene for a California tourism commercial. Or maybe one of those car commercials where the main point is to show off a car, but at the same time it advertises the beauty of driving that car down the California coast. Yeah, now that I think about it, it was actually more like one of those. I'd be like that lone cyclist on the side of the road that the camera pans away from before following the car down the coast. Just a prop along the side of road between the ocean and the hills. Of course, I would be watching the car drive away in amazement, like it was the sexiest car I'd ever seen. *Ah, daydreaming. It's so easy to do around here.*

The bright blues and muted greens of the giant Pacific Ocean contrasted sharply, but naturally, with the steep golden hillsides and cascading shorelines, the land spilling into the sea like they were destined to be together. As if the contrast wasn't stark enough between the two, the famous Pacific Coast Highway cut right through it all, the type of scene you might find printed on post–World War II tourist postcards and old wooden citrus boxes. Everything majestic about the California coast came together that morning, and it was just the right combination of events to pull every tourist in the area out onto Highway 1 to enjoy the view. I didn't blame them at all, really. Who wouldn't want to take a drive along the California coast on a lazy Saturday afternoon? I would, and I was. I just happened to be enjoying the view while "riding" down the highway on top of a bicycle. Don't be fooled, however. I may have been on a bike, but I was definitely driving, not riding. My quads could assure you of that.

The view of the coast today was truly breathtaking. *Huh. There's that cliché again.* But breathtaking views lead to distracted driving, and I wanted to make sure I made it through the tight turns as fast, and safely, as possible. Remaining seated kept my "bike print" as compact as possible, eliminating the inevitable sway of the bike into traffic when pedaling out of the saddle. The narrow shoulder on this part of the highway, combined with the fact that the two panniers strapped to the back of Jezebel doubled her width—*don't tell her I said that*—made it even more important that I kept myself visible and on a predictable trajectory. Keeping that in mind, I rode diligently and cautiously, but quickly, glancing over my left shoulder every time I heard a car engine approaching me from behind, just to make sure they knew I was there. I was heading south, so I was riding on the west side of the highway, where the shoulders spanned about twenty inches, twelve in some places. If I was heading north, I would be riding twelve to twenty-four inches away from the jagged rocks of the mountainside, with no turnouts for an escape.

If you think about it, I guess I was actually on the "safest" side of the road. A general term, for sure, considering the environment. One mistake, by me or a distracted driver, and I was going to slip over the edge, tumble down the cliffs, and get swallowed up by the ocean. Consequently, every movement I made on this stretch of highway was calculated. I was constantly moving when in traffic, but I pulled over at every turnout, waiting for a large clearing before rolling back onto the highway.

*   *   *

The iconic Bixby Creek Bridge finally came into view after a while, and that brought me some relief. I'd seen it occasionally through the distant haze, blinking in and out of sight as I maneuvered the snakelike turns along the rugged coastline. For the past several hundred yards, however, I fixated on it as a solid "beacon of beckoning," a goal of some sort. For what? I don't know, nothing of substance really. Most likely just something to concentrate on, a break from the stress and monotony of keeping myself alive and uninjured over the past several miles of dangerous road conditions. I arrived soon enough, and did feel a certain level of relief, mainly that I had rolled onto the bridge unscathed. Ironically, I felt safer standing on a 360-foot-long man-made bridge built in 1932, towering 280 feet above the ground, than I had traveling on the highway the past hour or so.

Traffic was the main challenge of the morning, but at least the highway was cut into the solid rock of the mountain, providing an assurance of sturdiness, integrity, and security. The Bixby Creek Bridge, on the other hand, was old and gave off the illusion that it was floating over the deep ravine below it.

It was time for another break. The shoulders on the bridge were just as narrow as the ones on the highway, but I was able to tuck myself and Jezebel into one of four small outcroppings built into the bridge piles. I took a couple minutes to absorb the picturesque scene. The view was dramatically different in all directions. Chaparral-blanketed mountains to the east, a sapphire ocean to the west, slowly crumbling cliffs to the north, rugged coastline buried in mid-day haze to the south, a deep ravine of green under the bridge, and blue sky above it all. I peered over the edge of the bridge and into the fertile drainage. There were no trees, only densely packed shrubbery, the taller plants swaying back and forth in the light breeze. The wavering abyss gave me vertigo, the same feeling I get when peering over the railing of the Golden Gate Bridge in San Francisco, so I didn't look too long.

Pulling my eyes away from all that lay under the bridge, I marveled at the ocean, as I frequently do, appearing vast and endless. I can't tell you how many times I've stared out over the great Pacific and gotten lost in its illusion of infiniteness. Its horizon always appeared to be the crest of a waterfall, a fast track to another place. *Hawaii's out there somewhere... imagine that. Now that's a place I'd like to be right now, especially if Mo was there with me.*

To my left, the upcoming challenge loomed in the distance. The highway's profile cut diagonally into the hillside before me, and I was going to need to climb it. I closed my eyes and, forcing the Hawaii fantasy out of my mind for the moment, filled my lungs with clean, salty air. I held it in for several seconds and then exhaled slowly, opening my eyes and sighing with the release. Pedaling up mountains is not something that comes naturally, or easily, to me, regardless of the time I put into it. At 185 pounds, plus the weight of the bike and all my gear, a tough time was guaranteed. But if I wanted to reach Mo, I had to push through it. So I needed to get in the right frame of mind for what lay ahead, as there was a lot of climbing to conquer in the next several hours. The mountains of Big Sur were fast approaching.

Climbing, whether on a bike or in running shoes, has always been a challenge for me, as I'm on the heavy side for distance and endurance sports. My athletic endeavors, mostly anaerobic in nature, required me to develop quick and explosive power, and use it over relatively short durations. Football, wrestling, baseball, track (as a sprinter), and swimming (again, as a sprinter) were my athletic activities of choice. None of these sports required the development of endurance necessary to be proficient at long-distance activities, like long-distance cycling or cross-country running. Never was this more apparent than when I had to perform the Marine Corps Physical Fitness Test in boot camp.

The Marine Corps PFT consists of three events: pull-ups, sit-ups, and a three-mile run. Achieving a perfect score of 300 points requires you to perform twenty dead-hang pull-ups, complete eighty sit-ups in two minutes, and run three miles in less than eighteen minutes. I scored perfect on the pull-ups and sit-ups. I even did several extra, because, well, "Oh Rah!" The run, on the other hand, was a different beast altogether. A drill instructor leads the run a rabbit once the gun goes off, wearing a red-and-gold USMC shirt, the rest of us in our Marine Corps green. He maintains a six-minute mile pace for the entire three miles. If you wanted a perfect score on the run, you needed to cross the finish line with him, or in front of him. I was able to keep the rabbit within a "reel-in" distance for about the first mile, and then, even with max effort, he gradually slipped further and further away, soon falling out of sight completely. I couldn't keep the pace and didn't see him again until I crossed the finish line with a respectable, although not perfect, time of 19:40. That's a pace of 6 minutes and 33 seconds per mile. And, at that time, I was eighteen and in the best shape of my life. No perfect 300 for me, but good enough to be in the top 10 percent. *Enough reminiscing, Matt. Let's go.*

Having spent plenty of time with my thoughts already—too much, really—it was time to get moving again. Daylight was burning. I picked Jezebel up and set her back on the highway shoulder, hopped on, and pedaled on down the road. Riding with the same caution as before, I stayed in the saddle and frequently gazed over my shoulder for dangers. I hugged the outside edge of the white line while climbing and became one with the traffic on the downhill portions, moving into the middle of the lane. As long as I was able to maintain a reasonable downhill speed, it was much safer to ride with traffic than along the shoulder. This zig-zag, up-and-down pattern continued all the way down the coast until I reached the redwood-laden forest of Big Sur.

The unofficial beginning of the climb up to Pfeiffer Big Sur Campground started in Andrew Molera State Park. From there, Highway 1 turned inland and slowly started to gain altitude, gracefully meandering through a narrow valley nestled between two long mountain ranges running north to south, parallel to the coastline. These ranges make up the Big Sur forest area, pushed up and out of the ocean millenniums ago, the result of an ongoing stalemate between the Pacific Plate and the North American Plate, neither willing to give up ground as they push against each other.

As I gradually climbed inland, I found myself in familiar territory, ecologically speaking. The valley floor supported various species of coastal oak trees and drought-resistant shrubbery. The grassy oak terroir, mountainous in its topography, reminded me of my mountain bike–riding days, bringing to the surface satisfying memories of tearing up the trails in the Fremont hills. Over the next several miles, as I struggled up the climb to the Big Sur summit one laborious pedal stroke after another, the terrain transitioned into an environment more adept for Coastal Redwoods than Coastal Oaks.

As I slowly reeled in the miles, my weakness for climbing became uncomfortably apparent, as I knew it would. My quads and calves burned as gravity started to take its revenge on the gradual, yet continuous, incline. There was no way to rest without stopping completely, but that would be disastrous. I had to maintain whatever momentum I was able to earn. Earlier in the day I made it over steeper climbs in the Carmel Highlands, but they were much shorter in duration, and my muscles found rest on the descents. Here, there were no downhill sections to speak of, only a constant trek upward. I was either climbing or pushing through a level section on my way to another climbing section, spending about 70 percent of my time in the saddle and 30 percent standing on the pedals, mashing the gears.

Gravity can, and will, make things difficult whenever it can, but you can use it to your advantage if you know how. Pedaling out of the saddle allows the rider to use weight and gravity to maximize the efficiency and power of each pedal stroke. But you also burn more energy using this technique, as you not only push down with your front foot and pull up with your rear foot, you also rock the bike back and forth. More energy is consumed moving your upper body around than if you remain seated and spin, but the trade-off can be beneficial. When in the saddle, I can maintain a more consistent pedal cadence and adjust the gears as necessary to conserve energy, providing an opportunity of rest for my upper body. This allows me to maintain a more relaxed, efficient, and aerodynamic position on the bike.

I was no Miguel Indurain, not by a long shot, so it was to my advantage to stay in the saddle as much as possible and set a pace that I could comfortably maintain for a while, especially since I had such a long way to go. When the highway ticked up a few degrees, I would drop the gears and increase my RPM's, reducing my speed but at the same time conserving energy and increasing the circulation of blood through my legs. I would do the reverse when the road leveled off, using the level sections to stand up, build up speed, and "stretch the legs."

*   *   *

The miles ticked by, much slower than I would have liked, but one pedal stroke after another brought me to the summit, near the entrance to Pfeiffer Big Sur Campground. Now that the most difficult part of today's ride was finished, it was the perfect time for a much-deserved break. I pulled over alongside one of numerous massive redwood trees growing a couple of yards from the side of the road.

Pacific coast redwoods, the tallest trees in the world, are finicky conifers. They grow slowly, flourishing inside a very small sliver of ground running north and south that follows the coastline of the Pacific Northwest. It's a unique patch of earth about five hundred miles long and twenty to thirty-five miles wide, spanning from southern Oregon to the southern end of Big Sur. Geographically speaking, this is a very tiny piece of land, and I was standing at the end of the line. Or maybe it was the beginning. Who knows? I guess it depends which way you're traveling. I was heading south, so it was the end for me. Regardless of my direction of travel, the micro-climate of this area allows for a predictable marine layer most of the year. This provides enough seasonal moisture for redwoods' dense canopies of branches and needles to pull water right out of the air. Quite an ingenious way to grow so tall, really. These tall, straight, and fast-growing trees are remarkable both in appearance and structure, especially when you compare them with the coastal oaks they share the ground with. The coastal redwood stands tall among the coastal oaks, lean and strong, like an NBA player. In contrast, the oaks seem perfectly content growing slow and low to the ground, like a short and stalky NFL running back with large, round, bulging muscles.

The redwood tree's rapid growth allows for the development of a delicate, but resilient red-hued bark. Surrounding the younger trees, it's soft to the touch, like a roughly made wool sweater, extremely resistant to fire and bug infestations. The bark on the oak trees, however, is sturdy, strong, and rough.

Spanning the mid-day hours, sunlight finds its way through the thick tree canopy, scattering bright streaks of light against the trunks of redwood trees. The fibrous bark, now bathed in pastel hues of crimson and gold, illuminates the forest floor, providing warmth and embellishing all that is there. When conditions are right, the trees take on the appearance of a towering stick of cold fire. The older redwoods show their age not only by their height, but also by the color of their bark. Time, the destroyer of all life and thief of all things, hardens their shells and dampens the vibrancy of their hue. Exposure to the harsh environment tarnishes the vivid color of youth, commuting its armor to the dark browns and grays of ancient maturity. Immersing yourself into a forest as special as this is humbling, and it takes courage to fight off the sense of insignificance that follows you in. There's no debate who the true kings and queens are in this place. I was just one of many living things here, and, confusingly felt slightly out of place, while at the same time harboring an undeniable and strong sense of belonging.

I duck-walked a few steps into a grove just off the edge of the highway and lay down on the forest floor. I was hot and sweating from exertion. The air was dry and warm, but the ground felt refreshingly cool and damp, the pine needle bedding soft and welcoming. I removed my sunglasses and gazed up into the needle-laden canopy. The redwood trees, although crowded among other ground-dwelling vegetation along the forest floor, were the only occupants of the sky, their tops rocking slowly and erratically in the coastal breeze high above all the others, drawing invisible pictures on the clear blue canvas. High-pitched creaks and deep bellowing groans emanated from their trunks as they swayed, some of the sounds coming from trees rubbing gently against each other in the dense forest. If I was patient and listened carefully, I could hear not noise, but music.

I closed my eyes and again thought of Mo . . . and food. The hunger pangs came on sharply at rest, as if a pinecone fell from one of the surrounding trees and hit me right in the gut. I was starving! Mo knew how to fill my heart, but not my stomach. I wished so hard at that moment that we were hanging out together eating lunch somewhere, maybe on Pier 39 in San Francisco, as we had done nearly three months ago on our first actual date.

* * *

After our meeting in Disneyland, Maureen and I spent the following weekend together. I drove across the bay to hang out, all the way from Fremont to her hometown of Cotati. She opened the door with a smile and, over the barking of her not-all-that-intimidating dachshund, Beanie, introduced me to her mom, Jan. After a brief get-to-know-you discussion with her mom, we spent our first day together, a typically hot July day, cooling off at Windsor Waterworks.

The following day around noon we took off to San Francisco in her shiny new green—*teal, Matt, teal, not green*—Geo Storm hatchback. On our way there we got caught up in bumper-to-bumper traffic while waiting our turn to cross the Golden Gate Bridge. Normally a frustrating endeavor we found ourselves not bothered by it at all. We were young, carefree, and had nowhere to be except where we were at that very moment. And the view? Stunning. *And I'm not just talking about the woman in the driver's seat either.* No marine layer, no smog, no haze. Just clear blue skies and the San Francisco skyline. We were able to see all the way to the East Bay foothills. Getting caught in traffic while descending out of the Marin Headlands and onto the Golden Gate Bridge is a blessing in disguise, especially on a day like that. I don't know of a more picturesque place to be driving an average of five miles an hour. We just turned up the volume on the Green Day album we had spinning in the CD player and got to know each other. We even made new friends in other cars as we slowly moved along.

We spent the entire afternoon and most of the evening being tourists, hanging out on Pier 39 and walking the surrounding streets. We took in the bounty of the tourist shops, exploring the plethora of music boxes for sale in a store that sold music-related San Francisco–themed items and other chotchkes. We snacked on Ghirardelli chocolates, watched a magic show at the end of the pier, and treated ourselves to a loud performance of sea lion theater, watching them sun themselves on nearby docks and lazily groan when one of them got too close to another. We even convinced a tourist visiting from another country to memorialize our day by taking a picture of us sitting on the railing with Alcatraz Island in the background.

When the sun began to set, the hunger for a "real meal" settled in. We decided on the Franciscan Restaurant for dinner, an upscale dining establishment located between Pier 39 and Fisherman's Wharf, with wide-angle views of San Francisco Bay, the city, Alcatraz Island, Angel Island, and The Golden Gate Bridge. It was the first fancy dinner we shared together as a couple. We sat and talked. I don't think either one of us shut up at any point during the meal, let alone the entire weekend. A woman more comfortable in conversation than silence, Mo instinctually knew how to brighten up the dimmest of exchanges with interesting stories told not only with her voice, but with drama and pizzazz. She was, and still is, a radiant soul: beautiful, mesmerizing, and enchanting. She had so much happiness in her perfect freckle-dotted face, and her eyes lit up like fireflies when she smiled. And she smiled a lot, like a woman who harbored only happy and hopeful thoughts.

The view from the restaurant was worth the cost of the expensive meal, or so they tell me. I wasn't paying much attention to the view beyond the windows, to tell you the truth. I was too consumed with this amazing woman I had just met. I couldn't take my eyes off her. Something told me this girl was special and she might be worth some effort.

I don't remember what she had for dinner. But I remember enjoying the halibut with cream caper sauce, made even more enjoyable with the endless supply of San Francisco–made sourdough bread, served alongside room-temperature salted butter. Delightful! Oh my God, what I would do to have that right now! *Dude, stop! Why are you thinking about that right now? Stop, you're just making it worse.*

CHAPTER FIVE

My eyes flashed open at the sound of a woodpecker hammering the point of its beak into a nearby tree, abruptly putting the brakes on my daydreaming. I forced myself off the ground and heel-walked back to the highway shoulder. I needed to get moving again and find some real food to throw down my gullet, and soon. The PowerBars and Gu packets weren't cutting it. But right now, I didn't have much of a choice. While I hobbled over to Jezebel, I squeezed the entire contents of a Gu packet into my mouth. It wasn't halibut with cream caper sauce or sourdough bread with salted butter, but it would have to do for now. These Gu packets aren't much more than pure liquid sugar, but they would hold me over until I could get some decent food in my belly. It would also bring my blood sugar back up a bit. I could feel it dropping with every passing mile.

The highway took on a slow descent from here, so the riding was easy, comparatively speaking. I coasted down the mountain for countless miles past the last of the redwood trees, where the land opened up into rolling hills of rocky grassland. Most of the ride from the summit back to sea level was smooth and fast. With minimal traffic, I was able to position myself in the middle of the lane, avoiding the dangers of the shoulder during speedy descents. After I settled onto the flats, a sign on the side of the road attracted my attention. It pointed west, off the highway, and had "Nepenthe Restaurant" written on it. *Should I?* I really couldn't spare the time, but I was so hungry that I couldn't help myself. *I'll make it quick*, I whispered to myself. *I can eat fast, just ask my Marine Corps buddies.*

Without slowing down to give myself the opportunity of talking myself out of it, I turned toward the ocean and pedaled down the short driveway to the restaurant's front entrance. I hopped of the bike, pushed open the front door, and clumsily dragged Jezebel into the quiet lobby. The restaurant sported an open floor plan where almost the entire inside seating area, including the bar, could be seen from any point within the interior. It was larger on the inside than it appeared to be from the parking lot. Broad beams of timber supported high-vaulted ceilings and large windows lined the restaurant's perimeter, providing panoramic views of the Pacific Ocean and surrounding Big Sur area. Every table had a view, and none of them were terrible. There was even outdoor seating for the adventurous souls, as long as you didn't mind the onshore breeze and the occasional yellow jacket joining you for lunch. The air inside the restaurant was cool and smelled of cooked food. I lifted my nose and breathed in a lungful. *I'm so hungry!*

"Hi there," I said to the hostess.

A professionally dressed woman in her thirties was standing at the counter cleaning menus and organizing the greeting stand. She welcomed me with a friendly voice and a genuine smile.

"Good afternoon, sir. How can I help you?"

I grimaced playfully through a closed-mouth smile.

"Sir? Is my father here?" I said, looking around playfully.

Not finding my comment nearly as amusing as I did, she politely smiled again and leaned her head to the left. Her blond hair, all tightly pulled back into a ponytail, slipped from behind her left shoulder and fell heavily over her nametag.

"How many in your party?" she asked.

"Oh, it's just me, thank you," I replied, sheepishly. "Hey, um, before I get seated, I really don't want to leave my bike unattended outside and I don't have a lock. Would it be okay if I left it leaning up against the wall over here while I eat?" I asked with a pleading puppy dog look on my face.

"I don't see why not," she said. "It's a little early for us to have too many guests anyway. Go ahead and put it over there in the corner." She pointed to a windowed corner near the entrance. "Just make sure it doesn't block the door."

"Okay. Thank you so much. God, I'm so hungry, I can't even tell you," I said. I wasn't sure what kind of response I was looking for, but from the look on the hostess's face, I don't think she gave a shit about how hungry I was.

I wheeled Jezebel as far into the empty corner as I could, leaving as much room as possible for the door to swing unencumbered. I removed my helmet, sunglasses, cycling shoes, and gloves and laid them down on the ground underneath the frame. The hostess took a quick glance down at my socked feet but didn't say anything.

"Thanks so much," I repeated. "I really appreciate it."

"It's my pleasure, *sir*. Please follow me." It was her turn to cast a sarcastic smile.

Shessh! Tough crowd, tough crowd.

She sat me down at a small two-person table near the entrance. I appreciated that as the location allowed me to keep an eye on Jezebel.

"Awesome. Thank you," I said, taking a seat.

"You're welcome. A server will be with you shortly," she replied, then turned away.

I perused the area. It looked like the bartender might be the only server in the restaurant this early in the day as I didn't see many other people walking around. My suspicion was soon verified when the hostess waved at him as she walked away from my table and back to the greeting stand, giving him a heads-up that I needed service. Not that she really needed to. I made so much of a racket stacking all of my gear in the corner a few minutes before sitting down that I'm sure everyone in the restaurant knew I was there. A few minutes later, he came over. I knew exactly what I wanted even before I saw the menu: a burger, salad, fries, and a Coke.

"Hey. How you doing?" he asked casually as he approached, drying his hands on a white towel draped over one of two large pockets in his black waist-apron.

"Hi. I'm good. Thanks."

"Good to hear. Can I bring you something to drink?"

"Coke, please. And I'm ready to order food too, if you're cool with that."

Like he'd been doing it for years, he pulled a notepad out of the other pocket of his half-apron and, at the same time, slipped a pen from his breast pocket.

"Great. What'll you have?" he asked with a smile.

I pointed at the menu and leaned it in his direction.

"I need that burger and fries. And a side salad, please."

The waiter leaned over and looked briefly at the menu, then turned away to write the order down in his notepad. He looked up a few seconds later.

"Sure thing. Anything else?"

"Nope. I think that will do. Thank you."

"Ok. Let me put this order in and I'll bring out your Coke."

He clicked his pen shut and reached for the menu. I picked it up off the table and handed it over.

"Great. Thank you," I said.

He tucked the menu under his left arm and hurried back to the bar.

The Coke came out first, and I dumped it down my gullet as fast as I could, stopping periodically to breathe and let the stinging in the back of my throat subside. With the exception of the ice cubes, I drained the entire glass before he made it back behind the bar. The rush was almost instantaneous, as though the sugar diffused directly into my bloodstream the moment it hit my stomach. And it was wonderful. Every sip delicious and rejuvenating. *No wonder people get addicted to the stuff*, I thought. By the time the waiter came by a second time, I had been reduced to chewing on the remaining ice cubes. I'm a known ice-chewer, even though I know I shouldn't be.

"Need a refill?" he asked with a look of all-knowing certainty.

"Oh. Yes, please. How'd you guess?"

"Eh. You know. The ice crunching kinda gave it away."

"Hmm. Yeah, you're probably right." I handed over the glass. "Thanks."

"No problem. I'll be right back."

It seemed to take forever, but when the waiter brought me a full refill, he also had my food with him.

"Here you are."

"Ah, thanks. That looks amazing," I said.

"It's a customer favorite. We sell a lot of these burgers. Enjoy."

"Thank you."

Hardly a few seconds after the waiter left the table, I had a mouth full of burger. I devoured it first, so quickly that I thought I might choke, every so often slipping in a fry or two between mouthfuls. The salad finished off the meal, and I did it without choking, thank you very much, washing it all down with the last of the Coke. Then I sat silently in the mostly empty restaurant, trying not to reveal my impatience. However, I wasn't doing too well with my restraint. I loudly placed my fork and knife on the glass plate and, instead of picking the plate up and setting it down like I usually would, I scooted it into the center of the table, creating a minor racket in the process. A few seconds later I wadded up my napkin and precariously put it in the middle of the plate next to the dirty utensils. He must have caught me out of the corner of his eye from the bar and recognized the hints. As soon as the napkin hit the plate, he quickly walked over, discreetly dropped the check on the table and took the plate away.

"Thank you for coming in, sir," he said politely. "I hope you enjoyed your meal."

I knew it was the polite thing to do, but it felt so awkward when people called me "sir." The only people in my life that warranted the term, to me at least, were my Marine Corps drill instructors and my father, and maybe an older stranger. It made me feel old, and more important than I was. Shoot, I was nineteen, way too young for people to make me feel elderly by attaching a term to me I reserved only for my elders or superiors. But hey, I got it, he was only doing his best to earn a decent tip.

"Yes, very much so. Just what I needed. Thank you," I replied.

"Outstanding," he said and backed away from the table. "Have a good day."

"Thanks. You too."

"I will."

The waiter walked back to the bar and continued his prep for the inevitable dinner rush later in the evening. I paid in cash, which I left on the table next to the bill, and was out the door before he could return. I still had a lot of miles to cover, so there was no time to waste. *No MORE time to waste. Shit ,Matt, you're burning too much daylight. Get out of here.* Thank goodness the hills of Big Sur were behind me.

I paused in the parking lot for a couple of minutes to adjust my gear and check my laminated maps. All I needed to do was follow Highway 1 all the way to San Simeon, a no-brainer really. But, just to be sure, I checked them anyway. I pulled all of them out of my left pannier, found the one that detailed the section of Highway I was riding on, and gave it a once over. Sure enough, I was on course and heading in the right direction. No significant distractions from here to my first checkpoint.

I pedaled up Nepenthe's driveway on a full stomach and rejoined the highway. *Ah, man, that is exactly what I needed. Good stop, Matt.* I coasted for the next several miles, letting lunch settle and enjoying the downhill relaxation. My next landmark was McWay Falls, one of only two picturesque waterfalls that flow directly into the Pacific Ocean. I arrived at the trailhead to the McWay falls vista point a little while later and realized that I would actually have to hike down a short trail to watch it splash into the Pacific. I didn't have time for that, or the proper shoes, for that matter, nor did I want to maneuver Jezebel down a narrow dirt trail. What a bummer. So, unfortunately, I had to miss out on this experience and continue down the road. *There will always be another time.*

As predicted, the highway leveled out after my descent from Big Sur and made for smooth riding. Traffic thinned to a minimum, and my ride was uneventful all the way into San Simeon. The miles between McWay Falls and San Simeon were a mix of rolling hills and long, flat stretches of road, every mile gracing me with the glory of the beautiful coastline; desert mountainside to my left and the massive turquoise water of the Pacific Ocean to my right.

While periodically stealing a few glances over the ocean as I rode by, I found the contrast between its deep blue and the pale white of the afternoon sky stark, and mysterious. Its mystifying presence begs one to question what's beyond that distant horizon. I'm not the seafaring type, which is ironic considering I joined the Marine Corps, a department of the Navy, but I understand the gravitational-like pull the ocean can have on people. Humans are curious by nature. It's how we learn about our surroundings and build trust in our relationships. The wanderlust of early explorers and adventurers must have been extreme for them to brave the unknown in search of what lies beyond the vastness of great oceans. Many of these adventurers succumbed to the torrent of the ocean's fury, however. Evidence of her unparalleled power and relentless force is scattered all over the seafloor just offshore from where I was riding.

I was far beyond the end of the redwoods now, and the terrain slowly began its transition from a Pacific Northwest marine-influenced environment to a coastal desert one, consisting largely of dry, rocky soil that supported the growth of rugged, drought-resistant plants. Many grew from cracks in the land, their straggly roots holding rocks and boulders together. Or maybe they were slowly splitting the rocks apart. Looks can be deceiving.

But the rocky environment only lasted for a short while, just a few miles, gradually transitioning into golden hillsides of dry grass and white rocks. Here, majestic birds of prey circled high above the rippling landscape, unflapping and floating weightless in the late afternoon updrafts, their heads cocked downward, waiting for careless prey to slip out from the protective camouflage of dry grass. I even spotted a few cows grazing in the distance. *You all keep your distance. You understand me? Stay off the road!*

The terrain may have been rugged, but the road was smooth and well maintained. For a two-lane road, it was wide compared to those cut into the mountains of the East Bay. Along this stretch of highway there was plenty of room to ride safely along the shoulder, unlike the precariousness of the highway I pedaled over earlier today before the climb up Big Sur. Location is everything when it comes to road width, I guess. It was smooth sailing now.

Speaking of sailing, earlier in the day as I was riding past Carmel, I observed several boats floating around under a gentle wind about a mile offshore. The further south I traveled, the fewer of them I saw. The few that stuck around, which my imagination convinced me were following me down the coast, moved at a pretty good speed, especially as the afternoon weather began to materialize. Sporadic whitecaps danced in the water around them, warning me that wind was on the way. That turned out to be true, and soon enough the boats became tiny dots in the distance. This change in weather would affect me as well, just not as beneficially. I knew it was coming and I was prepared for it. Miles of slow, tricky riding, that's what I had coming. Gusty onshore breezes are common along the California coast, a daily afternoon phenomenon in most parts, especially where mountains meet the sea. They're always expected, but when riding a bike, hopeful avoidance is the state of mind. I'll admit it, I harbored a similar mindset that afternoon, too. But it didn't take long for me to realize I wasn't avoiding any of this predictable reality.

Onshore winds gradually increased with the passing hours. These, combined with the setting sun and cooing temperatures, drastically slowed my progress. My ego did its best to push the challenges aside as mere annoyances, but I was not immune to these natural torments. Energy output and concentration increased dramatically as I was forced to make erratic corrections to keep Jezebel in a straight line. That's one thing about being on a bike; you become highly observant of things you're usually privileged to ignore when sitting behind a steering wheel and glass windshield. Out in the elements I was exposed, a land-sail incapable of transferring wind energy into speed. Here, wind only hindered me. Leaning westward from time to time was necessary to offset the push of the crosswinds and prevent them from blowing me into the middle of the road. The protection of the redwood trees in Big Sur and the shielding provided by buildings I'd past in the coastal towns this morning were far behind me now, and nothing stood between me and the ocean to dim its intensity. I expected all this and would likely be dealing with these annoying crosswinds for the rest of the ride into San Simeon.

Fortunately, although bothersome, it wasn't as bad as it could have been. I was holding my own. The wind could have very easily been blowing twice as hard. It was October and the weather was mild, pleasant really. If it were summer, I would have been dealing with not only the cool wind blowing in off the ocean, but also the added diurnal effects of rising warm air off the mountains, as air from the ocean would have raced up the mountainside to fill the gap opened up by the ascending air.

CHAPTER SIX

After a few more hours battling crosswinds, autumn's seasonally abbreviated timepiece of ensuing darkness took control, escorting me into San Simeon under a colorful blanket of costal twilight. I was tired, but happy about achieving my goal for the day and relieved that the winds had died down several miles outside of town. The lights of San Simeon would guide me in with an easy finish to my full day of adventure on two wheels. After a long and difficult day of riding, I was able to check day one off the list. Success! From the beginning I knew it would be tough, but now it was over.

I arrived unscathed, except for some annoying numbness between my legs and a few of my toes. Note to self: loosen cycling shoes when feet get hot and swollen, and maybe buy one of those saddles with the center cut out of it. *Guess I need to give that guy John a call, or was it James? I don't remember. All I know is that he made bike saddles that prevented penile numbness.* I currently wasn't suffering from any of that craziness, but you never know. I still had two days of riding ahead of me, after all. *I wonder if I still have his card somewhere? Whatever, I'll worry about that later.* I had other things on my mind.

Mentally, I was ready for a change of pace. Ready to settle down in a hotel room, take a shower, prepare for tomorrow, find a payphone to call Mo, and get some rest. *Don't forget to call your mother too, dumb dumb, or you'll never hear the end of it.* Oh, and food. I needed that too. I was starving again. Remember that amazing lunch I had at Nepenthe, hours ago? Yeah, that meal was filling, but I'd burned up those calories miles ago.

The sun had been below the horizon for a while now, and evening had settled in. Only a thin band of crimson and gold outlined the edge of the world to the west, the last trace of day hanging on before sleep. *Got here just in* time, I thought. All the effort I put into pedaling through the crosswinds produced ample amounts of sweat. The salty breeze quickly dried it up, leaving salty lines of white where streams of sweat had previously run down my arms and legs. I was really looking forward to washing all of that away under a nice, hot shower.

The temperature had noticeably dropped over the past hour, and a chill was creeping in. As long as I kept moving, I stayed warm enough, but when I stopped, I got cold. And stop I did. I coasted into town and immediately became tangled in traffic, something I wasn't expecting in this small town, especially in October. Confused, I pulled over to the side of the road for a minute to assess the situation. I didn't see the flashing lights of emergency vehicles or anything else indicating that there was a car accident or something. It looked like San Simeon was simply crowded. Cars and people were everywhere. *What's going on?* I asked myself. *I thought this was a small, quiet town.*

Vehicles were waiting at every intersection to cross the highway, their brake lights accenting the misty twilight with a diffused glow of artificial red, the stop-and-go flashing of so many of them mimicking the erratic behavior of flickering campfire embers. The putter of car engines and playful screams of children splashing around in a nearby hotel pool drowned out the restful sound of waves lapping against the sand behind me. Every parking space in front of each hotel appeared taken. People were walking in all directions, carrying luggage and tiny humans. I watched all this craziness unfold in front of me as I straddled Jezebel on the side of the highway with a bewildered look on my face. Nervousness started to creep in. *Well, this isn't looking good. I hope I can find at least one available hotel room for the night.*

I entered the craziness and pedaled over to the Motel 6 on the southern end of town, looking for the cheapest bed. I walked inside the front office area, Jezebel in tow, and stood in line behind three parties waiting to check in. The line moved fast and I walked up to the front desk, my shoes clicking on the tile floor. The man behind the front desk greeted me as I rested my left arm on the counter between us.

"Good evening. Can I have your last name or reservation number please?"

I smiled nervously.

"Hi there. Actually, I don't have a reservation. I was hoping you had a room available for tonight," I raised my eyebrows and widened my smile.

"I am sorry, sir. We are completely full for the night. It's very busy," he said, placing both of his hands on the counter in a way that conclusively said, *I really can't help you.*

"I can see that," I said, trying to use a tone of understanding but surely sounding disappointed. My eyebrows settled back into their natural places and my smile receded. "Huh. I assumed it was going to be easy to find a room here in October. It isn't always like this, is it?" I asked.

"No. Not here. Usually we have plenty of vacancies this time of year. This is just one of those odd weekends where the entire town fills up with visitors," he explained.

"Why? What's going on?"

"They have the evening tours of Hearst Castle going on this weekend. Tonight's the opening night for the autumn season. It's always busy like this on the first weekend of these events. Kinda makes things crazy around here for a couple days."

"Oh, wow. I didn't even think to look into anything like that. I had no idea."

"Well, you might have some luck at one of the other hotels in town." He raised his right hand, gesturing out the window. "It would be worth it to check them out. I mean, you're already here. Might as well poke around and hope for the best."

"Yeah. Sure will."

"But you should make your way around soon. I've already had a few other people come by looking for rooms too," he said politely, shooing me away gently with a wave toward the door.

"Dang it," I said, discouraged. "Okay, I'll go check out the others. Thank you."

"Good luck, sir," he said as I clumsily made my way outside, pulling Jezebel along with me.

"Thanks," I said as the door shut behind me.

Jezebel and I rolled from hotel to hotel with no luck. Every single one of them said the same thing as the first guy. "I'm sorry, sir, we are all booked for tonight." "I'm sorry sir, we have no rooms available this evening." "I'm sorry. We're full." There are eleven hotels in San Simeon, and not one of them had an available room. *What the hell, man? Really? This is crazy.* I visited all of them. Yes, every single one of them. Nothing.

Understandably frustrated and crabby, I rolled up to the front entrance of the San Simeon Lodge and Restaurant, disengaged from my pedals, straddled Jezebel's frame, and tried to think about other reasonable options. It was way too late in the day, and too dark already, to safely ride anywhere else. Besides, I was beat, and a little irritated to say the least. I gave some serious thought to checking out what was available in West Village, another town just a few miles south down the highway, but feared all the hotels there would have the same responses for me as the ones here. Then I would be stuck there, instead of here. No real benefit gained in that scenario. I'm sure most of the other unsuccessful "hotel room hunters" had headed that way already and snatched up all the available rooms there too. And riding there in the dark would have been far from the safest decision of the evening.

Ravenously hungry again, I parked Jezebel inside the front door of the San Simeon Lodge and Restaurant and sat down for some grub. I think better on a full stomach, anyway. *Maybe some other grand plan will come to light while I bask in the comfort of a warm restaurant.* I passed a payphone as I walked in, but thought better of calling. Best to do that a little later, after I figured out what the heck I was going to do for the night. Always better to come to the conversation with solutions, not just a bunch of "I don't know's."

Well, no great ideas came to mind while I was eating, only fatigue and complacency. The situation was what it was, and, unless something miraculous happened, it looked like I would be treated to a night of sleeping under the stars. *I guess that's why I brought the emergency gear, right? An occasion such as this will, at the very least, validate lugging around the extra weight.* That wouldn't be the worst thing in the world. I'd slept overnight on the beach countless times before. And I'd save me forty bucks, too.

I paid for my meal and left the crowded restaurant. I got back on Jezebel and slowly rode around looking for a safe place to lie down for the night, preferably a location with one way in and out, and close to one of the hotels. *Is this really happening?* The fact that it was happening amused me, but I would take it in stride. I wasn't a novice to sleeping outdoors, not by a long shot. Having bivouacked plenty of times in the Camp Pendleton back country and spent many weekends of my childhood and teenage years camping with the family, I was confident that I could hold my own. But this was a little different. I would be out in the open, alone, exposed, and vulnerable. I thought about spending the night on the beach but wanted to avoid its darkness and seclusion. Although the beach would seem like the ideal place to lie down for the night, I thought it might not be the safest place, considering all the expensive gear I had with me.

Up the street from the restaurant where I ate dinner, I found a large swath of shoulder-high, ground-hugging shrubbery growing under the low-hanging branches of a large tree. This small plot of foliage lay in an undisturbed lot of sand, dirt and grass on the other side of the fence next to the Quality Inn parking lot. With a slow, bewildered nod of preliminary approval, I thought, *This just might work.* I had only the final moments of dwindling twilight and the subtle glow of the nearby lighted hotel signs to work with at this point, so I pulled my battery-powered handlebar light out of my pannier and used it as a flashlight to inspect the area.

My expectation was that a homeless person had already claimed the territory and I would need to move on to find another spot. But my initial inspection didn't tip me off that anyone had ever slept among these bushes before, let alone called this place their home. Other than a few pieces of trash, the place was pretty much untouched. *Yep. This will work,* I said to myself, chuckling out loud at the circumstance. *It will have to do.* Well, At least it wasn't raining. *Oh, lucky me!*

CHAPTER SEVEN

My hopes of a long, hot shower and comfortable bed quashed, I set out to make the best of the situation. Of all the places I'd slept under the stars, this was actually not that bad. As far as I could tell, the threat of being startled awake in the middle of the night by a snake slithering inside my sleeping bag or a tarantula crawling across my face was slim to none. Don't roll your eyes thinking I'm being overly dramatic; it's happened before. Not to me, mind you, but I've heard stories. I was banking on the assumption that rattlesnakes and tarantulas don't like the damp environment near the beach. Whether that was true or not was not up for discussion between the voices in my head. Bivouacking deep in the desert hills of Camp Pendleton, where these horrible visions are not just the stuff of nightmares, made this place look like a picnic. For the sake of my own sanity and a good night's rest, though, I decided that everything would work out fine, and that was that.

Before I got busy settling myself into my beachside camping spot for the night, I needed to find a payphone. My nightly "need to call" list consisted of only two people, but I couldn't bed down for the night without checking both off the list. There would be hell to pay if I brushed this obligation off as a "maybe if I have time" sort of thing. My reasoning for breaking the oath wouldn't matter either. The scorn would be swift, and harsh. No worries, though. None of this "oath-breaking" was going to be of any concern tonight.

It didn't take me long to find a phone. Lucky me! Just a short walk over to the entrance of the Quality Inn, the first hotel I came to after crossing over to the "civilized" side of the fence, and there one was, attached to the outside wall. I sat down sideways, side-saddle style, on Jezebel's top tube. I picked up the receiver and wiped both ends down with the bottom of my jersey. Those things can get pretty nasty, you know. Once I deemed them both to be of "acceptable" cleanliness, a loose standard by any measure, I dropped a quarter into the phone and dialed up her number. She picked up after the second ring.

"Hello?"

It was Mo. I was happy she picked up and not one of her roommates. This didn't leave open the chance that she wasn't there.

"Hey."

"Matt?" she asked confirmingly, her voice alert and a little louder than her initial greeting. "Is that you? You sound so far away. Speak up a little."

"Yep. It's me. How are you?" I answered, raising my voice a level.

"Oh! Hi! I've been waiting for your call. You okay? Where are you? How's the ride going?" She fired off the questions in such rapid-fire succession I couldn't begin to answer one before the next was in progress.

I chuckled.

"I'm fine. Made it to San Simeon. In one piece too. But it's been, let's just say, interesting."

"Oh, good. How was the ride? Did you just get there? It's been dark for a while now."

"I got in about an hour and a half ago and had some dinner after looking for a room. I'm having trouble finding a place to stay, though."

"Really? I thought you said there were plenty of hotels. They all booked?"

"Yeah. Crazy. There's eleven hotels here. All of them full. I went around to each one to see if any of them had a room. No dice. There are so many people here tonight. It's crazy," I said, my voice growing increasingly frustrated with every word.

"Oh no. Why is it so packed?"

I began to answer but was cut off when the phone clicked over to a recording: "To continue, please insert another twenty-five cents." That's right, long distance. *That'll cost me. But it's worth it.*

"Just a second. I need to add another quarter." I reached into my jersey pocket and grabbed a handful of quarters. I dropped four of them in the payphone's coin slot, listened for the chime of acceptance, and got back on the line. "Okay, we're good for a while now."

"So, why are so many people there? Something going on?" she inquired.

"One of the hotel front office workers said it's the first weekend of the night tours at the Hearst Castle. It's just up the road from here, up in the hills. I passed it on my way into town. I guess it's a popular event and they only host them in autumn and spring."

"Ah, honey, I'm sorry. What are you going to do? You're not going to continue riding in the dark, are you?" she asked. I could sense concern in her voice.

"No way. I'm done for the day," I said excitedly. "And I'm way too beat for that. It was difficult enough riding today when the sun was out. I don't want to risk riding after dark. I'm actually going to lay out under the stars in my emergency sleeping bag. I already found a good spot."

"No, you're not!" Mo exclaimed.

"Don't worry." I chuckled. "I'm going to be fine. It will be like I'm camping on the beach," I said in a jovial tone. She read right through it.

"But what about your bike? Where are you going to put it while you're sleeping, so it's safe?"

I could sense her concern turning to worry.

"I found a spot next to a well-lit hotel behind a fence and next to a tree. Nobody can see me from the road, and I will lean Jezebel up against the fence and sleep right next to her." I did my best to make this sound as safe as possible.

"Really?" she said with a "are-you-fucking-crazy" tone to it. Maybe there was some truth to that, just maybe.

"Sounds crazy, I know. But I'm going to be fine, really. The weather is great. It's not cold. It's not raining. It's not even foggy. I'll be alright."

"Oh God, Matt." She sighed into the receiver. "I'm hardly going to sleep tonight worrying about all this," she said. My explanation didn't help alleviate much of her anxiety. Note to self: *Learn to say things without saying things that make the original thing sound bad.* I'm still working on that one.

"Well, at least you don't go to bed until the early morning hours. So you'll only have to worry for a couple of them. I'll be getting up about 6:30."

"Ha. Real funny, Matt," replying in sing-song sarcasm. "Come on, that's not helping," she continued, dropping her voice back to her normal tone.

"Sorry," I said. "Trust me. I'm going to be fine, Mo. Really."

"Will you call me when you wake up, before you start riding again?"

"Of course I will, Mo. Just keep the phone close to your bed. Speaking of bed, I need to get some sleep. I did a lot of riding today and I'm really tired. I'll call you in the morning before I leave and when I get into Santa Barbara tomorrow night."

"Okay, Matt. Please be careful. I can't wait to see you."

"I can't wait to see you, too! Good night."

"Good night," she said softly.

I stayed on the line and let her hang up first. Such a dopey thing to do, but hey, I was a hopeless romantic then. Still am too. Keep that to yourself, will ya? *Oh yeah, wouldn't want to ruin your street cred now, would we Matt? Sure, sure. We'll keep it on the down-low.* After hearing the click of disconnection, I pushed the receiver handle down, held it there for a couple seconds, waited for the coins I dropped in earlier to crash into the phone's coin receptacle, let it go, waited for a dial tone, and dropped in another dollar's worth of quarters. Might as well, it will cost me at least that much. This time I called my home number. After a couple rings, Dad picked up.

"Hello," he said, more as a statement than a question.

"Hey, Dad."

"Hey, Matt!" he said excitedly.

In the background I heard my mother scream.

"Is that Matt?"

"Yep," Dad said, barely audible.

His muffled answer convinced me he'd turned away from the receiver and yelled into the bowels of the house to let Mom know it was me on the phone. A second later, his voice came through in a normal volume.

"Hold on, Matt. Mom's picking up the phone in the bedroom."

Before I could even get a word of acknowledgement out to Dad, Mom joined in with a click in the receiver.

"Hi, Matt!" she said happily. Mom quickly took control of the conversation, dropping Dad's status to that of an eavesdropper. "Are you okay? Where are you?"

"I made it to San Simeon, safe and sound. It was a long, hard day of riding, but didn't have any issues," I said.

"You must be tired," Mom said.

"Yep. Pretty beat. Went up and down a lot of hills today. I'm ready for bed."

As soon as I said it, I knew I shouldn't have. We would have gotten around to talking about it anyway, but I was secretly hoping the issue wasn't going to come up. Immediately after the word "bed" came out of my mouth, I knew where the conversation was headed and took a deep breath to prepare myself.

"Where are you staying?" she asked, as predicted.

"Well, there's a story about that," I said.

I spent the next several minutes detailing the same situation I'd laid out to Mo a few minutes prior. As expected, Mom was worried sick. All of my reassurances didn't help either, they never do. Maybe it's a "mom thing." Hard to believe it would just be a "MY mom thing," to worry so much, that is. Even after I reminded her that I lived with snakes, tarantulas, and a bunch of crazy Marines for two weeks in the desolate hills of Camp Pendleton during Marine Corps combat training and turned out just fine, she still wasn't satisfied.

"That's different," she said, her voice sulking.

As if to balance out the emotions, I could almost feel Dad rolling his eyes through the phone receiver.

"Not really," I said. "Mom, come on, don't worry so much. Please?"

"I can't help it. Do you want me to call all the hotels and see if I can find a room for you?"

"No, Mom. Look, I told you already, I went around to every single hotel, even the expensive ones. There literally isn't a room available in the entire town tonight."

"Okay. I just want to help, if I can."

"I know you do, Mom. Thank you. Okay, I do need to get my little make-shift place set up and get some sleep. Tell you what, I told Mo I would call her when I wake up tomorrow morning. I'll call you too. That way you'll know I'm okay. Sound good?"

"Alright. Just be careful, Matt. Please," Mom said, pleading.

I heard the worry in her voice. I didn't like her worrying about me, but I understood. Every new experience I went through was a first for her too. I was the first born of four children, the first to drive, the first to have a girlfriend, the first to graduate high school, the first to leave the house, the first to join the military, and, of course, the first to ride a bicycle down the

California coast to visit a girl.

Of all the things I've done in my life, my enlistment in the Marine Corps was the hardest for her to accept. Not because she was anti-military, not by a long shot. Quite the opposite, actually. She met my father while he was serving in the US Army, fighting on the front lines with the First Cavalry during the Vietnam War. They started conversing after my father read an open letter she penned to service members in the local paper during his first tour of duty. My dad got hold of the paper several weeks later, after receiving a care package from his mom containing the newspaper. They wrote back and forth for months, until his first tour of duty ended, and he came home. That was when they met each other for the first time. It was 1970. After communicating only through letters again while Dad served a second tour of duty, he came home, married my mom a few years later, and they've been together ever since. The worry and heartache she felt for my dad while he was in combat must have been excruciating. I'll never fully comprehend that level of anguish and enduring uncertainty. The thought that her son could also end up in combat gave her anxiety and restless nights. I wasn't fighting in any wars tonight, but I was sure it would be one of those restless nights for her regardless.

"I will, Mom. Good night. You too, Dad. Good night."

Both of them tumbled over each other in my ear with their "good nights" and "I love yous."

"I love you, too. I'll call you in the morning," I said.

I gently hung up the receiver and, as with the previous call, waited for the quarters to jingle into their final resting place inside the phone. I backed Jezebel up and away from the phone. I was so close to where I was going to stay the night that I didn't even bother to ride over there. We walked and rolled, just Jezebel and me. As I passed the fence, I took a precautionary look around before stepping off the sidewalk and into the shadows. I definitely wasn't trying to attract any unwanted attention this evening. It helped that the empty field was a sizeable lot and at the tail end of a line of hotels. Set away from the town's hustle and bustle, it was quiet and empty. At the other end of the lot was the southern limit of the town, marked only by the Motel 6 where I started this crazy evening.

Holding Jezebel by the top tube and handlebars, I walked as far into the field as I could, guided only by the light of the moon and the faint bloom of pink neon light emanating from the hotel sign next door. I was surprised by Jezebel's weight, or lack of it, really. As bulky as she appeared with two panniers straddling her backside and a sleeping bag strapped to the top of the frame behind the saddle, one would have expected her to weigh more than she did.

Once I reached the rear of the shrubs, next to the tree where I would hopefully be sleeping the night away, I set Jezebel down and turned on the handlebar light. Aided by the additional illumination, I inspected the area more thoroughly than I did a while ago and found a clear space next to the tree and against the fence where I could wedge her for the remainder of the night, a corner that would protect her from two directions. I would then lie on the ground next to her, protecting from the other two directions. If anyone were to come into this area and try to cause any problems, I was sure to hear it.

Stealth and safety issues out of the way, it was time to get some shut eye. After struggling through an excitement-induced restless night of small naps the night before, I'd been up since 4 a.m. I'd exerted a lot of energy since then. My eyes were starting to burn from tiredness. I rubbed them gently for a few seconds to cool them off, getting little relief. Better than no relief, I suppose. I pulled my boxer shorts and T-shirt out of the panniers and draped them over Jezebel's top tube while I prepared my sleeping area for the night.

After squeezing Jezebel into the small opening between the fence and the tree, I unstrapped my sleeping bag, yanked it free of its stuff bag, and rolled it out on top of the dry grass. The bag was bright blue in the sunshine but appeared gray and dark under the muted light of the moon. I slipped off my shoes and used the sleeping bag as a barrier between my feet and the ground while I got naked under the stars. Relief from the all-day compression of cycling clothes came instantly, but evidence of its constriction remained. Even under the faint glow of moonlight, my eyes having adjusted to the darkness by now, I could easily make out the crisscross pattern impressions on my waist, thighs, and upper arms, pressed into my skin by the seams of the tight-fitting Lycra. My naked body, now unprotected in any form and exposed to the cool night air, felt the chill, and I quickly slipped into my dry, loose-fitting boxer shorts and oversized T-shirt. Amazing how much a simple thin layer of clothing can fend off the cold bite of night. It felt wonderful to get out of the skin-hugging clothes and into some comfortable dry ones.

Man, I needed a shower, though. *Dang, you stink, bro.* Oh well, maybe tomorrow, nothing I can do about it tonight. Well, I guess I could go take a dip in the ocean. *Yeah, I don't think so.* If I was lucky, maybe the smell would help keep the bugs away.

The night was not only cool, but clear, and I didn't see any indication that fog was going to move in before morning. The light of the moon drowned out much of anything else in the eastern sky, but the heavens to the west, above the dark, charcoal-colored ocean, were sparkling with brilliance.

So much so that the western horizon, usually indistinguishable under a cloudy nighttime sky, was easily identifiable.

The clear sky meant I was in for a cold night's sleep, but at the same time it gave me a comfortable level of confidence that I wouldn't be sleeping outside in the fog. So I turned my cycling clothes inside out and laid them over Jezebel's handlebars and top tube, hoping they would dry out by morning.

I set the alarm on my Timex digital watch for 6:30 a.m. That would get me on the road by 7. I flicked the watch off my wrist and wrapped it around a couple of spokes on Jezebel's front wheel, keeping it close to my head and allowing me the best opportunity to hear it go off in the morning. This final chore complete, I didn't waste any more time getting my tired ass to sleep. I slithered my body into the tight-fitting bag and zipped it all the way up to my chin. It was a lightweight mummy-style sleeping bag, complete with a hood. The bag was cold to the touch when I first climbed inside, but warmed up quickly as I settled in. I pulled hard on the drawstring to cinch down the hood and shuffled around for a bit, trying to find the most comfortable piece of ground. One rock in the wrong place can make all the difference for a good night's sleep, trust me. Same goes for little nocturnal critters, too. I might have been nervous about snakes making their way into the bag during the night, but now that I was snuggled up inside, it felt like there wasn't enough room inside for a mouse, let alone a slithering reptile.

*　　　*　　　*

The first night on my road to Mo, and I was sleeping next to Jezebel alongside Highway 1 in a one-man sleeping bag on top of cool dirt, dry grass, and wind-blown sand. It was quite comical if you thought about it. At least I thought it was, and it made me smile, despite the discomfort of the uneven ground.

How funny I must have looked all snuggled up with only my face showing through the open hole in the sleeping bag, sandwiched between a bicycle propped up against a fence and some shrubbery growing just off the side of the highway, next to a hotel, one hundred yards from the Pacific Ocean. Mo would have laughed if she saw me. And I smiled while I lay there, thinking of her laughing at me.

All tough talk aside, I was a little nervous about what the night had in store for me. The unknown always makes me weary. I thought it might keep me from sleep, at least the restful sleep I desperately needed if I was going to recuperate from my long day of endless pedaling. But I tried to let these concerns slip from my mind, trusting that all would be fine when I woke up in the morning. The loud roaring of the normally quiet town had subsided, and the music of the ocean returned. I closed my eyes and listened to its ancient lullaby. I allowed myself to concentrate on its rhythm and sing me to sleep, but I couldn't stop Maureen from slipping into my thoughts between the hissing of each wave as it rolled against the sand. I yearned deeply to be lying next to her instead of Jezebel. It was the most wonderful thought that could have entered my mind at that moment, the perfect vision to lead me into my dreams. Not long after that, all my concerns floated away as I drifted off to dreamless slumber.

A sign near Marina State Beach, heading south. The journey just began and there's still a long way to go.

Looking back on Bixby Bridge after riding past.

Self-portrait in the late afternoon of day one, riding the relatively flat
road into San Simeon.

The sun sets on my first day. Taken just north of San Simeon.

PART FOUR

A Day of Challenges

San Simeon ⟶ Santa Barbara

Matthew Koehler

CHAPTER ONE

I woke up with a jolt after what felt like a twenty-minute nap and, after a brief moment of confusion, remembered the unusual situation I was in. My lower back spasmed as I shifted around in the sleeping bag, attempting to relieve the tingling in my right arm.

What the hell? How long have I been asleep? Oh my God, Jezebel.

I immediately turned to my right from inside my blue cocoon. I could see the outline of her frame, backlit by the light from the hotel next door filtering through the slits in the fence. She was as I had left her last night, still obediently wedged between fence and tree.

It was still dark, but I could tell it was morning as the sky was beginning to brighten with the rising sun. Or was it the moon? It was tough to tell as the whole sky was bathed in the same soft light. *That's odd,* I thought in my post-wakeup delirium. It only took a few moments of evolving clarity to realize that clouds were beginning to brighten, not the sky. And from my position on the ground it was impossible to know whether they were being illuminated by the pre-dawn sun or the moon. "Damn it," I whispered, quickly emerging from my brain fog and realizing that I was certainly wrong in my assessment that the marine layer was not going to roll in overnight. *You should have known better, Matt. Come on.*

As my cold, wet face indicated, the marine layer had in fact, silently made its way on shore while I was sleeping. *Damn you!* "Ah, man. Shit," I muttered quietly into the mist, remembering that I left my cycling clothes laid out on Jezebel to dry overnight. Well, I didn't even need to feel them to know that didn't happen. *So much for that.* Worrying about wet clothes would have to wait though. I needed to get myself out of this sleeping bag and take a piss, like right now. My bladder felt as full as a high-flying hot air balloon, and it was going to explode if I didn't take care of business.

As quickly as I could manage, I loosened the drawstring holding the hood securely around my face. I expanded the opening as wide as the fabric would allow and, like an earthworm, wiggled my body free from the bag. As with the marine layer, the ramifications of yesterday's efforts had settled in overnight, and as I slowly brought myself to a standing position, the extent of my overexertion revealed itself with every muscle contraction. My legs felt heavy, like bags of sand, and most of the muscles below my waist were tight as stretched rubber bands. The spasm in my back had calmed down, though, so at least I had that going for me. *I'll worry about that in a minute,* I thought. *Right now, I need to pee.*

I clumsily high-stepped out of the sleeping bag and allowed it to fall at my feet as a crumpled mess on the soft terrain. Holding in the urge to let loose right there, I hobbled on my heels across the damp ground and dew-topped grass to the edge of the shrub line, stood in the dim light of dawn, and went from full to empty in about twenty seconds.

"Shit, it's cold," I murmured to myself as I finished up. "And where did all of this fog come from?"

The dampness in the air sucked the heat right out of me as I stood motionless, unforgivingly exposed to the elements and ostensibly alone in the heavy mist and gloomy dawn twilight. My eyes squinted for detail into the distance, hopelessly searching for a break in the fog. Finding nothing but random shadows, I tilted my head back and stared blankly into the sky, letting loose a long, frustrated sigh into the grey nothingness. As I finished "nature's call" and turned around to face my camp, the urge to climb right back into that sleeping bag and warm up again nearly overwhelmed me. *Not a chance, Marine. You're up now, so get moving.*

To keep the wake-up process moving along, I tip-toed back to my crumpled sleeping bag, stood on top of it to get my feet off the ground, and took several minutes to stretch the tightness out of my legs and adjust to the morning climate. All I really wanted to do was get dressed and find some breakfast, but with my muscles as tight as they were, it was going to take me a while to get warmed up. They needed a little love before the day got started. Goosebumps be damned, after a few minutes of contorting myself in the frosty air, it was time to get dressed.

I rose up onto my toes again and stepped carefully across the damp grass to Jezebel. I opened both panniers and rooted around for my second set of cycling clothes and all my cold-weather gear. I found them without much effort as there wasn't much in the panniers to sort through. As fast as I could manage, I ripped off my boxer shorts and T-shirt and immediately stuffed them into the panniers. Not thrilled about standing naked along the side of the road in the chilly fog, I quickly yanked up my cycling shorts and pulled down my jersey, slid on my leg- and arm-warmers, slipped into my jacket, and zipped it all the way up to my chin. I put my full finger gloves in my right jersey pocket and my damp fingerless gloves in the left jersey pocket. Sitting down on the dry interior part of my sleeping bag, I pulled the T-shirt I'd slept in out of the pannier and dried off my feet, soaked and freezing from the bath they'd just taken as I shuffled through the morning dew. After wiping them down to a reasonably dry state, I pulled my socks on and quickly slipped my feet into my shoes.

"Okay, that's better," I said under my breath.

Now I could get organized. Since I was down on her level, I took my watch back from Jezebel and glanced at the time: 6:20. I turned off the alarm and strapped it back on to my wrist.

I stood up, gingerly, and peeled yesterday's wet clothes off Jezebel's frame and handlebars, folded them, and placed them in one of the spare plastic bags I'd brought along for situations such as this, and then stuffed the whole thing in the left pannier.

"What dumb fucking luck," I murmured into the thick mist, the fog nearest where Jezebel lay glowing a dull pink from the light of the nearby hotel sign.

I picked up the sleeping bag, now twice as heavy as it was when I laid it out on the ground yesterday evening, and shook it vigorously, getting rid of as much water and dead grass as possible. While stuffing it back into its stuff-bag, I mumbled into the mist once again. "Man, what dumb luck. I had better get a hotel room tonight."

I looked to Jezebel for confirmation while I strapped the now-stuffed sleeping bag back down to the top of the pannier frame, but got nothing. She was perfectly content leaning against the fence. Tiny beads of water were slowly settling out of the air and onto the dry strips of top tube where my cycling clothes laid just a few seconds earlier. Surface tension formed them into mostly-spherical blobs, and they too took on some of the aura that surrounded us, making them stand out like pink polka dots against Jezebel's dark frame.

I pulled my handlebar light out, flicked it on, and used the extra light to scan my surroundings. The brightness of the lamp illuminated the water in the air, turning its single beam into a globe of light, drowning out all of the pink in the air. *Yep, looks like I got everything.* Jezebel was packed, and I was ready to go. First thing first, however. I needed to place a couple of promised phone calls.

I pulled Jezebel away from the fence and carried her over to the sidewalk, noticeably heavier than she was the previous night. Not by much, but even a few extra pounds makes a big difference when you're pedaling hundreds of miles, and I think the fog added just enough to pack on a bit of irritation to today's ride. On the bright side, it had become noticeably brighter in the short time I had been awake. Not exactly daylight yet, but bright enough to keep me from kicking something or stepping in a hole as long as I was paying attention. Accordingly, I walked carefully on my heels so I didn't get any dirt or sand in the pedal cleats, glaring attentively at the ground with each awkwardly landed step.

Jezebel and I sounded like ticking clocks as we clicked and clacked our way over to the payphone, each of us ticking out a different rhythm. Jezebel with her freewheel clicking as she rolled, me with my pedal cleats slapping the sidewalk with every step.

Arriving at the front door of the hotel several seconds later, I leaned Jezebel up against the window outside the Quality Inn lobby, next to the payphone and underneath a dimly lit "Vacancy" sign. I stared in disbelief. *Vacancy? What? Did somebody check out in the middle of the night? Vacancy? That sure would have been nice to know last night! Eh, whatever, I saved some dough and maybe someone cancelled late into the night while I was sleeping. Who knows, and who cares? It's too late to care about it right now anyway.*

I picked up the receiver and placed it against my ear. No dial tone. I slapped the cradle a couple time to reset the phone. Still nothing. *Are you kidding me? Really?*

Frustrated, I hung up the phone and walked inside the hotel. I was met with warm, dry air that felt rejuvenating and welcoming. My fingertips instantly seemed to get some of their dexterity back, and all was forgiven in regard to the broken phone. *Well now, would you look at that, Koehler. A blessing in disguise. Isn't that nice?*

"Good morning," the front desk lady said as the door shut behind me. Her cheery tone helped further brighten the dreary morning.

"Hi there. Good morning," I replied, forcing a smile. I stuck up my right thumb and jabbed it toward the window behind me. "The, um, payphone outside isn't working. Do you happen to have another one around?"

"Sure. There's another one right over there."

She raised her hand and pointed to the back corner of the lobby.

"Oh, great," I said. "May I?"

"Of course."

"Thanks. I'll just be a minute."

I walked to the back of the lobby. Other than the lady at the counter, I was the only one sharing the space, and the sound of my shoes click-clacking on the tile floor echoed sharply off the mostly bare white walls. The woman behind the counter didn't seem to mind, though. She went back to whatever she was doing before I walked in the door. I picked up the receiver and put it to my ear. This one had a dial tone. *Wonderful.*

I called Mo first. She picked up after the third ring and spoke in a whisper.

"Hi. Is that you, Matt?" she asked.

"Hi, Mo," I replied softly. "I just got up and I'm getting back on the road. All was good last night. The fog rolled in, so everything's a little damp, but I'm fine," I explained.

"That's good. Glad you're okay," she said, still whispering.

I imagined her lying face up on her elevated UC Irvine college bed with the phone to her ear, eyes shut, barely conscious; her roommate, Laurie, asleep on the other side of the room in her own elevated bunk bed. Mo doesn't do mornings very well, but I knew she would at least be able to sleep better now that we'd talked.

"I'll call you tonight," I said.

"Okay. Be safe," she said, still whispering.

"I will. Bye."

"Bye."

I listened for her to hang up. The call disconnected with a "click," and I pulled the phone away from my ear. I'm almost positive that before I even returned the receiver to its cradle, she was already fast asleep again.

One down, one to go. I picked up the receiver again and dialed home. Mom would be waiting impatiently for my call, I was sure of that. It was Sunday, so she was probably close to getting up anyhow.

"Hello?" she said, picking up in the middle of the first ring.

"Hey, Mom."

She wasted no time getting right to the point.

"How are you? You okay?"

She spoke clearly, like she had just finished drinking a large glass of water, and I could hear the familiar concern in her voice. It sounded like she had been up for a while already.

"I'm fine, Mom. The fog came in overnight, so everything's a little damp but nothing that won't dry out after a few miles of riding."

"Oh good. I was worried about you last night," she said, finally sounding relieved.

"I know, Mom. But everything's alright. I need to get on the road, though, if I'm going make it to Santa Barbara tonight. There's a lot of miles to cover between here and there."

"Alright. Well, be careful, Matt. Love you," she said.

"Love you, too, Mom. Say hi to Dad and the rest of the Koehler clan for me."

"I will."

"Thanks."

I hung up the phone and made my way outside, trying my best to walk quietly across the lobby floor, without success. As I clip-clopped across the hotel lobby, I happened to pass the continental breakfast area. The smell of freshly brewed coffee and hot breakfast food billowed from the small nook. I stopped outside the open door and stared fervently at the spread of hot cereal, waffles, scrambled eggs, bacon, and all sorts of snacks. I wasn't feeling hungry, until now, and my nose beckoned me to enter.

The lady at the front desk soon broke the silence.

"Go ahead, sir, it's open now."

I looked over my right shoulder and saw, to my astonishment, that she was actually speaking to me. She must have thought I was a guest at the hotel.

"Okay. Thank you. Don't mind if I do," I said.

See, things were looking up. And I hadn't even been awake for thirty minutes. Score!

I hurried into the breakfast nook before she figured out that I was currently running on vagabond status and not a guest at the hotel. She didn't seem suspicious and didn't give off the vibe that she cared anyway. I filled my plate high with flavorless eggs, thin bacon, fruit, and pastries, then sat down at one of the small tables. While I ate my fill, I guzzled down two cups of coffee, a glass of orange juice, and a glass of water. It didn't take long for me to arrive at a level of contentment, my body having warmed up from the cool morning and now my stomach full when it should have been empty. *What luck*, I thought.

Not wanting to delay the start of what was destined to be another long day in the saddle, I'd mentally prepared myself for the reality that I was going to throw a PowerBar down my throat just so I could get rolling, maybe finding a better place to eat somewhere down the coast. And here, good fortune fell right in my lap in the form of a breakfast buffet inside the hotel that had rejected me last night, forcing me to sleep in the weeds along the edge of its parking lot. Glorious! I took two bananas for the road and headed for the door, shooting a thankful smile and a wave at the lady behind the front desk.

"Have a good day, sir," she answered, waving in-kind.

"Thank you. You too," I replied.

With a belly full of breakfast and hot coffee, my mood was now as warm as my body. With an appreciative sigh, I pushed the front door open and stepped out into the cool morning air, the coastline still buried in fog, and took care of the final preparations for the day's ride. I unslung my helmet from Jezebel's handlebars and pulled the cold, dew-covered brain protector down over my head. I told myself to ignore the smell of the sweat-stained foam pads lining the interior of the helmet as they passed by my nose. But you know how that goes. I breathed in the stench anyway.

Afterward, I pulled the full-finger winter cycling gloves out of my jersey pocket and slid those on. They weren't padded in the palm, but they were dry and would keep my fingers warm and functioning properly until I made it past the fog bank or it burned off with the rising sun.

I plucked Jezebel away from the window and walked her the short distance to the Highway. With the marine layer limiting my field of view, everything took on the nostalgic appearance of a 1970s polaroid landscape photo: slightly out of focus and somewhat faded, with too much of a magenta hue to appear natural. The chilly coastal breeze was calm but erratic and bit sharply into my exposed skin. The gentle push of wind carried the fog around me in eddies and swirls. Granting a certain level of credence to this phenomenon of movement, the melody created by the gentle slapping and hissing of waves against the nearby beach became more audible the closer I got to the ocean, but I still couldn't see them through the soupy fog.

After crossing over to the western side of the highway, I straddled Jezebel and pointed her south. The longer I stood over her frame, the more keenly aware I became of the weakness in my leg muscles from the fifteen hours of riding I put in the day before. The number of miles, and the difficulty of the terrain took a lot out of me, more than I anticipated it would. All the hills, crosswinds, and dangerous road conditions had taken their toll. *You're thinkin' you should have made this a four-day adventure, aren't you, Matt? Just start pedaling, man.*

I knew once I started riding things would loosen up and I'd feel better, so it was time to go. With a full belly and a cold face, I pushed off down the highway and into the mist. As I slowly started to roll down the road, the little Jiminy Cricket in my head had something to say about the recent events. *Next time, Matt, it might do you good to train a little harder for a ride like this. Oh, and maybe call ahead for hotel reservations. Just a thought.*

The first several miles of the day passed slowly, by design, and I was thankful the road was flat. It took a while for my legs to warm up and the soreness in my ass to subside enough that sitting on the saddle was bearable. Sitting on that skinny saddle most of the day yesterday had done a number on my backside. I didn't even realize there was going to be an issue down there until I sat down on it for the first time this morning, feeling like I'd set myself down on a solid steel pipe. *You'll manage. Just keep riding.*

Disregarding the dangers of riding down a highway in heavy fog on the brightening, but still dark, side of dawn, it can be a pleasant experience. I was pedaling slowly anyway, so keeping to the right of the white line was easy enough to do. Riding at a more relaxed pace gave me the luxury of enjoying the slowly passing, partially obstructed scenery, while at the same time granting me a better chance at quickly responding to dangerous events. You must pay incredibly close attention to your surroundings when sharing the road with 3000-pound bricks of steel and rubber, all traveling at crazy speeds, two feet from your armor-less body.

As if the universe were sending me a warning about these "road beasts," I soon rolled up to a recently killed snake lying in the middle of the road. Its mangled carcass was barely visible against the yellow center line and hidden in the fog until appearing abruptly in front of Jezebel's front wheel. Poor guy. *Huh, so much for the "snakes don't like hanging out at the beach" argument I made last night.* Well, it won't be there for long. As soon as the fog pulls back, it will be gone. The buzzards around here are relentless and spend all day riding the onshore breezes with their massive wingspans, gliding high above the highway looking for roadkill just like this. One of these birds would enjoy eating this guy for breakfast as much as I enjoyed eating the hotel buffet.

Dangerous possibilities aside, it's nice to be able to take it all in, especially when traveling alongside such a beautiful stretch of coastline. As I sliced through the fog, it waxed and waned, tumbling over the highway and climbing effortlessly up the adjacent hillside. Momentary holes opened sporadically inside the fog bank, widening my field of view for a short while until they collapsed back in on themselves. Every so often, one would open large enough to grant me a glimpse of the shoreline, where I could watch, not only hear, the waves crashing into the beach.

*　　　*　　　*

Another nine miles down the road I came to the relatively large mid-state coastal town of Cambria. The highway turned inland here and headed southeast, cutting diagonally through the middle of town in the shape of a giant "S."

The further east I traveled, the thinner the fog became. By the time I made it past Cambria's southern border, the ground-hugging cloud had given up its grasp on the coastline and all but disappeared. Despite losing its grip on the landscape, the marine layer still hung high in the sky, blocking out the rising sun and casting a gray aura over the local ambience. But that's better than dealing with it hanging out on the ground, at least while riding a bike. I was invisible enough to drivers as it was without being hidden in a cloud.

The riding was easy as I continued south toward Estero Bay. The closer I got, the faster the resilient marine layer receded. Soon hardly any remained at all. As blue took over and slowly filled the sky, the sun came out and instantly began to warm everything up, including me. So much so that after riding a few miles under the full morning sun, I deemed it necessary to pull over and remove my cold-weather gear. That finished, I settled into the warmth, ready for the day to officially begin. My ass, having finally come to the realization that we weren't even close to being finished, settled into the saddle for the long day, the soreness progressively subsiding with the ticking away of miles. I was cruising and making great time.

That was . . . until I wasn't.

Matthew Koehler

CHAPTER TWO

Two miles north of the small town of Cayucos, just past Estero Bay, the morning took a drastic turn. For the most part the highway was smooth and the traffic light. After the fog cleared, the breeze died down and the weather turned mild and beautiful. I took advantage of the relaxing atmosphere and lowered my head to stretch out my tight neck muscles. This, of course, is exactly what you shouldn't do while riding a bike. I knew better, and I should have just pulled over for a minute or two, but I just kept pedaling down the highway. Right in the middle of one of these stretches, head bowed, my eyes staring down at Jezebel's top tube, Jezebel's front wheel slammed hard into a wide crack in the pavement. It might well have been a curb. The entire bike shook from the impact and threw me way out of balance. The front wheel jolted sharply to the right, yanking my arms along with it, almost jerking my hands free of the handlebars. If Jezebel had been able to scream, she would have. She couldn't, so I did it for her.

"Ahhh! Damnit! No!"

Reacting instinctually, I somehow managed to regain control and pull Jezebel back to center, successfully regaining my center of gravity. How I managed to stabilize myself without being thrown off my bike and into the right lane of the highway, I will never know.

Full of adrenaline and relief after avoiding a faceplant into the highway and a tumble into traffic, I slowed to a stop on a flat front tire. The tire went flaccid immediately after the collision, so I knew right away I had a blowout to deal with. After a few choice words let loose into the otherwise calm and quiet surroundings, I disengaged from the pedals, dismounted Jezebel, and stared down at her injured wheel. My eyes, hidden behind the dark tint of my Oakleys, squinted in concentration, and I suddenly became aware of how shallow and rapid my breathing had become. I was shaken, and that made me nervous. My primary concern for this journey, the thing I feared the most but refused to admit outload to anyone, was being hit by a car. This impact could have thrown me right into traffic before I even realized what was going on. I lucked out, but there was a lesson to be learned here. *Pay attention, man.*

Well, other than the flat tire it doesn't look too bad, Matt. You might have lucked out there, kiddo. Hoping my intuition was right, I laid Jezebel down on her left side in the tall, dry grass along the side of the road to take a closer look at the damage. Frustrated but hopeful, I spun the wheel and inspected the rim and spokes for damage. No wobble, and no broken spokes. *Wow. Dodged a bullet there, Jezebel.* I left the wheel alone to slowly spin to a stop and stood silently next to her while I contemplated my next move.

Finding the pinch-flat was simple. It only took one methodical rotation of the wheel to find the fibrous hairs of the tire protruding out of a gaping half-inch hole in the sidewall. *Ah. There you are, you son of a bitch,* I thought. They flared out like a bunch of nipple tassels on a gaggle of burlesque performers. Not good. This meant unrepairable damage.

"Don't worry, Jezebel, I'll have this fixed in no time," I whispered.

I removed the wheel and laid it on the ground while I pulled my spare tire, tube, bike frame pump, and tools out from their respected places and took a seat on the ground. I removed the blown-out tire and tube from the rim and tossed them aside, then inspected the rim for damage. We lucked out for sure. I only found one scratch on the outer part of the rim, and it didn't look deep enough to cause braking issues or impact the seating of the new tire. *Whew. Dodged bullet #2.*

Satisfied with the roadside assessment, I replaced the damaged tire and tube with new ones and screwed the repaired wheel back on the forks. *Good as new.*

Jezebel looked like she'd just gotten outfitted with a new pair of shoes. Well, at least half a pair, anyway. I put all my tools away, and in a matter of minutes I was pushing off down the road again. The stop was a nice rest, all things considered, and while I worked on the tire replacement, I ate both bananas from the hotel. Back in the saddle, I quickly got over my anxiety about the near-catastrophe and concentrated on finding my rhythm again. Feeling good on the bike for the first time that morning, I stood up on the pedals and pushed hard, accelerating quickly. After settling into a relatively fast pace, I lowered myself back down on the saddle and cruised down the flat, sidewinding road.

The late-morning sun, now unencumbered by stubborn fog, played peek-a-boo with me as I rolled in and out of long shadows that lay across the highway like dark fingers. The great ball of fire in the sky appeared to be dancing in the open spaces to the east, welcoming the day by momentarily disappearing behind brown grass-covered hills and reappearing a short time later in steep tree-lined valleys, like a slow-blinking fog beacon warning incoming ships of the dangerous shoreline.

Easing into one of the sharper bends in the road, I lightly feathered the brakes. Immediately my spidey-sense went into high gear. Something in the feel of the brakes was just not right. The instant the brake pads encountered the rim of the front wheel, the most horrible sound filled the air. *Pffft, pffft, pffft, BANG!* It happened so fast I couldn't do anything to prevent it. In a matter of three revolutions after applying the brakes, my emergency tire went flat from the second blowout of the day. Two blowouts in less than a mile? There's only one thing you can say about that. *Fuck me!* I couldn't believe it. Really?

Somehow, I avoided yet another crash and was able to coast to a stop on the side of the highway, again. And there I stood, straddling Jezebel with my hands clasped behind my helmet in disbelief, helplessly stuck between two small towns on Highway 1, having just blown out two tires and two tubes. Unbelievable. *What the hell, man? Is this really happening?*

Looking north, I could literally see where I had suffered the earlier blowout. I had another tube in my emergency stash, but I was shit outta luck on the tire. I don't know for certain what caused it to blow, but I'm sure it had something to do with me not paying enough attention when I seated the tire bead inside the rim. Bicycle tires don't just blow out for no reason, especially brand-new ones. My weight on the newly seated tire, combined with the stress of actually rolling on the pavement and the friction of the brake pads squeezing against the rim could have caused the partially seated beading to break loose, releasing all of the contained high-pressure air at once and blowing the sidewall. Or . . . maybe I should have been paying more attention to the business at hand and less to stuffing my face full of bananas. *Shit, you got to be kidding me. This is ridiculous.*

The simplest option available was the obvious one. *Occam's Razor for the win, man. Don't think too hard about things, or you'll complicate everything.* So, after yet another volley of choice words, again screaming in no particular direction, I took off my cycling shoes, placed them in one of the panniers, unsnapped the chinstrap holding my helmet in place, and, in socked feet, started pushing Jezebel down the highway toward the small town in front of me. I didn't know the name of the town yet, but it was shimmering in the morning sunshine like a beacon of hope.

My "walk of shame" now underway, I couldn't help but reminisce about the time, years ago, when I had no other choice but to push the remains of my bike down the back side of Mission Peak after having an unfortunate confrontation with a cow. At least this time I wasn't bleeding, and all Jezebel needed was another new tire. Pushing Jezebel down the highway was definitely not in the plans for the day and, needless to say, I was not happy about it. Nor was I happy about extending the ride. I had a schedule to keep, damnit! From the look of things, I knew this little "snafu" may force me to add another day to the trip. The thought was frustrating, and it occupied a substantial part of my brain capacity as I walked. I hated thinking about it.

The town appeared to be only a couple of miles down the road as the crow flies, so at least I had that going for me, a bright moment in an otherwise dark hour. It's easy to get caught in the middle of nowhere on this section of Highway 1 as there's a whole lot more open space than urban areas. That's part of what makes this part of coastline so majestic. There's just enough human intervention to allow enjoyment of the land and access to the sea, but not so much that the area loses its character. My current situation placed me in the middle of one of these spacious territories between towns, but within walking distance of possible salvation. A blessing, for sure. I needed to look at it that way, otherwise I would drive myself mad with frustration and anxiety. Born an optimist, Mo would have looked at it that way too. This accident could have happened further north, closer to San Simeon. If it had, I would have been screwed. I knew for certain no bicycle shops resided in that town, only hotels and restaurants. But what about this town? Would they have one? Would luck be on my side? *Oh, luck be a lady, today!* I sang to myself. It seemed like an appropriate tune. *Come on, Frankie, help me out here.*

From where I was on the highway, the town ahead of me looked very similar to San Simeon; small, coast-hugging, and out of the way. As I walked, I prayed it would be not so similar though and have more than just hotels and restaurants. But most of all, I prayed there would be a bike shop in town and that it would be open on a Sunday morning. That was lot to ask of a small town abutting the sea, I know. The possibility was there, but the probability of finding what I needed in a small beach town along the sparsely populated coastline of Northern California, on a Sunday, was as slim as the white line I was following down the highway. Needless to say, I wasn't feeling too optimistic about my chances. But it was the only lifeline I had, so I latched onto it.

After walking about a half mile down the highway in socked feet, I came to a city marker on the side of the road. It read "Cayucos, population: 2000, elevation: 75 ft." I paused and gave it a quizzical look. *Huh. How the hell do you pronounce that name?* I looked to Jezebel. No response. Her silence led me to believe she didn't have a clue either.

About a quarter mile past the sign, my brain still occupied with the challenge of deciphering the proper pronunciation of the town I was walking toward, digging deep into my latent grade-school phonics lessons to assist me, a maroon-colored pickup truck loudly rumbled by in a blur, pulling me free from my mental gymnastics. Other than its initial "fly by," I didn't give the truck much of a thought until I saw its brake lights come on a little further down the road and watched as it pulled off the highway and onto the shoulder, kicking up dust and flattening the dry grass with its large, knobby tires. This piqued my interest, and I stopped walking after he finally came to a stop about fifty yards up the road. The transmission clunked as the driver threw it into reverse, white backup lights replaced red brake lights, and the rear end of the truck slowly weaved back and forth along the shoulder in my direction, finally coming to a stop a few yards in front of me. Another cloud of dust filled the air as the driver threw the truck into park. A baseball hat-covered head and left arm of a man leaned out from the open driver side window, and he glanced back at me.

"Hey there. You okay, man?" he yelled.

"Yeah, I'm alright. Just got a blowout on the road back there."

I thumbed over my left shoulder to show it happed "up yonder."

"Bummer. Need a ride somewhere?"

"Uh, that would be awesome, man. I'm making my way into that town over there," I said, raising my arm and pointing toward Cayucos.

"Sure, man. No problem. Throw your bike in the bed and hop in."

He pulled his head back into the truck, leaving his elbow to hang out the window.

I didn't waste any time. I flipped down the tailgate like I owned the thing and gently laid Jezebel down on her side in the mostly empty truck bed as hot exhaust from the tailpipe blew across my hairless right leg. The familiar aroma smelled sweet, almost organic, and reminded me of what the garage smelled like when my dad was out there working on one of his Mustang engines. Something must have been off with the truck's fuel/air mixture, meaning complete combustion wasn't taking place and some of the fuel was being released with the spent exhaust. I may not enjoy working on vehicles as much as my father does, but some of his lessons on car maintenance have stuck with me.

Through the rear-view mirror and open rear-cabin window, the driver watched me load Jezebel into the bed of his truck, his right arm resting comfortably at the top of the steering wheel. I slammed the tailgate shut after I finished loading everything and walked over to the passenger side door, opened it, and slid my Lycra-wearing ass onto the cracked black vinyl passenger seat. The cracks bit into the flesh on the back of my thighs, but even with that annoyance, it was a hundred percent more comfortable than Jezebel's saddle. He pulled down on the column shifter without saying a word and threw the truck into drive.

"Dude, are you kidding? You're a lifesaver. Thank you so much!" I said, leaning over and extending my hand after pulling the door closed.

He grabbed it tightly and gave it a firm shake. His grip was strong, and without my gloves on I could feel the roughness of his hands.

"Hey. Andrew," he replied, letting go of my hand.

"Matt. Nice to meet you," I said.

"No problem, man. You said you needed to go into town?"

Andrew raised the index finger of his right hand, currently resting at 12 o'clock on the steering wheel, and gestured toward the glistening town down the road.

"Yeah. I need to see if I can find a bike shop," I said, turning my gaze toward Cayucos, scanning the area through the bug gut–streaked windshield.

"Oh, Cayucos? Okay."

Andrew shuffled in his seat and shot a glance over his left shoulder out the windowless door. With no traffic on the highway, he pressed down on the accelerator and merged onto the highway in a cloud of dust.

"Yeah. That'll work, hopefully," I replied.

"So, what happened? Get a flat?"

"That would have been manageable. Believe it or not, I got two blowouts in less than a mile," I explained, my voice taking on a defeated and somewhat embarrassed tone.

"No way," he said, snickering through his nose. "Ouch. That sucks, man."

"Yeah, tell me about it." I raised my eyebrows from behind my sunglasses and nodded toward Cayucos. "So, I'm hoping this town over here has a bicycle shop so I can get another tire. That's all I need, really. If not, I don't know what I'm going to do. Next town is Morrow Bay. That's some ways down the road."

Andrew shook his head and breathed in through closed teeth.

"Uhh. I don't know, man. That there is a pretty small town," again pointing toward Cayucos with his right index finger, leaving the rest of his hand resting at 12 o'clock on the steering wheel. "Don't know if a town like that would have a shop like that," he added.

"Yeah. I'm hoping that's not the case, but you're probably right. It's the best shot I've got at the moment though."

"You know, I'm heading further south if you want to keep going. You might have a better shot finding what you need in a larger town, like San Luis Obispo or someplace like that."

"I appreciate that, but I need to make sure I ride as much of the highway as I can. Crazy as it sounds, if I did that, I would have to find a way back here to continue." I shrugged. "I've committed to riding every mile. It would drive me nuts if I didn't."

"Alright. Suit yourself."

"Thanks for the offer, though. I appreciate it," I said.

"Sure thing. So, where you riding to?"

"Tonight, the goal is Santa Barbara. The end goal is Irvine. If I get this tire situation figured out soon, I should get there tomorrow evening."

"Irvine? By tomorrow evening? On a bike?"

"Yep," I replied with stern, but questionable certainty.

Andrew turned to the right and shot me a look from under the brim of his hat that silently communicated only one thing. "Really?"

"That's the plan, anyway," I replied. "All depends on how this whole debacle works out, though."

Andrew turned his gaze back to the road.

"Let me guess. You're chasing a girl?" he asked, speaking out the windshield now.

"You could say that. Going to see my girlfriend. She goes to UC Irvine"

"I knew it. It's written all over your face." He let loose a one-breath chuckle. "I've done that before. Not on a bike, but I've definitely chased my share of tail in my day, that's for sure."

"Is it that obvious?"

"Eh. Not really. I was just kidding. But you aren't riding with anyone else, so I figured you're chasing something, or someone. I guess if you need to chase something, a girl is one of the best things to run down, no?"

Anthony laughed through his nose as if he was flipping through memories of previous girlfriends, and that made me chuckle, too.

"Yeah. I guess so," I replied.

By car, Cayucos was a short sprint down the road. We exited the highway after only a couple minutes of driving and made our way into the center of the downtown area, nearest the beach. I thought this would be the most likely place to find a bike shop if there was one to find. If there was one close by, it would be here.

"So, wha do ya think man? Where you want out?" Andrew asked. "This whole street is lined with random stores and stuff."

"I guess this spot's as good as any, no?"

"Sure, this should work for ya," he agreed. "It's kinda the beginning of the touristy area. Because of that, this is where you'll probably find some help, if you were going to find any at all in this town."

"I'll ask around and see what I can find," I said, looking out the open window and scanning the area. "What a cool town."

"Yeah, this place is great, especially if you're the beach bum type. I personally think it's the best beach around here. It's a lazy, laid-back place. A good place to hang out after a hard day's work. The surf is nice too. And if you're really into chasing tail, the girls are pretty too. Careful, though, don't stay too long. You might never leave. Ha ha!"

I looked over and smiled. He snickered and raised an eyebrow.

"Good to know, good to know," I said, nodding in amusement.

"Most people just drive on by, too," Andrew added. "Everyone seems to be on their way to somewhere else. Crazy really. But at least it keeps the crowds to a minimum."

"Sounds like a blessing, and a shame."

Andrew pulled over and slammed the truck in park. The engine rumbled at a high idle, causing the old truck to shake.

"Alright, Matt. Well, there you go. Good luck."

"Thanks again, Andrew. I really appreciate it."

"Any time, man. Take care, and I hope you find what you're looking for."

We shook hands again, and I hopped out of the truck, hitting the pavement hard in my socked feet. I walked to the back of the truck and threw down the tailgate, lifted Jezebel out of the truck bed, and gently set her down on the sidewalk. I slammed the tailgate shut, and Andrew waved at me through the driver side mirror. I waved back, and he was off.

Matthew Koehler

CHAPTER THREE

U nfamiliar with the town, I paused to find my bearings. Cayucos is laid out as a long, narrow strip on the western side of Highway 1, densely packed with homes and business between the highway and the beach, making good use of the coastline. The eastern side of the highway contrasts starkly with its western counterpart. Other than the Whale Rock Reservoir and a few scattered ranches, there is not much of anything on the inland side.

As crowded as it is, Cayucos doesn't feel cramped. It's a quaint, picturesque beach town, sectioned off with wide streets lined with old buildings, some bloated with so many layers of paint you couldn't make out the grain of the wood anymore. Ocean Avenue, the main strip, runs the entire length of the town. If you were so inclined, you could exit Highway 1 onto Ocean Avenue and follow it all the way through town and merge right back on to Highway 1 without making any turns or that many stops. This thoroughfare is lined with shops, restaurants, and hotels, ready to serve the California coast's tourists' every desire. Well, most of them, anyway.

Sprouting out like branches off a tree trunk, miles of easily navigable streets intersect the avenue, most sporting high-value residential properties and vacation rentals, many bathed in cliché California beach décor.

I supposed, considering my current pass-through status, the residents of Cayucos would classify me a tourist. I wouldn't argue with them about such an assessment, even though I tend to equate tourism with fun and excitement, neither of which I was experiencing at the moment. From my perspective, I was an uninvited guest who, circumstance as they were, didn't want to be there either. I was supposed to blow right by this town like it didn't even exist, just as Andrew was mentioning to me before I got out of his truck. But there I was, standing on the sidewalk supporting a bicycle with a flat tire, looking worried, walking around in my socks on a mission to find the lone superhero in this town that would rescue me.

*   *   *

The first hotel I came to as I walked down the sidewalk was the Shoreline Inn. I clumsily staggered inside to ask if they knew of any bike shops in town. I walked right up to the front desk and was greeted by a man wearing a nametag that said: "Jared 'The Merman.'" *Oh, look, this guy's got a sense of humor.* He greeted me with a smile and in an overly friendly voice.

"Welcome to the Shoreline Inn, sir. How can I help you today?"

"Hi, Jared," I said, adding in a wave for good measure.

"Hello. I hope you're having an amazing morning," he replied excitedly, emphasizing the word "amazing."

"Huh. Well," I began, looking around the hotel entry area. "I'm working on it. You might be able to help me with that."

"Okay."

"I was riding down the highway this morning and suffered a blowout on my front tire here." I pointed to Jezebel's front wheel. "And now I'm stuck."

I took a deep breath. I still had more to say, but before I could get another word out, Jared cut in.

"Stop. Just stop," he said authoritatively, the exuberance making me jerk my head back a little bit. "Oh no. That's terrible! I am so sorry to hear that."

His tone was way too exaggerated to be genuine, or was it? It was tough to tell, really. Was he being rude or, at the very least, extremely sarcastic? It seemed like it had to be one or the other. If the look on his face hadn't been bleeding concern, I would think he was making fun of me.

"It's okay, really. I'm in desperate need of a bicycle shop, though. I need a new tire. I can't continue my ride unless I find one." I sighed, then continued in a pleading tone, "Do you happen to know of a bike shop in this town?"

"Oh, honey," Jared responded wistfully. He leaned forward, resting his forearms on the counter, and looked up toward the ceiling as if in deep thought. "Hmmm. I don't know. Hold on a minute." He pushed away from the counter and raised the index finger of his left hand. "I'm going to see if I can get you some help." He started walking away, his finger still hanging in the air. "Stay right there. I'll be back in a sec."

Jared disappeared into the back room behind the counter. A door creaked open, and I heard him talking to someone but couldn't make out what they were saying. *Did he just call me 'honey'?* I asked myself. *Well, that's a first.* It felt good to find some humor in my stressful situation. Up till now I hadn't been in the happiest of moods. While waiting patiently for "the Merman" to return, I let go of Jezebel and allowed her to fall against the outside of my left leg. I placed both of my hands on the low counter and leaned into them, stretching out my shoulders. My clavicles popped as my shoulders reached my ears. It felt so good that I continued with the skeletal adjustments by leaning my neck from side to side, rattling several vertebrae. About a minute later, Jared returned to the front counter, shooting me a frustrated "I wish I had better news for you" kinda smile.

"Well, I'm not really sure," he said. "I don't know if there are any bike shops in town or not, and neither does my manager. I'm thinking there isn't. I've been working here for a while and I don't think I've ever seen one. But I don't ride bikes very often, so I would never be in need of one either. Sorry."

"Ah, bummer. Okay."

"But all hope might not be lost, not just yet, anyway." Jared cracked a smile of hopefulness.

"Oh yeah? How so?" I asked, intrigued.

"My manager did have a good idea. She thinks you should go down the street to the hardware store and ask them. It's obviously not a bike shop, but maybe they will have what you need. They do have a lot of random stuff, stuff you would never think would, or should, be in there. I'm sorry. I know that doesn't help you very much, but it might be worth a shot to go check them out."

I gently grumbled at the long shot of the idea, hoping it wasn't audible outside of my own head.

"Thank you so much for checking," I replied, forcing a thin smile.

"It's worth a shot, right? The hardware store, I mean. They're probably your best bet."

"Yes, yes. definitely. I'll check pretty much anywhere. I don't have much of a choice. Is the hardware store this way?" I pointed out the door toward the center of town.

"Yes. Just go this way, down the avenue . . ."

Jared leaned over the front desk and pointed through the front hotel window and down the street. "Oh, shoot. Hold on a second, it will be easier for me just to show you."

As Jared started walking around to the front of the counter, he called back, presumably to his manager, "Christine, I'll be right back! I'm just going to show this man where the hardware store is! Two minutes."

A muffled reply came from the back room, presumably a gesture of acknowledgment.

Jared finished making his way around the counter and into the main lobby where I was standing.

"Right this way. Follow me," he said, waving his hand toward the front door.

I followed, and he held the door open long enough for me to roll Jezebel through it and onto the sidewalk.

"Thank you," I said.

"My pleasure," he said, grinning.

Man, this guy really likes his job, I thought.

He walked out to the edge of the curb, leaned up against a newspaper machine, and pointed south toward the center of town. My gaze followed his finger.

"Okay. You see that intersection there, two blocks down?"

"Next to the flagpole?" I asked, squinting in the bright sunlight at the surrounding buildings. I raised my hand to my brow to shade some of the sunlight. *What, did you forget you had sunglasses resting on your head, bro?*

"Not over there. That's the firehouse. You need to be on the other side of the street. The hardware store is two buildings down after that," he said.

"Oh, alright. Great. I'll go see what they got. Thank you very much."

Jared dropped his hand back to his side, and I finally brought my sunglasses down over my eyes.

"I don't remember their names, but the couple that owns the place are really nice people. If they can figure out a way to help get you all fixed up, they will," Jared said, once again more friendly than necessary.

"Wonderful. Thanks again, Jared. I really appreciate it."

I lowered my hand from my sunglasses and held it out in his direction. He took it and we shook hands.

"No problem at all. I hope you get your bike fixed and have a great ride," he said excitedly.

Jared turned and walked, some would say strutted, back inside the hotel. I really wanted to stop him and ask about the merman thing, but I held my tongue. In hindsight, I should have asked. I have a feeling that I would have been treated to a funny story. He waved as the door shut behind him, and I waved back.

Before heading down the street, I took another look around. *Cool town,* I thought. Music and a growing crowd of people, and seagulls, drew my attention to the north end of town. Sprawling out in front of the large dolphin statue at the entrance to the pier, some kind of festival or farmer's market seemed to be taking shape. Multitudes of people were scurrying about, busily setting up tables and chairs underneath partially assembled white pop-up tents. I didn't give the budding festivities more than a cursory thought and instead redirected my attention toward the hardware store. Taking off my socks to preserve what little was left of their integrity, I started pushing Jezebel down Ocean Avenue along sand-dusted sidewalks in bare feet, amused by the diagonally parked cars jutting out into the wide coastal boulevard.

After walking a couple blocks south, I crossed the street and found the hardware store Jared was talking about, right where "the Merman" said it would be. Frustrated, but not all that surprised, I found it closed. Inside, lifeless shadows of random items lay hidden among the aisles. Filtered sunlight from two large street-facing windows illuminated the walls with such a measly amount of light I couldn't make out much of what was in there. I even tried the door handle. I mean, why not, I was already there. Locked.

"Shit," was all I could say to myself as I peered inside the windowed door through cupped hands. In the meager light, a store stocked with hardware supplies, fishing gear, and beach stuff slowly took shape. But, no humans were to be seen. Past all the beach stuff, however, hanging from nails high up on the right-side wall, could be my salvation. *What is that? Could it be?* My eyes widened when I recognized bicycle tires; suspended between light and shade and only partially visible from my location. But when you know what you're looking for, you know when you see it. An involuntary "Ahh!" escaped my lips and my hands went from cupped to slapping flat against the glass in exaltation. One of the tires looked like it might fit Jezebel's front rim too.

Desperate, and now very determined to get into this store, I pulled my face away from the glass and looked frantically around for someone who might work there. No luck. Leaving Jezebel to keep watch at the front, I walked around to the rear of the store to see if there might be an open back-entrance. No luck. So, I returned to the street-side and tried the doorknob again. Ya know, just in case it magically unlocked itself while I stepped away for a second. No surprise, still locked shut. But this time my eyes settled on something I'd missed the first time around. Posted above the door handle, behind the glass, a small hand-written sign read "Closed today, please come visit us tomorrow."

My shoulders, and all hope of salvation, sank into the shallow pool of sand beneath my feet. My initial thought upon arriving at the uninhabited building was that they were going to open late, and I would just have to sit around and wait for a while. It was Sunday, after all. Reading the sign taped up behind the glass window shattered what little optimism I had left. I slowly turned my back to the store, put my hands on my hips in hopeless frustration, and stared out at the beach, contemplating my next move. *Now what? Maybe you should have given Andrew's offer to drive you to a larger town a little more thought, Matt.*

Deep in thought and still hanging out in the breezeway of the hardware store, Jezebel helplessly leaning up against the door like an injured horse, I saw a woman pass by. Sparked by pure amusement, or concern for my well-being after seeing me in my current state of despair, she engaged me in conversation. She was interesting enough, and friendly, but she did seem a little curious as to why I was hanging out in the doorway of the shop the way I was. *I must look a tad bit out of place. You think?*

My initial impression led me to believe she was a local. Her demeanor, and outfit, seemed to fit in well with the quirkiness of this little town. Her long, dark, curly hair draped down over broad shoulders, and her skin appeared artificially dark from too much time spent laying out under the California sun. She was wearing oversized—like, obnoxiously oversized—yellow sunglasses, with lenses so dark I couldn't see her eyes, and a matching tank top, the bottom of which hung slightly north of the bottom of her cutoff jean shorts. Her feet slid to a stop next to Jezebel's rear wheel, the scattered bits of sand beneath them grinding between her flip-flops and the sidewalk.

"Hey," she said with a quizzical tone to her voice.

"Hi," I replied. I was too frustrated to laugh, and that was probably a good thing. Under any other circumstance her outfit would have at least forced a smile to my face. Not this time, though.

She pointed toward the door.

"You looking to get into the hardware store? Shop's closed today. Owners are running a booth down at the local festival on the pier," she said very matter-of-factly, now pointing north, toward the dolphin statue.

"Yeah, I was hoping it would be open. I just saw the sign." Turning halfway toward the door, I tapped on the glass in front of the hand-made sign with my right index finger and huffed out a disheartened laugh. "The shitty thing is, I'm kind of in a bind here. My front tire blew out on the highway, and I need to find a new one. I see one hanging on the wall in there that might work," I said, now turning the other direction and tapping on the window with my left index finger in the direction of the tires hanging on the wall. "So that's why I'm here looking in the windows." She didn't immediately say anything, and I took the opportunity to suck in a deep breath. "I literally just saw the closed-all-day sign and was thinking about what I was going to do next."

"Ahh. Well, shit. What a bummer, man. About the bike, I mean," she said, turning her head and glancing back down the street toward the pier.

"Sorry. Sometimes I talk too much, especially when I'm frustrated."

"Oh, no worries," she said. "I get it."

I stuck my hand out to the third stranger of the morning.

"I'm Matt, by the way."

We exchanged a brief handshake.

"Ziggy."

Ziggy. Of course. A name as interesting as her outfit.

"Nice to meet you, Ziggy. Do you happen to know if there is a bike shop in town where I can get a tire, or any other shop that may sell tires for a bike like this?" I asked.

Her gaze migrated down to Jezebel's blown-out tire as I rambled. When I finished asking the question, she looked back up at me, and I tried with all my willpower not to laugh or smile. Her yellow tank top and matching sunglasses against the blackness of her hair made me feel like I was having a conversation with a bumblebee. Suddenly, I found myself amused and developed an urge to smile, maybe even laugh a little. *Don't do it, Matt. Not even for Ziggy the bumblebee.*

"No. Not really. There might be a place around here that can help you out with that, but I don't know where to send you." She paused for a second and glanced toward the pier again. "You know what? Why don't you just wait here for a couple minutes. Can you do that?"

I shrugged, comically.

"Yeah, sure. All I have is time at the moment."

"Okay, cool. I know the owners of the shop and I know they're manning a booth down at the pier. I'm walking down there anyway, so I'll see if one of them can come and open up the shop for you. Cool?"

My hands fell from my hips as hopefulness filled the air once again.

"Really? You would do that? Oh, man! Thank you. That would be so nice of you," I said with obvious excitement.

"No problem. I'll be right back, or . . . one of them will. Don't go running off though. If you do, it'll make me look bad. Know what I mean?"

"Yeah, yeah," I agreed excitedly. "You got it. I'm not going anywhere. Thanks again!"

Yes! Yes! Thank you, Ziggy the bumblebee. Now let's hope for the best. Cross your fingers, Matt.

And with that, Ms. bumblebee was off, sliding her flip-flops against the sidewalk like she had given up on the art of picking up her feet as she walked. I watched her slowly make her way to the pier and, even with all the bright yellow clothing, she disappeared easily into the ever-growing maze of people and pop-up tents.

I took a seat on the concrete next to Jezebel and leaned back against the building's façade. I was anxious, but I allowed the late morning warmth and coastal views an opportunity to lift my spirits. It worked. The longer I sat, the better I felt. People shuffled on by, apathetic to my presence and situation; most making a beeline across the road to the beach while others slowly meandered over toward the pier. I don't know if it was my need to get back on the highway as quickly as possible, or what, but everyone here seemed to be *not* in a hurry. Maybe it was just the way people got around in this town; easy, laid-back. *I'll get there when I get there, man. Just chill.* I'm sure if you hung out in a place like this long enough, you'd slowly meld with its character, over time become a part of it, and realize that slowing down to enjoy a less stressful pace of life has merit. There is value in that philosophy, and I had a feeling that I could blend into it without much effort at all.

Well, it sure seemed like there was a lot of that "laissez faire-ness" going on here today, because it felt like I waited forever for someone to return. Feeling more relaxed, but still nervous, the anxiety of missing out on my goal started to creep back into my psyche. Realistically, the wait was only about fifteen minutes or so, *but who's counting? Me, obviously.* I was deep in thought when a lady I guessed to be in her early seventies walked right up to me and opened up the conversation by getting right to the point.

"You must be the guy looking for a bike tire," she said, peering down at me and shooting a few glances in Jezebel's direction.

"Oh, yes, ma'am. Hi. Did my disabled friend here clue you in?"

I snapped out of my trance and put on a smile as I rose to my feet.

"Maybe a little. But your outfit kinda gave you away too."

I was standing now and brushing sand from my shorts.

"Ah. Yes. This kind of outfit usually lets everyone know exactly what I'm up to."

"Yep. That'll do it," she said, smiling.

Not wanting to put an end to my morning of shaking hands with strangers, I stuck my hand out in greeting for the fourth time today.

"Good morning," I said, quite formally too, which was weird. But I didn't want to sound to young, or disrespectful. "Is this your shop?"

"Yes. Yes, it is." She gently grabbed my hand and refused to let go for a moment.

"Can I give you some advice right away?"

"Sure," I said, confused.

"My name isn't 'ma'am,' it's Dorothy. Please don't call me that again, or our conversation will end as quickly as it began. Capeesh?"

"Okay. Um, sorry. I . . ."

She snickered, then let go of my hand and smiled.

"Oh, stop. Just kidding. Call me Dot, everybody does," she said.

"Hi, Dot. Matt. Thanks for coming over. I'm kinda in a bind here."

"Looks like it. Well, we don't have too many bike tires here, only what you see on the wall in the corner over there, but I can show you what we have and you can tell me if it's what you need or not."

"That would be wonderful. I saw one through the window that I think might work," I said.

"Okay. Well, let's find out."

I moved to the side as she walked up to the door and opened it with her key. The door squeaked as it swung open, ringing a bell along its arc, indicating to currently non-existent employees that someone had entered, or exited, the shop. Scents of old wood and fertilizer puffed out of the open door like an invisible cloud. I paused and waited to be invited in like I was visiting Dot at her house.

"Well, come on. Hurry up." Dot held the door open and gestured for me to come inside. "Bring your bike in here so I can shut the door. I don't want people thinking we're open for business today."

"Sure thing."

I wheeled Jezebel into the store and leaned her up against the front counter next to the cash register. Dot shut and locked the door behind us and started walking down the last aisle of the store where the tires were hanging high up on the wall. I followed.

"Okay, Matt. It was Matt, right?"

"Yes, Matt."

"Sorry, at this age memory isn't one of my strongest traits."

"Well, you did good. Shoot, you can call me any name you want right now. I won't be complaining, that's for sure."

She laughed.

"Okay, well, let's see if we have what you need. Come on over here."

"Alright."

I followed her over to the bike parts display and we both looked up at the tires.

"Now, I can't reach that. Think you can pull those down off the nail?" she asked as we stood together beneath the tires.

"Of course. This is the only one that could possibly fit my bike, so I'll just bring this one down," I said.

I reached as high as my five-foot-eight frame would allow, standing on my toes to reach it. I barely got enough of my hand wrapped around the bottom of the tire to inch it away from the wall and off the nail. Even with that I had to give it a couple nudges. After pulling it away from the wall, I turned to face the front of the store for light and spun the tire around in my hands looking for the size. I couldn't find anything except some generic manufacturer name on the sidewall. I turned back to Dot, standing quietly in the middle of the aisle.

"I don't see a size on here. Do you mind if I try and install it to see if it will fit?" I asked. "It won't wake long, promise."

"Of course. Go right ahead," she said.

Feeling hopeful, I walked over to Jezebel. The tire was thin and lightweight, probably of low quality. But I was a beggar at the moment, so being a chooser wasn't an option. My only hope was that it would fit. *That's all I need. It just needs to fit.* I pulled the front wheel off and let Jezebel's naked forks rest on the well-worn linoleum floor. This is usually frowned upon, but the floor was so smooth that I wasn't too concerned with damaging the far ends of Jezebel's forks.

I stripped the damaged tire and tube from the wheel with a couple of quick jerks of my hands. As I did this, I noticed that the rubber tags running down the center, leftover from the manufacturer, were still present. What a waste. I didn't even put enough miles on it to knock these thin pieces of rubber off. *That's pretty pathetic, Matt. You know that, right?* Whatever. I could only laugh about it now.

Tossing the now worthless tire and tube aside, I pulled my last spare tube from my under-the-saddle tool/emergency bag and began my attempt at installing the new one. *Please let this work.* After some careful prying with tire levers, a little pushing with my thumbs, and ample prayers, I was elated to watch the new tire snap into place and seat snuggly onto the wheel. The comforting "thud" of the stretched tire bead releasing against the inside of the rim assured me a perfect fit. I couldn't believe it. My day had been made, right there on the worn-out floor of a closed hardware store in a town I didn't even know existed until an hour ago. *Oh God, thank you! And, thank you Dot!*

I shrieked into the muted shadiness of the store as if a crowd of people were watching me. "It fits!" Through eyes filled with equal amounts of relief and excitement, I glanced at Dot while I continued working on the tire. "Thank you, thank you," I said, my tone softening some as I worked. She was smiling and had her arms crossed at her chest, her keychain dangling from her right index finger. "You just saved my day Dot. No joke."

"Well, I'll be damned. It worked. That's wonderful," she said, sounding relieved. Her voice now thick with sarcasm, she continued. "Now, hurry up. I have other things to do today."

I finished with the tire installation and seated the assembled wheel back onto the forks, double-checking the rim and tire this time. Everything looked good. While immersed with the repair, Dot had walked around to the other side of the counter and waited for me to finish up. When Jezebel was back to riding condition, I stood up, wallet in hand.

"What do I owe you, Dot?" I said.

I had never been so happy to pay for anything in my life.

"Fifteen dollars," she said.

"Fifteen dollars? That's it?" I said, looking confused, an I-don't-believe-you look on my face. "That can't be right."

"Yep. That's the price of the tire," she said.

"Well, what you did for me is worth more than that. Are you sure that's all I owe you?"

"Yep. Fifteen dollars," she said again. "Now, are you going to pay me so we can get the heck out of here, or what?" she said sarcastically. "Come on now. I have a festival to attend to."

"Absolutely. Here you go." I handed over a $20 bill. "Money well spent. Wow. You're an angel, Dot. Please keep the change for yourself," I said.

"No, no, no. I don't do business like that. But thank you for the gesture."

Dot reached into the till and pulled out a $5 bill. She smiled at me as she handed over the change. "How about you just pay it forward? Karma works wonders, you know."

"I wish I could share with you how much you saved my day. Thank you so much. It was very kind of you to open up the shop," I replied, sliding the $5 bill in my wallet and securing it in the bottom of the right pannier.

"It was no problem at all, really. Glad I could help. Now get out of here so I can get back to my booth on the pier," she said, laughing and shooing me away from the counter.

"Okay, I'm out. I have a long ride ahead of me anyway. I need to be in Santa Barbara by sundown," I said as we both made our way out the front door.

"Oh, dear," Dot said. "That's a ways away. You better get going. Ride safe now."

With that, we walked outside together. The bell above the door dinged as we left the shop and she locked the door behind us. We waved at each other as she started her slow trek back to the pier. I walked over to the nearest trash can, which happened to be right in front of the hardware store, and tossed the worthless tire into the void. *Man, what a waste. That was a really good tire, too.* Too late to worry about that, though. I had some serious time to make up.

I sat down on the curb and hurriedly put on my socks, shoes, helmet, sunglasses, and gloves. I made a conscious effort to remember that, even though I just bought a new one, I would need to hit up a real bike shop as soon as possible to buy another high-quality tire, just in case this stupid situation happens again. Standing up, I hopped back on to Jezebel, complete with yet another brand new, albeit non-matching, front tire. *You need to let that go, Matt. This is no time for vanity.* I pushed off, heading south on Ocean Avenue, stopping once more in the center of town at a small supermarket to resupply my rapidly depleting stash of snacks.

CHAPTER FOUR

Rescued, but still low on some of Jezebel's emergency gear, I rode attentively through Morrow Bay and into San Luis Obispo. I was determined to stay on the road as much as possible. No more long breaks or side trips. The Cayucos detour had already eaten up all my break time for the day. The goal was Santa Barbara before dusk. Even though the distance from San Simeon to Santa Barbara was less than the distance from Capitola to San Simeon, I would be traveling through some larger, more populated areas, and I expected that to slow me down. Besides, I already lost an hour and a half finding a new tire for Jezebel. That alone was probably going to push me into twilight come dusk.

With Jezebel's supply issue fresh on the mind, I pulled over at the first gas station I came to after rolling into San Luis Obispo. My father attended college here at California Polytechnic State University, class of '74. It's a mouthful to say, so everyone just calls it Cal Poly. It's also the largest campus in town. Every time we took a family vacation that brought us within a hundred miles of this town, all six of us had to stop for a visit and check out the engineering building. We all loved it . . . the first time. After that first visit, us kids figured out all we needed to do was survive a couple hours of Dad nostalgically romping through memories of his "BC life" (life before children), happily reminiscing about college days and time shared with my mom after they first got married. When those escapades were over, we would move on somewhere else. Somewhere exciting, like the beach or lunch.

I coasted up to a lone attendant working on a car in the garage, again reflecting on my dad's stories of his time in San Luis Obispo. Dad worked his way through college as a gas station attendant, and rolling up on one of these guys painted a mental image of what he must have looked like working the same job back in his college years. Manifesting a mental image like that wasn't really a stretch for me, though. My dad was always working on cars, as long as I could remember anyway. I don't think I ever saw him without grease under his fingernails, swollen knuckles, or scrapes on his hands and forearms.

Stopping a few feet in front of the man, I nodded a greeting of hello as I slowly rolled to a stop and unclicked my shoes from the pedals. He didn't say a word or even nod back. He just looked at me through squinted eyes and wiped his hands on a dirty towel he pulled out of his front pocket. Confused, but undeterred by this gesture of disinterest, I asked if he knew of a bike shop somewhere in town close to the highway. San Luis Obispo is a college town, so I expected there would be several, and it was an easy enough question to answer. *Just point the way, man, and I'm outta here.*

"Bike shop." He said it as a statement, like he was insulted by the question or something. "Like, for motorcycles? Or one of those?" he asked through a questionable grin. He leaned his head to the side like he was peering around a corner and pointed at Jezebel.

I thought it was somewhat obvious what kind of "bike" shop I was asking about. I was standing in front of him straddling a bicycle, wearing what he probably thought was a pretty ridiculous tight-fitting outfit, smooth shaved legs sticking out of the end of my shorts and a goofy-looking Styrofoam helmet on my head. Most people would have understood what kind of shop I was looking for. This guy, apparently, was not one of those people.

"Um, I'm looking for a bicycle shop. I need some things for my bicycle here," I said, responding as politely as I could while patting Jezebel's handlebars.

"Oh. Nope." He responded quickly with sharpness in his tone, like someone would when they knew the answer to a question but did not want to admit it. "Not off hand. I know where a motorcycle shop is, but nothing for those bikes. I ride bikes with engines, not ones I have to power myself," he said, pointing at Jezebel again, smiling sarcastically. "Makes things easier, if you know what I mean."

"Yeah. That's not going to work for me," I replied.

"See there?" He turned to face the second garage bay, nodded his head, and then turned back to me. The dented bay door was closed and had been for quite a while. By the look of all the used tires and discarded car parts lying on the ground in front of it, it hadn't been opened in a long time. Parked there in front of the door and next to all the mess, hiding out in the last hurrah of morning shade, was a gently used Harley-Davidson motorcycle. "That's mine," he said pridefully.

"Ahh. Nice-looking set of wheels, man," I said, nodding my head in appreciation.

"Thanks. Original owner. Fast too."

"I bet."

He fell back into silence, and I thought for a second that he was making fun of me. He most likely was, but he also might have just been accentuating his point, making sure I understood that he liked riding bikes that didn't require him to work very hard or wear ridiculous outfits, funny shoes, and goofy helmets. Shit, anyone who cared at all about their "street cred" wouldn't be caught dead riding their motorcycle with any form of brain-bucket on their head. Bandanas were an acceptable accessory of course, especially along the California coast, where freedom meant casually cruising up and down Highway 1; wind in your hair, sun on your face, and motorcycle tailpipe exhaust echoing off nearby mountains. Motorcycle helmets save lives, but get caught wearing one, especially on a Harley Davidson, and you might as well toss your social standing into the great Pacific and start all over. Sensing this conversation was going nowhere fast, at least in the direction I needed it to go, I decided to move on. I would find a bicycle shop soon enough.

"Okay. Well, thanks for your help, sir. I'm sure I'll find one along the way," I said, clicking into Jezebel's pedals. I waved and pushed off.

"See ya," he said, and watched me roll out towards the gas station driveway. He had gone back to wiping his hands on the towel.

I passed by several gas pumps and noticed a man staring at me from between his car and one of the pumps. He was standing next to his small red compact car, holding the gas pump nozzle in his right hand, his left hand resting on the frame of the back passenger door above the open gas tank. We made eye contact as I slowly rolled by his front bumper, so I greeted him with a nod.

"You lookin' for a bike shop?" he yelled.

"Yes, sir, I am," I said, circling back and coming to a stop in front of his car. "One close to the highway, if you know of one."

"There's one right up the road here on Foothill. About three blocks up on the left," he said.

He pointed me down the road in the direction of the shop. I followed the gesture and squinted down the street.

"Oh, awesome!" I said excitedly. "Thank you. That's a big help."

"No problem." He lifted his hand from the car and waved me off. "See ya."

I took off down Foothill Boulevard and rolled up to the front door of Foothill Cyclery in a matter of minutes. I dismounted and walked inside, Jezebel in tow, like a pet owner walking into a pet store with his dog. *Only Jezebel won't pee on anything.*

Clip-clopping up to the parts counter, I was greeted by a salesman about my age standing behind it. Bike shops are one of the rare places where I feel right at home walking in wearing nothing but Lycra with my shoes ticking on the floor. I fit the part, and this gave us an instant rapport. I shared an abbreviated version of my morning adventures, and we shared a few laughs at my expense.

"Dude," was his initial verbal reaction. "I've been working here for years and I haven't heard any kinda story like that before. Now I think I've heard them all. That's one I might have to share."

"Yeah, the whole thing sucked balls, but I kinda lucked out. So at least I have that going for me," I said as optimistically as possible.

"Yep. The kindness of strangers. It's kinda like that cigar you have once a year, or that extra piece of cake on your birthday, ya know? It doesn't happen to you all that often, but when it does, you don't forget it. Right?"

"Right," I agreed sharply.

"Wicked!"

He shot me a shaka sign, thumb and pinky finger extended out in perfect proportion like he'd been doing it for years. I returned the gesture, but mine looked a little out of place in my fingerless gloves.

"Yeah. For sure."

So . . ." He slapped his hands down on the counter and stood up straight. "What do ya need, man? Let's get you situated."

I asked for the most durable foldable tire they had and two spare tubes. That would get my emergency stock up to where it was this morning, before the blowouts.

"You sure you don't want a formed tire? They tend to sit better inside the wheel in my opinion. Don't have the tendency to pop loose during installation, like what you had happen earlier, ya know what I mean?"

"Yeah, that would be ideal, for sure. But it needs to fit in my panniers, and there's limited space as it is. So, I think the only option is for me to get a foldable one."

"Well, if that's the priority, then I'll be right back with what you need," he said and walked into the heart of the store.

"Thanks," I said.

From somewhere in the store I heard him ask, "How many you need? Just one?"

"Yeah. One is fine. Thanks."

He returned a short time later with a new foldable tire and two new tubes.

"All right. There ya go, bro. That should do ya. Anything else?"

He laid the items on the glass countertop and started walked around to the back side of the cash register.

"Might as well fill up on more of these while I'm here. My resources are quickly dwindling," I replied, reaching for snacks.

I grabbed a handful of Gu packets and a six-bar stack of original flavor PowerBars, all neatly organized by flavor in their display boxes next to the register. I paid for everything and was out the door and back on the highway in a matter of minutes. It was a good stop. I felt relieved, and a lot less nervous about the road ahead.

*   *   *

The ride west from San Lois Obispo to the coast went through the Johnson Ranch Open Space. Traversing the narrow valley that split the reserve in half, the gently sloping descent allowed for a quick cadence, and the wide shoulder gave me a safe lane to ride in. Good thing too, it was time to work and reel in the miles. I didn't take time to enjoy the scenery, even though that would have been nice. There was plenty of it to enjoy, that's for sure. I was determined to make up some of the time I'd lost earlier, so I limited myself to what I could enjoy from the bike. Taking a short nap was out of the question. I wasn't going to make it to Santa Barbara by nightfall if I didn't spend some serious time in the saddle.

After cutting inland through the coastal mountain range for several miles, the highway turned west, dumping me back against the coastline after a short time away from the water. I was happy to have the ocean in my sights again and savored the last view of the coast I would see for the rest of the day.

The further south I traveled, the more zig-zaggy Highway 1 became, breaking away from the coast for miles at a time before meandering its way back to where it belonged, outlining the western edge of America. It was right about here where a change in the topography and climate became noticeably apparent, the environment taking on more of a "Southern California coastal" vibe; arid and desert-like.

Here in the southern part of the state, when fog wasn't hugging the ground, the air was dry, notably different than northern California where the relative humidity remains comparatively elevated. I could feel the change in my nose and throat when breathing heavily, constantly needing a swig of water to keep my dry mouth moist. Carmex also came in quite handy when the torrid air cracked my lips. It could have been my imagination, or just fatigue, but the air felt thick, and pushing Jezebel through it made me tired. After hours of non-stop riding, it felt as if every molecule of air was pushing just as hard against me as I was pushing against them, trying to keep me from moving forward. It was like they didn't want me to continue. Their persistence was an annoyance, but not a deterrent, so I persevered through the shoving contest and kept moving, one pedal stroke at a time.

The numerous trees covering the coastal hills of northern California slowly thinned out as the miles ticked by, the landscape continuing its slow transition from a forest-centric environment into more of a coastal desert terrain. The ecosystem followed suit, supporting more shrubbery and drought-resistant trees in lieu of the water-guzzling Redwoods and Coastal Oaks of the north. Sandy beaches ballooned in size, contrasting starkly with the crumbling boulder graveyards and ocean-feeding landslides common along the central coast.

The first prominent Southern California shoreline I came to was Pismo Beach, bordering a long, thin strip of picturesque shoreline. Its popularity comes from the land's rich history of clam fishing and, oddly enough, a monarch butterfly–loving grove of Eucalyptus trees. Every year, from October through February, this small grove becomes saturated with migrating monarch butterflies. It's a sight like no other, or so I'm told. I've never experienced the phenomenon but seems like an amazing sight to behold. Eyewitnesses say so many butterflies fill the area that the tree trunks turn into a sea of orange and black. The slowly flapping wings of thousands of butterflies clinging to bark paint the illusion that the trees are moving in place. Sounds crazy cool. *Yeah, I need to add that one to my bucket list.*

Almost comically predictable now, Highway 1 took another jaunt to the interior just south of Pismo Beach and made a beeline for the farming community of Guadalupe. To the east was Los Padres National Forest and seemingly unending farmland. To the west, the coastline polished off the scenery with gently rolling dunes of sand, eternally changing shape as they drifted silently toward the ocean only to disappear beneath her waves. The highway continued south and east for several miles, outlining the western edge of the agriculture-centric Santa Maria Valley. I followed its lead and let it escort me and Jezebel along the edge between contrasting landscapes of mountains and flatlands. We hugged the foothills for miles, playing leapfrog amid fields of green, brown, and gold.

To the west the mountain range rose sharply, topped with peaks rounded smooth by wind and time, their surface covered in various shades of brown, painted by the naturally arid landscape and dying grasses. It was Mother Nature's grand finale after a long summer without a drop of rain. Miles down the highway to the east, these same mountains gradually leveled off, opening up to another valley of fertile land. Appearing just as wide as it was deep, the valley had been fragmented into a mosaic of every shade of green and brown the human eye could manage. Acres of vegetables and seasonal fruits as far as my eyes could see sprouted from every square inch of dirt, the roads the only obstacle slicing up the landscape.

One advantage of these roads, however, was the multitude of farm stands dotting the highway, offering up the bounty of the area to passing motorists—*and cyclists, thank you very much*. Unlike the fruit stands I passed by yesterday in Watsonville and Castroville, these were open, fully stocked with fresh produce, and ready to serve. I took advantage of this fortunate opportunity and pulled over at several of them, stuffing my constantly starving face with fresh strawberries and citrus fruit.

Exiting the valley, I pedaled for the next several hours through the lowland areas, the jagged peaks and steep hills of the wrinkled landscape rising high on each side of me, past Vandenberg Air Force Base and across the lonely stretch of highway between Lompoc and the US Route 101/Highway 1 interchange. Here, at a place called Las Cruces, I had two choices: turn left and continue inland to the town of Buellton and on to Solvang, or turn right and head west to the coast. I had already made my choice long before I even began my journey. I had promised myself that I would ride the coastline as much as possible, so my choice would be the latter. I was looking forward to following the relatively flat coastline all the way into Santa Barbara for a sunset arrival, where certainly an empty hotel room was waiting for me with a reasonably comfortable bed and, even more importantly at this point, a nice, hot shower.

And man, did I need one of those. My profuse sweating and constant consumption of sugary, electrolyte-laden Cytomax and PowerBars, was taking a toll on my clothing. I snacked while riding, and that made for unstable eating. Drippings from the water bottle and pieces of food tumbled from my mouth and frequently ended up down my often-unzipped jersey, festering with my drying sweat and salt-stained skin. Yeah, I was starting to stink. So much so that I was beginning to smell myself. And when you can smell yourself, that's when you know it's bad.

And the bed. Oh, the bed! Just thinking about it made me want to lie down and sleep for two days. I was late into the second day of my journey, and the mounting strain on my muscles was becoming a consistent companion, reminding me yet again that I should have trained properly for a trip like this. Relying only on a self-imposed timeline, sheer will, and my history as a multi-sport athlete did not guarantee success. Pedigree alone will not bring triumph. Time in the saddle is what I needed more of, and I surely didn't spend enough time there before embarking on this challenge. Accordingly, I was paying the price. My legs screamed when I climbed, and even though I had aerobars clamped to Jezebel's handlebars to rest my hands and forearms during long stretches of flat roads, my shoulders ached from so many hours of being slumped over them. My neck and the palms of my hands weren't happy, either. It didn't help that my gloves were consistently damp from sweat, and they had stretched out a bit over the miles, enhancing the discomfort. Why I didn't buy another pair at the bike shop in San Luis Obispo is beyond me. *Damn, Matt. I didn't know you were such a little bitch. Shut up and keep riding.* Complaining aside, all this agony was a temporary inconvenience, I knew, and would be relieved soon enough. Just a few more hours of riding, easing my way into Santa Barbara along the coast during the twilight of day. No problem. *I wonder what I'm going to have for dinner?*

CHAPTER FIVE

About a mile out from the US 101/Highway 1 interchange I noticed a faint cloud of smoke rising from the mountains ahead of me. It didn't look too bad, almost like a couple of large ag fires going off, something not uncommon in agricultural communities like these during the cooler months. They're frequently used as an efficient way to dispose of the collected trimmings from trees, shrubs, and vines after harvest season and the fields have been cleared. As I got closer, however, the distinctive smell of burning grass hung in the air, growing more pronounced the further south I rode, as did the plume of white smoke. A "situation" seemed to be brewing, one possibly more involved than I initially thought.

I found out exactly how involved it was as I rolled up to the stop sign at the interchange. The smell of burning grass was unmistakable now. It appeared the local hills were on fire, and there was a grass fire to deal with. A thin but growing cloud of smoke rose from the canyon to the west, thinning out and filling the sky above me with a veil of white mist, one that varied in intensity depending on the way the air was moving. Currently, the winds were calm, so the smoke drifted slowly eastward, riding up the mountainside in front of me with the help of a gently blowing onshore breeze and then casually, but deliberately, sinking into the valley on the other side.

"Not too bad," I whispered to Jezebel. "We can handle this."

Maybe we could. Actually, I knew we could. But local authorities had other ideas. I pulled up alongside a couple of other cars, already stopped at the interchange waiting to turn west on 101. Needing to turn right as well, I coasted up and stopped near the front bumper of a police car deliberately parked diagonally across the highway, blocking traffic heading toward the coast. I listened in on the conversations the drivers were having with the lone police officer, authoritatively standing next to his squad car. He informed all of us, much to our dismay and frustration, that there was an active vegetation fire burning along the highway in nearby Gaviota State Park and that the road would be temporarily closed to all non-emergency traffic. After a little back-and-forth between driver and cop, the two other cars took off to the east and I went to talk to the officer alone.

"Hey," I said as I approached, straddling Jezebel and duck-walking over, not bothering to pedal for such a short distance. Anticipating the inevitable route change, I had already reached into my panniers and pulled out my laminated maps.

"Hey there," the officer said.

He leaned back against the hood of his car, his right hand resting on the butt of his sidearm, safely holstered in his duty belt while his left hand fumbled with the knobs on the portable radio attached to his shoulder.

"So, this route's closed, yeah?" I asked, knowing the answer but feeling the need to ask anyway.

"Yep. Sorry," he said, obviously distracted.

I kept quiet for a bit, picking up on the fact that his concentration was in another place. He tried again to listen to his radio with no luck.

"Stupid radios. These things never work right," he whispered. I don't believe the comment was aimed at me, but I overheard it anyway. Shaking his head in disgust, he continued, this time louder and more directly, but calmly enough. "Until they get this fire under control, I can't let any vehicles pass," he said matter-of-factly.

The tone of his voice led me to believe traffic control was not on his list of favorite duties.

"Any idea when the road will open?" I asked hopefully.

As I spoke, a crackle of a human voice came through his radio, distracting him once again. Without answering me, the police officer cocked his head back to the left as though he didn't even hear my question and continued listening in on the broken transmission. Squabble continued to make its way through the receiver, making it impossible for me to understand what the dispatcher was saying. Apparently, he didn't either. The transmission was garbled and came in spurts, separated by several seconds of silence. Aggravation getting the best of him, the police officer stopped fumbling with the radio and sucked in a frustratingly deep breath.

"I give up. These dumb radios. I can't hear shit in the mountains. They really need to upgrade these things. Anyway, sorry about that. No clue. Fire trucks started arriving about thirty minutes ago, so it may be a while."

"Shoot," I answered.

The police officer lifted his right leg, rested his foot on the bumper of his cruiser, and sat down on the hood, forcing the front suspension to sag under his weight.

"Sorry. You're more than welcome to wait it out. But if you want my advice, you'd be better off if you head into town. Where you headed, anyway?" he asked, seeming genuinely interested.

"Santa Barbara," I replied.

He looked up and around, like he was following a fly buzzing around his head.

"Santa Barbara?" he said in a snark-tinged voice, crossing his arms and looking at me all confused-like. "Hmph." He paused again, still looking around but not saying anything.

"Yep," I replied slowly.

"Oh. Kay," he replied sharply, making each syllable its own word. "Well, no matter which way you go, this way or that way"—he uncrossed his arms from his chest and pointed east on Highway 101, then west down Highway 1—"it's going to be hard to get there by nightfall, especially on a bike," he said, now pointing to Jezebel. He crossed his arms again and adjusted his butt on the hood of the cruiser. "You trying to get there tonight?"

"Yeah. That's the plan, anyway."

So many obstacles were piling up today, and I was starting to feel like my goal of reaching Santa Barbara tonight was merely a pipe dream at this point.

He uncrossed his arm again and pointed east, sticking with his original recommendation.

"Hmmm. You'd be better off stopping for the night at another one of these towns down the hill and waiting until tomorrow." He waved his right index finger east and into the valley below. "I don't see you getting to Santa Barbara tonight. Really, man, this road could be closed for quite a while. Realistically"—he glanced up the hill where the smoke was spilling over between two peaks, then slowly turned his head back in my direction—"it probably won't be opening until after sunset."

"Shit. Yeah, I figured that," I said.

253

My mind felt constrained, torn between goals and personal safety. *Something to think about, dude. It'll be dark in a few hours.* Slowly, the realization that I may not reach my goal for the day was beginning to take up real estate in my head, and that sucked. If I headed east, there would be a few towns where I could bail and hopefully find a bed for the night. Well, maybe. Last night was a good reminder that reasonable expectations aren't always a guarantee. *Shit, man. Let's just ride until we can't, and deal with whatever comes our way. Fuck it. If you have to camp out on the side of the road again, so be it. Yeah, I think that's the best plan. We'll see. It sure is a whole lot better than just sitting around here and waiting to see if the road will clear.*

"Sorry, man," the cop continued. "Sucks, I know."

Truthfully, I don't think he knew at all. It looked like he hadn't spent five minutes on a bike in at least ten years. *Come on man, who cares? Let's move on.*

"But if I still want to continue, could you show me on my maps here the best way I can get around the fire?"

I scooted closer to him and handed over my map of the area, trying not to give him another opportunity to discourage me from continuing. He stood up from the hood of his cruiser, took the map out of my hands, and started looking it over. About a minute later, after pausing to mumble something into his shoulder radio, he turned back to me.

"Sure, I'd be happy to." He turned the maps over in his hands, inspecting them carefully. "Nice maps. You laminate these yourself?"

"Yeah."

"Huh," he said, impressed. "Not bad." He nodded slightly, amused for some reason.

"Thanks," I said. "So, whadda ya think?" I asked.

"Okay." He paused, tracing a route on the map with his finger. A few seconds later he continued. "Well." He pointed to the spot on the map where we were standing while angling the map in my direction. "We're here. Fire's over here." He moved his finger just off the highway to the south. "That's why you can't head to the coast at the moment." He dragged his finger to Highway 1 on my map and traced the shoreline with it. "See that?"

He looked at me for acknowledgement.

"Okay," I replied in agreement. "Yeah, I can see that."

"Alright then."

He switched to tracing US 101 east on the map with his finger and continued.

"I recommend heading this way and maybe finding a place to stay in Buellton." He tapped on the map to show me where it was. "Or continue down here to Solvang. You could easily make it that far before dark." He traced the map and tapped again, this time on Solvang.

"Okay. Thanks. What if I wanted to continue on to Santa Barbara? Just keep going south?"

"Well, if you really want to try that"—he paused, raised his eyebrows, and looked me square in the eyes—"I wouldn't recommend it, by the way"—another pause while he dropped his gaze back down to the map—"head down 101 here into the valley." He looked up from the map and pointed east. "When you get to Buellton, you're going to want to turn right on 246. Follow?"

"Yeah. So far, so good."

"Okay." He leaned over and continued pointing on the map. "Take this road all the way through Solvang to highway 154. Turn right and head toward the coast. You following all that?"

"Yeah. Looks pretty straightforward," I said.

"Okay, good. That will take you over the mountain range and into Santa Barbara. But it's a long way to go before nightfall, and a bitch of a hill to climb. Probably not the safest plan this late in the day. You sure you want to do that tonight?" he asked, handing over the map. "Again, I wouldn't recommend it. Not the best plan."

"I don't know yet. I'll have to figure this out. But thank you for the directions," I said.

"All right. Well, good luck. Sorry about the road closure. On a bright note, the fire department should be here soon."

Just as he finished saying that, as if on cue, three fire engines buzzed by, lights on, speeding toward the increasing cloud of smoke. We waved as they passed, and the firefighters returned the gesture. As they disappeared between the mountains, I caught a glimpse of the sun, currently high above the horizon but setting nonetheless. Its natural intensity filtered by thickening smoke, it shone down on me as an orange ball of fire surrounded by a red layer of shimmering lava. *That's crazy cool.* I turned back to the police officer.

"Well, I got to get moving, or I won't get anywhere tonight no matter where I decide to stop," I said. "I appreciate your help."

"All right. Good luck."

"Thanks. Have a good night."

"You too," the officer said.

He waved me off and walked over to another vehicle that pulled up to the intersection. His conversation, along with everything else to the west, soon became lost in thickening smoke. My attention was now drawn to the east, the exact opposite direction I was hoping to go. *Wow. What a bunch of DFL. That's short for "dumb fucking luck" to all the innocent out there.*

I didn't have any other choice, at least in my mind. The previous dilemma I was having with myself about continuing on to Santa Barbara or cutting today's ride short was simply a memory now. My decision had been made. I was going to make it to Santa Barbara tonight or die trying. Screw stopping in Buellton or Solvang. If I did that, I would never make it to Irvine the following day. My legs were in no condition to pedal over another mountain range, but I forced my mind not to focus on that fact, which would only serve to plant doubt and discourage me. I just needed to get moving and deal with it when I got there, one pedal stroke at a time. So I sat my perpetually sore ass back on the saddle and made off down the road. "I guess we're going to pass through Solvang after all," I whispered to Jezebel.

Knowing my time under a sunlit sky was short and I had a lot of difficult ground to cover with the light I had left, I pedaled hard, as the great ball of fire kept creeping toward the horizon way faster than I wanted it to.

I approached Buellton soon after leaving the interchange, the smoke thinning as I approached. So at least the air was better to breathe. Having grown accustomed to the crispy, clean air I'd been enjoying along the coast, my lungs were not happy about the smoke, especially since I was demanding that they work hard in it. They coughed in protest every so often, but I ventured on anyway.

After turning south on Highway 246, I noticed that the eastern side of the hills to my right, the ones I would be climbing over in a few hours, were already swallowed in shadow. "Aggggg! God, what a day! First the blowouts, now I'm forced to ride miles out of my way AND up a mountain. Oh, and I have to do it before the sun goes down. Fuck me!" I was yelling my frustrations and resentments into the emptiness, a wasted expulsion of much-needed energy, leaving them only to dissipate in a wake of solitude. The wind was the only one to answer, and she only whispered. Was she mocking me? Surely, she was. *Shit, I need to stop verbalizing my thoughts*, I thought, this time keeping it in all in my head. I just kept pedaling, shaking my head periodically in disbelief.

The town of Solvang went by in a blur of windmills, restaurants, and Dutch-style buildings. It would have been nice to stop at one of their famous bakeries if I wasn't flying through town on such a tight schedule. What a shame. I genuinely enjoy the food there, and the atmosphere. It's a relaxing, secluded place; a place that appears to be full of visitors even though most people I speak to don't even know the place exists. Go figure.

Matthew Koehler

CHAPTER SIX

A n hour or so later I arrived at the Cachuma Lake Recreation area. It was here where the mountain I needed to scale started to take its scary shape. Currently I was traveling on Highway 154, having turned south onto it several miles outside of Solvang. Passing in and out of shadows hurled across the road by the nearby peaks, an omen of encroaching twilight, I thought often about turning around and calling it a night. Now would be the best time to do it if I was going to. Better safe than sorry, some say. *That's what the weak say, Matt, not the strong.* But I just couldn't bring myself to do it. I set a goal, one I was determined to meet. Sticking to the mission was my way of having some self-respect, a commitment to an objective where failure wasn't an option. Even so, anxiety about time and the dangers of riding over a mountain after dark started to brew. It became clear I wasn't going to make it into Santa Barbara by nightfall—there was no debate about that now. Even though I should have planned for such an event, I didn't bring enough resources to safely ride after sundown. Other than the reflector strips sewn in on my panniers and cycling jersey, and my one emergency handlebar light, I was not adequately prepared to ride safely after dark, let alone ride down a mountain after dark where visibility would surely be limited. The only way to realistically attack this challenge was to get over the mountain as soon as possible. Easier said than done.

The highway turned right at the southern bank of the Cachuma Reservoir, where the mouth of the Santa Ynez River empties into it, splashing over half-exposed boulders in its attempt at filling the currently half-empty basin. The river got no more than a cursory glance from me, as I concentrated on more pressing matters and made a beeline for the San Ynez Mountains.

Here we go.

I arrived at the base of the climb about a mile later and started climbing immediately, gradually at first but increasing in grade the further west I traveled. I was already exhausted from the day's trials, and the extra miles I had to put in just to get to this point were taxing my resources, both physically and mentally. My legs were toast, and even though the thought of quitting was beaten out of me during Marine Corps training, I was tempted to do just that. Small cramps started to develop in my quads under the increased energy demands of the climb, and when I stood up on the pedals to relieve the now-constant numbness between my legs during the few intermittent flat portions, they shook uncontrollably from fatigue and resentment.

The miles ticked away slowly, too slowly for my liking, and all the while the sky continued its persistent transition into twilight. The higher I climbed, the more famished and frustrated I became. I didn't want to expend any effort reacting to my emotions as I usually would, so I actively forced myself to ignore the urge to behave like an undisciplined teenager. I chose to act like a Marine. A "just get the job done" attitude was a much better approach in this situation. Thinking about how much closer I was getting to Mo with every revolution of my wheels was motivating enough to rationalize the suffering and discomfort. I thought about her frequently, and that helped some. But truthfully, I just wanted to lie down.

I'll admit, my pace was consistent, but embarrassingly sluggish. And that's saying something coming from someone who knows how bad of a mountain climber I am. I was moving so slowly on the steeper ascents that I frequently had to twist Jezebel's handlebars from side to side just to keep from tipping over. Slow as I was, at least I wasn't the slowest one on the mountain that day. I became aware about halfway up the hill that I was gaining ground on a vehicle with its hazard flashers on. It looked like it wasn't moving at all until I got close enough to see that it was making its way over the mountain as well, but very slowly at that. Closing in on the hazard-light-flashing vehicle, the ever-encroaching twilight illuminated a small figure on what looked like a very small bike, riding alongside an equally slowly moving van.

After several minutes of heavy breathing and out-of-the-saddle pedaling, I finally pulled up behind the rider to find he wasn't riding a bike at all. This guy was riding a three-wheeled wheelchair. I couldn't believe what I was seeing. He was pushing himself up this relentless hill like a champ, pumping his arms in unison with a well-timed rhythmic bend at the waist, keeping pace like a metronome. Push, coast, and recover. Push, coast, and recover. Push, coast, and recover. Over and over. He just kept going and going. It looked exhausting.

I sat back in the saddle and followed behind him and the van, waiting for a safe break to pull out into the road and push past. The amount of effort he was putting out was mesmerizing to watch, and humbling at the same time. *How in the hell can someone push a wheelchair up this mountain? That's just plain crazy.* All the while, the white van kept pace, shielding him from traffic. I knew I should have just waved as I passed, but the urge to stop and talk to this guy was overwhelming. I knew, though, that stopping would be risky and delay my game. Having a conversation with this guy, even a short one, would cost me way too much of the day's precious remaining daylight. *Ah, fuck it. This guy has a story to tell.*

I decided to put the ball in his court and let him make the decision to stop and have a conversation, or not. I would yell out as I approached, letting him know that I was closing in on him from the rear. If he kept his pace and waved me by, or didn't say anything at all, I would cycle past and continue up the mountain. If he stopped, I would stop.

"Hey there! Coming up behind you!" I yelled, announcing my presence between deep breaths.

"Okay. I hear you. I'm pulling over!"

He answered loudly, also between deep breaths, turning his head to the right and yelling into the mountainside as he slowly came to a stop.

Well, shit. Guess I'm stopping, too.

I watched him pull over and followed in behind him, coasting to a stop. I unclicked from my pedals and straddled Jezebel's frame. My legs shook from fatigue, and my body thanked me for the break. I rested my forearms on the black cork-wrapping of my handlebars as the driver of the van pulled over a couple yards in front of him and shut off the engine, leaving the hazard lights flashing.

"Hi there. You didn't need to stop and pull over on my account," I said.

"Oh, it's no problem, really. Me and the wife over there in the van were looking for a place to pull over anyway. This is tough going, this hill." He flicked both of his hands out in front of him over his outstretched legs as if he needed to show me the challenge ahead. "I needed a break," he continued, dropping his hands down onto his lap. He was breathing hard and sweating profusely. He reached down and set the brake, then leaned back in his bucket seat and looked up at me. "You provided the perfect opportunity for that. Thanks."

"Yeah, tell me about it. This mountain's a bitch," I agreed, glancing up at the unforgiving cliffside.

"You got that right," he added. "My hands are starting to cramp up, and my triceps are burnin' like fire."

"Dude, right? I understand. I'm beat, too. It's been a very long day for me."

"Oh yeah? How so?" the man asked with a frown, one that formed so abruptly I wasn't sure if it was legit. "Couldn't be too hard. At least you get to pedal with your legs. I have to make it over this mountain with these puny old-man arms." I didn't even know this guy's name, and I already started flushing with guilt. Thankfully, he was just breaking the ice the best way he knew how. He laughed, letting me know he was only joking, and I'm glad he did. I would have felt terrible if he didn't. Even so, I must have looked guilty. "I'm just kidding, boy. Go ahead, tell me about it."

"Okay, thanks," I replied sheepishly, still feeling a little awkward. "Well, I started the day in San Simeon, got two blowouts outside the town of Cayucos, and then got rerouted around this mountain range by the cops because of a fire in Gaviota State Park. The plan was to cruise into Santa Barbara this evening after a nice twilight stroll along the coast. But here I am, climbing this damn mountain." I don't think I could have sounded more pathetic if I'd tried.

I could have filled in my sob-story with more detail, but suddenly, even though he'd told me not to feel weird about it, a wave of embarrassment rolled through me. I was complaining about my day spent riding my bike when this guy was pushing himself up the same mountain in a freakin' wheelchair. *A wheelchair. This guy might not have the use of his legs, but he's got guts.*

The man laughed as he lifted a baseball hat off his head and dropped it onto his lap. It was once a white hat, or so I presumed, the edges now stained salty brown from sweat and dirt, the bill folded down on the sides, presumably to shield his eyes from the sun. He ran his gloved fingers through his damp shoulder-length hair, letting it fall heavily over his ears. It was oily and wet from sweating.

"Hey, don't feel too bad," he said, turning to look at me while pointing toward the mountaintop. "Not too much further, and you'll be over the summit. Then you'll be coasting down the other side and be in Santa Barbara, lickety-split. It'll be like going over a waterfall."

"Shoot, I've been climbing so long I'm beginning to wonder if this mountain even has a summit," I said, half joking.

He found that amusing and smiled, a large toothy grin that inspired me to respond in kind. Just then a door slammed shut on the van and I turned to see a woman walking toward us with a water bottle dangling from her left hand. She was tall and slim with long legs supporting a short torso. Locks of silver hair draped naturally over narrow shoulders and hung loosely against her back. It swayed effortlessly against her gait as she moved. Her youthful-looking face didn't match the color of her hair, but I didn't sense a bit of shame from her at the contrast, only quiet self-confidence; confidence that commanded your attention without even asking for it. Taking long slow strides, she quickly closed the distance between us and the van. The man in the wheelchair introduced her right away.

"This sexy thing here is my wife, Jane," he said, a prideful smile growing on his face. "Isn't she the most beautiful woman you've ever seen?"

A shy smile formed on her face while her eyes rolled with mild embarrassment. She offered her hand to me and in the same motion, handed over the water bottle to the man. He took it eagerly and drank it dry while we introduced ourselves.

"Hi. I'm Jane," she said in a friendly tone. "Pleasure to meet you."

I grabbed her hand with my fingerless glove–covered hand and gave it a light shake.

"Nice to meet you too, Jane. Matt."

After a few gentle shakes, I extended my hand to the man in the wheelchair. He set the now empty water bottle down on his lap and grabbed my hand immediately, and with surprisingly great force. I was taken aback at the power of his grip. It was like an octopus had just grabbed my hand. Both of us were wearing thick padded gloves, and when our hands were clasped together it looked as if we were congratulating each other for a good fight after an MMA match.

"Hi, Matt. Harold. Nice to meet you. Good lookin' set of wheels you got there."

"Thank you. Yours are pretty cool as well. Nice to meet you too, Harold." We unclasped hands. "That's quite a grip you got there. Careful, you can do some damage with that."

He laughed.

"Yeah, when you spend the last thirty years of your life pushing one of these puppies around, you get pretty strong in the hands. That's nothing, though. You should see my arms! Here, check this out," he said excitedly and started to take off his jacket.

Jane cut in.

"Harold, don't do that," she said. "That's really not necessary."

She spoke softly, but firmly. I could tell this was not the first time she'd had to curb some of his enthusiasm.

Harold heeded her request and let go of his jacket. Amused with himself, he burst out laughing, so loud a few nesting birds took flight in a frantic flutter from a nearby bush. It was so abrupt it made me flinch too. Jane shook her head in bewilderment and shrugged shyly.

"He loves when people pull over to talk," she said, trying unsuccessfully to hide the statement under her breath. "He thrives on the attention."

Still laughing, Harold responded playfully, "Hey, I heard that." Then he turned to me. "But she's right, you know. Thanks for pulling over. I love shootin' the breeze with new friends. Let me guess, you want to know what the hell I'm doing out here pushing a wheelchair down a highway when I could be riding in that comfortable van with that hot-ass woman over there. Am I right? I mean, that's what I'd be wondering."

Harold again burst into belly-shaking laughter like he'd just heard the funniest joke ever. Jane rolled her eyes and shook her head slowly from side to side, amused yet again. I was amused as well, and a smile cracked open on my face.

"Yes, as a matter of fact, that is exactly what I want to know. But please don't feel—"

Harold cut me off and dove right into his story. He spoke loudly, way louder than he needed to, unless he was looking to entertain the hidden wildlife too. *Okay. Well, if he's going to take the floor, I'm going to take a drink.* While Harold got started, I reached down and pulled my Cytomax-filled bottle from its holder and took a long pull, glancing nervously into the still light, but noticeably darkening sky.

"Well," he began. "I got shot up in Vietnam during an ambush at the ripe old age of twenty. Those fuckers almost killed me. And there are times in my life when I almost wish they had. They took some of the best years of my life away from me, that's for sure. And my legs. Obvious enough, right? They got me in the spine and a couple times in my legs. My fellow Marines killed all of those bastards and then took me to the back lines to get fixed up. Things get difficult when you're forced into a life-changing situation like this though. But, hey . . . they didn't kill me, and even though it took a while to adjust, I made a conscious choice to accept what happened and move on with the rest of my life."

I wasn't expecting this kind of story, and it forced me into a bubble of awkwardness. The smile disappeared from my face, and though I didn't know what to say, I felt an uncomfortable urge to say something.

"Ah, shit, Harold. I'm sorry," was all I could muster.

Harold continued as if I said nothing.

"I spent a year in the hospital recovering from what felt like endless surgeries, but even with all their efforts, they weren't able to fix my legs. So, I'll be like this forever. At least that's what they tell me. But"—Harold raised both index fingers out in front of him before continuing—"I'm an optimist and I'm holding out for a cure, or at least some kind of technological marvel that could give me at least partial use of my legs. I hear some progress is being made, but it seems life will go by without me ever walking again. But I will always hold on to some sliver of hope. It gets pretty depressing if you lose that. Sometimes that's all you have to keep you going, you know?"

He paused, dropped his head, and stared at his hands for a moment. Just when I was going to say something to break the momentary silence, Harold raised his head and continued.

"Jane here was one of my nurses while I was getting worked on at the VA hospital. Seems like I was the one who lucked out in the end, huh?" He smiled in her direction. "At least I think so! What do you think?" He looked at me and started laughing again.

"That's crazy. And I agree. Looks like it all worked out for the best."

"Well, you could say that," Howard said. "I think she's pretty awesome myself. She knew what she was getting, right from the start, that's for sure. And she still sticks around. Can you believe that shit?"

"Harold, please," Jane said.

"Sorry, dear," Harold replied with a grimace. Apparently, Jane was not a fan of swearing.

"Well, maybe that says something about you, no?" I asked, meaning it more as a complement than anything.

"Ha. I think she mostly likes all the benefits, if I'm telling you the truth. Ah ha ha!" Harold roared with laughter again and wiped away a bead of sweat that had dripped down into his eyes. Jane couldn't stay quiet after hearing that.

"Yeah. That's why I stick around. All those great benefits." She rolled her eyes in playful contempt. "Harold, please."

"So, you're a Marine?" I asked, confirming his story.

"Yep. Yep. Been a Marine longer than anything else in my life. Medically discharged decades ago, obviously." Harold flipped his palms up and draped them over his strapped-down legs like he was showing off a table full of

Thanksgiving dinner.

"Well, Semper Fi, brother. And thank you for your service. I'm . . . uhh. . . I'm really sorry you had to earn that Purple Heart."

"Yeah." He paused. "Well, somebody's got to do it. Don't want all those medals to go to waste now, do we? That would be a misuse of taxpayer money, you know," Harold said, sarcasm dripping from the statement. "We wouldn't want any of that," he added with a wink.

"And from my father, he would welcome you home, brother. He served in the Army during the Vietnam War as well," I said.

He paused again for a moment, his head drifting off to the side, staring blankly at the mountainside. All the sudden it seemed like he went all serious on me. I wasn't sure how to continue, or even if I should. I glanced at Jane. She uncrossed her arms and raised both of her palms, silently telling me to just wait a minute. I kept quiet and slowly turned my gaze back to Harold. A few seconds later a semi-truck lumbered by in a low gear, nudging him free from his trance. After the truck rolled far enough down the road to be out of audible range, Harold disturbed the following silence with softly spoken words of sincerity.

"Yep, a lot of us unfortunate souls had to go fight and die in that fucking shit hole. A lot of good men died over there, damnit." He wasn't smiling, or laughing, anymore. And no scolding came from Jane regarding the swearing this time.

"Harold, I'm sorry. I—"

He cut me off again.

"It's okay." He paused, pointing at me. "Matt, right?"

"Uh, yes. Matt."

"Sorry. Names are hard to keep straight sometimes." He tried to laugh and managed only a soft, breathy snicker. It came out sounding more like a weighty cough. "Even after all these years, I still get worked up about all that bullshit. I know the memories won't ever go away, I can only wish they would. I don't know if the pain ever will either. Sorry about that," he said solemnly. He seemed to be calming down a little bit, and that was good. "But I use those emotions to raise awareness about the mental and physical challenges combat veterans deal with after coming home from combat zones."

His expression gradually changed back into one of purpose and contentment. I even sensed a bit of hope in it too.

"Dude. Harold, that's great," I said enthusiastically, working to elevate the mood. "Do you raise money for a cause, or what?"

Harold began to talk again, and I finally felt comfortable enough to have another pull from the Cytomax bottle. While he continued talking, I emptied the remaining sugar water, every last drop of it. It wasn't doing me any good in the bottle, anyway, and I still had riding to do. *Speaking of that, you need to get going, Matt, like right now.*

"Well, not directly. I work with a few different organizations to help spread the word. I'm in the middle of a border-to-border ride at the moment. Pushing myself from Canada to Mexico. My goal is to talk to as many people on the trip as possible and ask them to look up local veteran assistance programs in their areas and see if they can volunteer time or donate money to help out. I visit veteran centers and hospitals along the way to show other disabled veterans that life doesn't need to end because you had a really bad day on the battlefield."

"That's crazy! You're crazy, in the best of every way. Border-to-border? And Jane is following you the whole way?"

"Yeah. Of course she is. She has to. This whole thing was her idea!"

"Really? That's cool."

"Yeah. Can you believe that shit?" Harold winced. "Woops. Sorry, dear."

Jane only rolled her eyes.

Harold seemed back to his jovial self now, and that made me feel better. "She gets the easy job, though. Sitting in that air-conditioned van while I have to suffer out here on the road," he said, laughing loudly now, again seeming completely amused with himself. "But don't worry about me. She makes up for it in other ways, if you know what I mean,"

Harold shot a wink in my direction and continued with his wild laughter.

I glanced at Jane, shooting her an uncomfortable smile. She just stood there shaking her head and smiling, immune to his playful banter. I got the feeling that at some time in the past, public comments like those might have embarrassed her, but the years had seasoned her resolve. She wore the "whatever" look very confidently.

"Yeah, driving five miles per hour from border to border. Sounds exciting, right?" she joked.

Having spent most of my day in solitude, the three-way conversation was a welcome one. I wanted to stay but really needed to get over this stupid mountain and find me a hotel and get some sleep.

"Harold, what you're doing is a wonderful thing, and I want to wish you the best of luck on a safe journey to the Mexican border. I wish we could chat some more, but I need to get to Santa Barbara tonight, and daylight is quickly disappearing."

"No problem, Marine." He fired off a salute in my direction. "I know you understand what I'm doing out here. Spread the word. Help me out, will ya?" he said, chuckling again.

"I will, Harold. Thanks." I turned to Jane. "Jane, it was wonderful to meet you. You are a special breed of woman, for sure," I said, smiling and with a single head nod of exclamation. That brought a close-lipped smile to her face and a single audible huff of laughter through her nose.

"Yeah, I guess I am. I need to be if I want to stay married to this crazy guy," she said, now laughing through a full open-mouth grin while shaking her finger in Harold's direction.

"You're damn right about that, dear!" Harold agreed, again with more belly-shaking laughter. "You're the best."

Harold would have made a great Santa Claus, except for the fact that he had straight salt-and-pepper hair, no beard, and wasn't fat. He did have the jolly aspect down. Well, okay, maybe he wouldn't make a great Santa Claus, but maybe he could rent out his laughter.

I shook both of their hands, said goodbye, and pushed off up the hill. I heard Harold yell at me as I rode away, giving me a verbal push up the mountain.

"Go, go, go!" he said.

I recuperated some during the break and now felt like I was riding a little faster than before. Maybe it was a good thing.

*　　　*　　　*

Another thirty minutes of heavy breathing and slow climbing delivered me to the summit, tired and hungry, but relieved. Relieved to see what I presumed to be a small sliver of Santa Barbara in the distance, faintly visible through a multitude of deep ravines sandwiched between softly rounded mountain peaks. Unfortunately, the city was already dotted with gleaming streetlights under the looming twilight, their tiny bulbs of glowing radiance taking over for the sun and illuminating the Spanish-style coastal town under a blanket of warm evening light. From where I was, perched atop one of many pinnacles in the Sant Ynez mountain range, Santa Barbara didn't look much like the "American Riviera" some say it is. At that moment, it was just a goal, a spot on a map that I had to get to, as soon as possible, on a bike, in the dark. Preferably in one piece. And I had to do it all in a minor state of exhaustion. *Ugh. Matt, you can be so melodramatic sometimes. You should be thankful I'm the only one in your head. Cry me a river, will ya?* Well, looking at it optimistically, as Mo would, the American Riviera, as it were, was closer than it had been all day. But it was still so far away, and I wished deeply that I was already there.

The sun was below the horizon now, and that let the butterflies loose in my belly. What I was about to do wasn't safe, and I knew it. I was running on fumes underneath a darkening sky at a time when I should be riding with complete confidence and under full sunlight. And now it was time to descend into the valley with only the remaining light of day, the random passing light from cars, and my little emergency handlebar light to guide me down the steep descent into the "Riviera" below. Sounds romantic, right? I can assure you it was not. This was no movie.

Speaking of all that, I yanked my jacket and handlebar light out of my panniers. I pulled the jacket on over my sweat-dampened jersey and clicked the light in place on Jezebel's handlebars, turning it to the brightest of three settings. I was nervous about the impending descent but grateful to let gravity take control for a while. Although welcoming, this presented its own set of challenges. Better than having to push down on the pedals anymore today, that's for sure.

As I descended the western face of the Santa Ynez my speed gradually increased, enough so that both index fingers instinctually found a permanent home resting on the brake levers, ready for action at a moment's notice. Navigation of the long, snake-like turns went smoother than expected considering the amount of forced concentration required. It helped that the road was well maintained, with ample room along the shoulder to comfortably ride faster than I had been for most of the day, a pleasant reprieve from the slow grind of the past couple hours.

The air was still, but riding through it so quickly created enough wind to press the jacket against my skin. Made of thin nylon, it provided minimal protection from the elements, and almost immediately a chill set in on my chest and arms. Sharp snapping sounds disrupted the consistent roar of the wind as the loose fabric slapped at the air behind my neck, muted every so often by the road noise of passing vehicles and the occasional fear-inducing clattering of a semi-truck's jack brake. Sunglass time was long gone, and the fast-moving air caused my unprotected eyes to tear to the point of blurriness, forcing me to squint and blink more frequently than I wanted to in order to keep my vision clear. Gravity did its job, pulling me quickly down the mountain as Jezebel's freewheel clicked wildly, almost gleefully, in response. I do admit, even though I was butt-ass tired, it felt liberating to be traveling at such high speeds without my legs having to put out much effort. *You definitely earned this downhill, Matt.* But for once, just this once, I didn't care. I just wanted the ride to be over.

I used the downhill as an opportunity to rest my ass a little bit as well. Not happy with all the abuse it was forced to endure sitting on a skinny saddle for most of the past two days, a reprieve from the discomfort was long overdue. It wasn't the only protester either. Everything between my legs hurt. My ass cheeks and inner part of my upper thighs were chafed from sweat and the rubbing together from the thousands of pedal strokes taken over the past two days. The muscles surrounding my pelvis were tight, letting me know they could cramp up at any moment. All of this was wearing on me, but I've dealt with that kind of pain and discomfort before, and I knew if I just sucked it up for a little while longer, I'd get through it. I really didn't have any other choice. All I needed was a little rest. Of most concern to me, however, was the partial numbness I was experiencing in my nether regions, likely the result of sitting on that damn saddle for so many hours. This, as any man would attest, was unacceptable. Everything else I could deal with. But a numb dick? No effing way.

To help alleviate my distress over this "very important" conundrum, I situated my body in a more aerodynamic position over Jezebel's frame, pushing my ass further back on the saddle and leveling my feet with the ground. I dipped my head down, closer to Jezebel's top tube, and loosened my elbows, resting my hands on the lower part of the downward-swooping handlebars.

This funky, unnatural position helps in three ways. One, the aerodynamics of the position allowed for less drag as I moved through the air, increasing speed with less effort. Two, it put my body in a different position over the bike that it hadn't been in much over the past two days, relieving various sore spots and engaging different muscle groups, at the same time resting others. And three, should I hit something, like I did earlier that morning, the impact most likely wouldn't cause as much damage as it would if I was sitting upright, where most of my weight would be concentrated over the rear wheel. My muscles and joints would take a lot of the impact, relieving some of the stress and damage taken by the bike. Considering I was currently speeding down the highway after sunset, under limited visibility, it would have been dangerous for me to ride any other way.

Tucked into this new riding position, I was halfway down the mountain in no time. The problem was, the easiest and safest part of the descent was over. The most dangerous section loomed ahead. The further down the mountain I got, the darker it became. Soon I was riding in this weird twilight zone where my eyes had a difficult time deciding whether there was enough light to see what was going on, or not. Some things were clearer in my periphery than if they were directly in front of me. It didn't help that the surrounding mountainsides were blocking much of the days remaining light. Meager as it was, it was light I'd been relying on to navigate down the highway and spot impending hazards beyond the reach of my headlight.

In the interest of personal safety, this ever-increasing descent into darkness forced me to slow down. I began feathering my brakes to keep my speed in check, relying on passing cars to illuminate the road ahead of me. Although the light they supplied was intermittent and quick to pass, I was able to use these brief, sweeping beacons of saving grace to scan the road. In my exhausted state, this exercise of diligence became increasingly stressful and mentally daunting the further I descended the mountain range.

To make matters worse, the closer I got to the valley floor, the more tactically challenging the road became, especially with the increase in debris littering the shoulder. Cracks in the pavement appeared more frequently, some of them long ago repaired, some new and not repaired. Regardless, when I rode over one of them, they sent a jolt through Jezebel—and through my tired, aching body—each time reminding me of the morning's unfortunate adventure.

I really needed this day to be over. I was done, so done. Maybe Mo could just come up and hang out with me in Santa Barbara. That wouldn't be too bad. It's such a wonderful place.

*　　*　　*

Through sheer guts and a little luck, I survived the descent and gracefully entered the less-dangerous foothills to the west. The highway leveled out some, and for the first time in many miles, I, very gently, sat back down on the saddle and started pedaling again. My legs protested, as expected, but I forced them to cooperate. A few miles later, the mountain began to open up, and as straight roads became more common than curvy ones, the outer limits of the city came into view. Finally, I felt comfortable enough to allow myself several deep breaths of relief. As a person who relishes his time in the great outdoors, I do have to acknowledge the contradiction of how happy I was to see the pale amber glow of city lights. They were so much closer now than they were at the top of the mountain, and I was thrilled to be within striking distance.

Civilization slowly materialized. It started with a few ranches I coasted past while descending the foothills. A little further down the road, as the pavement eventually leveled out, suburban neighborhoods popped up as if out of nowhere, and with that, streetlights began to shine along the roadway, welcoming me into town.

"Holy shit, Jezebel. We did it. We're finally here," I whispered. "Un-freakin' believable."

Jezebel was a champ today. We both took a beating but arrived safe nonetheless. Now we needed rest. A long one preferably, but any length would do.

Finally, after a four-hour detour around and over the Santa Ynez Mountains, I made a left turn off US 154 and onto State Street. *Take that, Mr. Policeman. I fucking made it!* At this intersection I could, if so inclined, hop back onto Highway 1. But, knowing I would like to leave Santa Barbara tomorrow morning via State Street, I turned off here instead to look for a hotel. *Welcome back,* I thought, shooting a lazy glance at a nearby Highway 1 sign, *we missed you. Sorry about the detour.*

CHAPTER SEVEN

About 9 p.m. I rolled into the Motel 6 parking lot on State Street. My head hung in relief as I slowly turned into the driveway and came to a stop under a red neon "vacancy" sign shining brightly in the main lobby window. *Oh, please let it be true.* My tired eyes scanned the lobby. It was small, too small for me and Jezebel to fit in there comfortably, so I gingerly dismounted, leaned Jezebel up against the window next to the door and walked inside.

Even with all the noise my shoes made walking across the tile floor, nobody came to the front desk by the time the door shut behind me, so I spoke into the empty room.

"Hello?" I said, leaning over the counter and peering through a slightly open door in the back of the room.

A voice called out from behind the door.

"Just a sec. Coming."

"Okay. Thanks."

I leaned against the counter and waited patiently, using the opportunity to remove my gloves and stuff them in my jersey pocket. The door swung open a short time later, and a man appeared. He walked slowly over to the counter and stood across from me.

"Hey there. Good evening," he said, greeting me with lazy eyes and a shallow grin, like he'd just woken up from a nap. "What can I do for you?"

His words were cordial enough but spoken in such a tone that led me to believe he wasn't very happy about someone interrupting whatever he was doing in the back room. *Tough titties, dude. I need a bed and a shower. Like now.*

"Do you have any rooms available?" I asked hopefully, trying not to appear desperate.

"Sure do," he replied. "How many in your party?"

His response confirmed the "vacancy" sign in the window. Hearing what I'd wanted to hear since rolling into San Simeon twenty-four hours earlier filled my shaking legs with relief and gratitude. *Yes! Thank you, Jesus!* Knowing that I was privy to a shower and a full night's rest, on a bed, mind you, was worth more at that moment than if both of my panniers were full of gold. I openly sighed.

"Ahh. It's just me, thank you," I said, noticeably famished.

I must have looked terrible, as a veil of apprehension fell over the man's face. He must have thought I was going to collapse at any moment.

"You okay, man?" he asked, sounding genuinely concerned. I watched as he cautiously studied me from underneath a slightly furrowed brow, brushing some of his long-hanging blond hair away from his eyes to get a better look at me.

"Yeah, I'm alright. Thank you. It's just been a long day. A very long, challenging day, that's all. I need a shower and sleep," I said, again in a tired tone. I couldn't help it.

"Okay. Well, let's get you checked in then. How many nights?"

"Just one, please."

I paid for the room, handing over the cash with helplessly shaking fingers, and he handed over the key.

"Here you go, sir," he said. "I hope you have a good night's sleep."

Fingers still shaking, I reached out and grabbed the key.

"Thanks. Me too. God knows I need it."

He flipped me a polite wave and a smile.

"Night," he said, dropping his hand back down to the counter.

"Good night."

My heavy legs managed to carry me outside. As the door slammed shut behind me, I bent over and slipped off my shoes. Free of the tight constraints of unforgiving Velcro straps, my feet splayed out to their natural shape on the cool concrete. To say it felt wonderful would be an understatement. I pulled Jezebel away from the window and walked down the corridor toward the room. Thank goodness it was on the first floor. The thought of asking for a first-floor room had crossed my mind, but it fluttered away, as many of my thoughts do, once I engaged the front desk guy in conversation. *I wonder if he did that on purpose? If he did, "Thanks, bro."*

I opened the door, walked inside, and flicked on the light. The room was simple, clean, dry and warm. Just what I needed, nothing more. I leaned Jezebel up against the box-shaped air conditioner underneath the window next to the door and dropped my shoes at the foot of the bed. I kicked the door shut, stripped off my helmet, pulled my gloves out of my jersey pocket, and dropped them on the floor next to my shoes. Then I spun around and, like a wet noodle, fell limply onto the bed and stared up at the ceiling. Oh, how glorious it felt to lie flat on my back. The bed was firm, and under any other circumstance, I would classify it as slightly uncomfortable. But it sure was a hell of a lot more comfortable than the bed of dirt I'd slept on the night before.

Every one of my muscles relaxed at once, like they had been waiting for this moment forever. I acquiesced, and my entire body sank as far into the shallow mattress as the mattress would allow. My eyes closed, almost instinctually, and I relished the euphoric sensation of not moving any muscles for the first time in two days. I lay so still that I could not only hear the hammering of my heart in my ears, but felt it pounding against my sternum as well. I was spent.

Snapping back to the land of the living after dozing off for a couple of minutes, I forced myself to sit up on the edge of the bed. My body ached for sleep, the primary driver of all things at the moment; so much so my eyes burned. But I also needed a shower, badly. I had three things on the agenda for the evening: sleep, shower, and call Mo. *And Mom. Don't forget to call your mother, unless you want something to regret tomorrow.* If time allowed, maybe even dinner. But in my condition each task felt like a chore, and if I wasn't diligent about which one I completed before the other, I would wake up the next morning still wearing the same cycling clothes. And I really couldn't forget to call Mo. She has no idea what kind of day I had.

Shower first. I leaned over and removed my socks, silently laughing at the tan line left in its place. I clumsily dragged my finger up my shaved legs, collecting a fingertip full of gunk and leaving a noticeably clean line where I had just wiped away two days' worth of coastal salt and road grime. This left me amused and disgusted at the same time. Most boys are by such things.

More concerned with taking care of my agenda than childish amusement, I stood up, stripped off the rest of my clothing and retrieved yesterday's clothing from Jezebel's panniers. As expected, it was still damp from the previous night's foggy adventure. Now liberated from the gentle constriction of cycling clothes, a feeble sensation of weightlessness brushed over me. I took a moment and stared at my comical-looking self in the full-length mirror hanging behind the bathroom door. *Damn!* I looked like an alien. Dirty rivers of dried sweat and filthy salt ran down my arms and legs while sunburn outlined the borders of my jersey, shorts, and socks. I snickered at the reflection. The elements had done quite a number on my face, legs, arms, and neck since leaving Capitola, but my chest and pelvic region appeared untouched; clean, free of dirt and white as freshly fallen snow.

The faint sunglass tan line surrounding my eyes and stretching over the top of my ears was intriguing, and my hair, despite being "USMC regulation," still bore the impressions from my helmet's ventilation gaps. Chafing marks the size of silver dollars glowed a dull pink between my legs and high in the crack of my butt cheeks, and the palms of my hands were red and sore from wearing wet gloves all day. *Ugh. Shit, Matt. You haven't looked this bad since you were out bivouacking in the Camp Pendleton backcountry.*

Tired of looking at all that, I turned away from the mirror and began the process of hanging my cycling clothes from various high points in the room in hopes that they would dry overnight. Bedposts, lamps, doorknobs, TV, towel rack, you name it. Pretty much anything that would support hanging clothing had something dangling from it when I was finished. The image spawned memories of my grandma's backyard clothes-drying rack. As a child, it fascinated me. When empty, it reminded me of an "old school" TV antenna. But when loaded down with laundry, my imagination would conjure up an earth invasion of aliens and monsters. Amusing myself with childhood daydreaming, I would watch sun-cast shadows dance on the backyard patio as gentle winds helped dry the plethora of clothes-pinned garments and hanging towels.

Clothing hung, I yanked my still damp sleeping bag free of its stuff bag and laid it out on the floor between the bed and the wall so it could dry out as much as possible before I left the next morning.

Finally, I was ready for the shower. I walked into the bathroom, turned the shower handle to hot, and let the water run. While it was warming up, I rummaged around and found my toothbrush and toothpaste. Eagerly, I brushed away all the PowerBar residue and latent sugar from between my teeth, something I didn't get around to doing the night before. I was thinking about getting some dinner but, surprisingly, it only rose to that level: just a thought. I didn't feel hungry, so I might as well clean my teeth. At this point my body craved only sleep, not food, a rare and somewhat confusing event for someone harboring such a healthy appetite. All this meant was, in the morning I was going to be ravenously hungry. *Fine, whatever. I'll eat then.*

I finished scrubbing my teeth and stepped into the steaming shower. It was like I'd just entered the gates of heaven. The hot water splashing against my skin felt wonderful, exactly the way I had been fantasizing it would; all the way up until hot water hit raw skin. The pain I felt after my big mountain bike accident on Mission Peak came roaring back as the hot water flowed between my thighs and over the palms of my hands, lighting a fire at each sensitive spot. I instinctually turned around to avoid the pain on the front part of my body, but, almost comically, the hot water ran between my butt cheeks and lit a fire down there too. I had no choice but to drop the water temperature to warm and slowly creep it back up as my body adjusted to the heat and adapted to the pain and discomfort.

After letting the water rain down for several minutes, I took to cleaning myself from head to toe, feeling like a new man when finished. It's hard to describe how wonderful it felt to be clean again and not smell like a piss-stained parking garage stairwell. The heat and steam encouraged my muscles to relax, providing a real sense of comfort. Morale was improving too, I could feel it.

Turning off the shower was an unfortunate necessity, but I got what I needed out of it. Steam filled the small bathroom as I pushed aside the shower curtain and stepped out of the basin, similar in consistency to the fog of this morning, but much better received. I opened the door, and it quickly tumbled out of the new opening, dissipating along the low ceiling and clouding up the highest portion of the adjacent mirror before disappearing. After drying off, I climbed into my boxers and T-shirt. Bliss.

I wanted to sit down on the bed, lay back into it, and say goodbye to the day. Ninety percent of my body and mind wanted to do just that. But 10 percent did not. I couldn't fall asleep before calling Mo, I just couldn't. It wouldn't be fair. After all, she was the reason I was doing all of this, the reason for all the pleasure and suffering. So, before the temptation became too strong to bear, I grabbed a handful of quarters from my bag and walked back down to the front office in bare feet, a T-shirt, and boxer shorts.

As I walked, I thought about why I was doing this. I never did anything like this for my other girlfriends. But here I was, riding my bike, pushing myself down the California coast from Capitola to Irvine, on a deadline, all for the love of a girl. *Why?* Because I loved cycling, and this was just an excuse for me to put four hundred miles on the bike? Maybe. That's part of it, sure. But I really don't think it was the main reason. I really don't think my ego was the driving force for this adventure. I mean, I could have taken a bike ride to Southern California whenever I wanted, girlfriend or no girlfriend.

Something else was going on here. Something I couldn't really explain was telling me she wasn't just any other girl. She wasn't just another run-of-the-mill girlfriend I would have for a couple of months before moving on to another. She was *special*. Maybe even *the one*.

Special? Well, shit. What the hell does that mean, Matt? And . . . "the one?" You're nineteen, bro, way too young to be entertaining such crazy thoughts. I quarreled with myself, as if the two sides of my brain were fighting with each other. Was it the drowsiness? Had the need for sleep made me delirious? I don't think so. One side of my brain was telling me what I was doing was too much, it was overkill. *Dude, chill out, man. Don't hurt yourself, bro.* The other side was pushing me forward. *I don't know, man, I think this girl is the one. Drop everyone else. Go see her!*

The "go see her" side screamed the loudest, so here I was. For some reason, I chose to make this trip in three days, no excuses. Common sense would have said to take as long as I needed, especially since I was not in the kind of riding shape that would predict success. Three days? Maybe. Four days? Sure. Five days? Who cares? Mo surely wouldn't, as long as I made it to her safely. She had school to worry about anyway. But the Marine Corps in me speaks too, and you know what? The Marine Corps is a loud obnoxious beast. *Damnit, Koehler, if you say you're going to make the trip in three days, then shit, boy, there will be no excuses. You will accomplish the mission in three days! Do you understand?*

"Yes, sir!"

The door-less phone booth was parked right outside the tiny lobby. I shuffled up to it and dumped a handful of quarters on the metal tray underneath the phone with a clatter. A well-used phone book dangled from a steel cable attached somewhere underneath. I picked up the receiver, exactly the way I had done so fifteen hours earlier, and the evening before that. Remembering my grandfather's cleanliness standards, I wiped down the receiver with the end of my T-shirt, then brought the phone to my ear. I dropped in several quarters and dialed up her number but got no answer. After seven or eight rings I hung up the phone and retrieved my unused quarters from the change return door. I waited a few minutes underneath the glowing Motel 6 sign, taking the opportunity to rub out my quads, and called again. This time, Priscilla, one of her roommates, picked up the phone and told me Mo wasn't home, but she should be back soon. I asked her if she would tell Mo that I got to Santa Barbara safely and I would call her in the morning before I left. She agreed and wished me luck. I thanked her and hung up the phone.

The day wouldn't be complete without being a good son and putting my mother's worry to rest. So I picked up the receiver and dialed up my home number. Mom answered right away, as expected, and wanted a rundown of the entire day. I told her I was too tired to do that right now but that I made it to Santa Barbara in one piece and I would tell her all about it later. Our conversation ended quickly and I hung up the phone and shuffled back to my room. After standing out in the fresh air for the past twenty minutes or so, my room smelled like I'd walked back into my old high school locker room. Ugh!

Only one more phone call to make, then my day was complete. Before laying my head down on the pillow I dialed the front desk and asked for a wake-up call.

"6 a.m., please."

"Yes, sir. Anything else you need this evening?"

"No. That's it. Thank you."

"Very well. Good night, sir."

"Good night."

I dropped the phone receiver back in its cradle and set the alarm on my trusty Timex for 6:05. I laid it down face up on the nightstand next to the phone and flicked off the light. It was 9:30. I had eight and a half hours of sleep coming. Not wanting to waste a minute more of this precious time, I laid my head down on the pillow and started to think about Mo and how excited I was to see her pretty face tomorrow. What a bummer she wasn't there when I called. I felt bad that I couldn't call her back, knowing she was going to feel horrible when she got the message. But I would make up for it in the morning, rudely waking her up around 6:30 before putting Jezebel's rubber to the road. This was the last thought I remember as my body became heavy between the sheets. My mind quickly pushing me away from wakefulness, I allowed one last wakeful desire. *Maybe, just maybe, I'll dream about her while I'm sleeping.*

Roadkill just a few miles south of San Simeon on the morning of day two. My previous night was a little out of the ordinary, but at least I woke up in a better state than this guy.

Approaching Las Cruces, where a fire in Gaviota State Park almost stopped me from getting to Santa Barbara by the end of the day.

Another view of the fire as I rode away into the Santa Ynez mountain range.

Harold putting me to shame riding his three-wheeled wheelchair. You can see the smoke from the fire in the background.

Matthew Koehler

PART FIVE

Completing the Circle

Santa Barbara ⟶ UC Irvine

Matthew Koehler

CHAPTER ONE

T he next morning began as I knew it would but didn't really want it to, with the loud ringing of the hotel room phone two feet away from my head. Startled, I jolted from slumber, rolling on to my right shoulder on a mission to snuff out the annoying mechanical clanging of the phone's ring. Swimming in a fog of sleepiness, I thought surely this must be a dream, and not the type of dream I was hoping for when I drifted off to sleep the night before. *There's no way it's time to get up yet.* If it wasn't for the thin slit of light shining into the room from between the drapes telling me otherwise, I might have believed the thought. My left hand fumbled around on the nightstand until I found the phone. I picked up the receiver and brought it to my ear in the dark.

"Hello?" I said, voice crackling.

A friendly and way-too-awake female voice came through the receiver.

"Good morning, sir. This is your 6 a.m. wake up call," she replied with an insultingly joyful voice, leading me to believe she was having the happiest day of her life.

Me? Not so much. *Six? How in the hell can it be 6 a.m. already? I just closed my eyes, like, a few minutes ago, didn't I?*

"Okay. thank you," I said softly, my voice hoarse and shaky from mouth-breathing most of the night away. I lowered the receiver towards the cradle when I heard the woman on the other end of the line start to say something else, so I brought the phone back up to my ear.

"What was that?" I asked.

"Coffee's ready in the lobby, sir, if you want some," she repeated, still cheerful.

Before responding, I tilted the receiver away from my face, licked my dry lips, and cleared my scratchy throat.

"Oh, okay. I'll definitely be needing some of that. Thank you," I said and hung up the phone before she could say anything else.

I stared blankly into the darkness for several seconds, slowly blinking between wakefulness and a heavy wanting of sleepiness. In an effort to fight off the foggy drowsiness, I flicked the covers to the side, slowly slid my legs over the edge of the bed. Hanging my groggy head and leaning forward at the waist, I clasped my hands together as if in prayer and rested my forearms against my knees. I knew Mr. Timex was going to sound off any minute, so my hunched position wouldn't endure for long. To avoid the inevitable beeping, I reached over and slid it off the bedside table. The last thing I wanted to hear before flicking on the lights was another loud noise. My brain tried desperately to convince me of the benefits of resetting the alarm and lying back down for another thirty minutes. *Come on, man. Just another thirty, dude! You'll feel so much better, I promise.* I might have considered that in my sleep-drunk state, but my full bladder thought otherwise and took control of my motivations for the next few minutes. *What is it with needing to pee so bad first thing in the morning? Uhhh!*

I sucked in a lungful of dry, air-conditioned hotel-room air before standing up from the bed. The window-mounted air conditioner ran all night, keeping the room cool, but not cold, just the way I like it. Normally, the sound of an air conditioner clicking on and off all night would keep me awake, but not last night. I didn't wake up for anything. Last night my mind chose sleep over food, and that said a lot. Once my brain shut down for the evening, the only sound getting me out of bed this morning was a ringing hotel phone.

I mentally prepared myself for the leg pain I was destined to endure once standing. I just wasn't sure how bad it was going to be. I gently rubbed my quads for a few seconds and could already feel the sensitivity and soreness in them. It seemed to run all the way to the bone. I took in another deep breath and slowly exhaled, emptying my lungs of air, and placed my feet flat on the floor.

Leaning forward, I cautiously brought myself to a standing position, supporting myself by tightly gripping the edge of the nightstand with my right hand. All of the soreness from the past two long days of riding came home to roost. Lactic acid had built up in my calves, quads, and glutes while I slept. All screamed in protest, informing me they were not in the mood to do anything today, let alone ride another 140 miles.

"Shit," I mumbled. *This really sucks. Oh my God. Suck it up, buttercup. We got shit to do today. Let's go.* Taking small steps, I duck-walk to the bathroom to relieve my screaming bladder. Thankfully, I hadn't dehydrated myself too much yesterday, and my body had plenty of water to spare this morning. And I wasn't peeing in the bushes while standing in the fog, so at least I had that going for me. When finished, I duck-walked back into the dark room and sat on the floor, purposely avoiding the comfort of the bed. All alarms had been tripped or turned off, and my bladder was empty. Lying back down on the bed would be a bad idea, a very bad idea, especially if I still wanted to get to Irvine by evening.

I spent the next fifteen minutes stretching my legs. They needed it. I should have done this before I went to sleep, but I was just too damn tired. I started with the hips and groin, then quads and ankles, deferring the calf stretches for later when I was on the bike. It's easy to stretch the calves when you're clipped into the pedals. After several minutes of leg-limbering, I sat up straight and twisted my body from side to side, stretching tightly wound lower back muscles. Pushing a little further than my natural range of motion released a fluttering of pops and rattles up and down my spine. *Ahh. Man, that feels wonderful.*

Legs still tender, but feeling limber and more awake now, I slowly stood up from the floor and turned on the lights. I squinted at the sudden brightness, but my eyes adjusted quickly. The mess I'd made of the room the night before materialized with the sudden bloom of light. Clothes were hanging from pretty much everything. Jezebel was in disarray, awkwardly propped up in the corner next to my sleeping bag, which lay crumpled like a deflated balloon on the floor. I'd even made such a mess of the tiny little bathroom vanity that it would be difficult to distinguish it from any number of truck-stop bathrooms I'd used in my life. *Shit, man. What a mess.*

Having neither the energy nor the time to worry about it, I took a deep breath, bent over at the waist to stretch my hamstrings, then got right into packing. Plucking my cycling clothes from their perches around the room and feeling them for dampness, I was damn near ecstatic to discover that my first set, the set that got wet laying out in the fog all night in San Simeon, had completely dried out overnight. Beginning the final day clean and wearing dry clothes was a huge boost to morale.

I tossed that set on the bed and began packing everything else inside Jezebel's panniers. I stuffed the (mostly) dry sleeping bag inside its stuff bag and strapped it back onto Jezebel's back frame. What a difference a day makes. My body was a little more beat up, but I'd had a better night's sleep and a shower. And my clothes were dry. Even the room was back to normal now. For some weird reason, that made me feel better. Things were looking up.

I got dressed and wasted no time getting out of there. With everything packed, I gave the room one last look around for any forgotten belongings, a habit I'd picked up as a child having to participate in a "policing party" when leaving a campsite, looking for trash and left-behind items. Finding none, I rolled Jezebel out into the pre-dawn morning and went immediately to the front office to check out and grab a cup of coffee. Outside, the air was unexpectedly warm and comfortable. Odd, because I wasn't used to such warm October mornings. In Northern California, unless it was Summer or the Santa Ana winds were blowing, the mornings were cool. But here in Santa Barbara, there wasn't a breath of wind to speak of and the sky was crystal clear. Maybe it was a local weather abnormality, or maybe this is just the way October mornings were in Santa Barbara. I don't know. I was just happy the morning wasn't sopped with fog. Without the marine layer hovering above me, blocking my view of the heavens, I was treated to a couple of early morning's brightest stars, still shining dimly in the brightening sky. It was shaping up to be a beautiful morning for a bike ride, I could feel it. *Well, well. Wouldn't this have been nice to wake up to yesterday morning?*

*   *   *

"You're leaving early this morning," the lady at the front desk said as I walked into the front office. *Um. Yes, I know. Please don't remind me.* I recognized the voice as the same cheery one that woke me up thirty minutes ago.

I immediately headed for the coffee carafe sitting on a small table in the corner. As I poured myself a cup, I looked around for some food. Nothing. No breakfast at the Motel 6 today.

"Yes. A little early, even for an early riser like me. But I need to get to Irvine today. So if I'm going to have any chance at making it, I need to get going as soon as the sun's up," I replied, then took the morning's first sip of coffee. *Ahh. Yes. Just what I needed.* "Trust me, I would love to hang out a while longer. This town is awesome."

I wasn't much of a coffee drinker in my teenage years, but I had been known to dabble in it from time to time. I hadn't made up my mind whether I liked it or not. Sometimes it was just what I needed, like today, but other times I would dump most of the cup down the sink, finding it unpleasant for one reason or another. My dad drank a lot of it, so I was used to its pleasant aroma. Growing up eating food that frequently contained an element of sweetness to it, I found the taste of coffee bitter and not easy to drink. But on a morning like this, its warmth was soothing, and the caffeine it dumped into my bloodstream was just the right kind of fuel I needed to jump-start the day. The more of that, the better.

"Are you going there on that bike?" she asked, her eyes inquisitive as she pointed to Jezebel, currently outside and leaning against the window.

"Sure am," I said and took another sip of coffee.

"Oh, wow. That's crazy. Why?" she asked, genuinely interested but noticeably put off by the idea. I sensed a little distain in her voice, too, like she was slightly offended by what I was doing. *That seems odd. Why do people care so much about the way other people do certain things, especially when it doesn't affect them at all?*

I chuckled through the first sentence of my response while staring down into my coffee cup, contemplating the next sip.

"Well, I like riding bikes, and my girlfriend is attending UC Irvine. So, I'm on my way to see her," I said, raising my head and smiling through a thin ribbon of rising steam.

Saying that out loud made me think of Mo and the fact that I was going to see her today. A rush of nervous excitement ran through my body at the thought.

"Oh. Okay." She shrugged. "You must really like her," she added.

"Sure do. You have no idea. She's pretty incredible."

I took another moment and sipped more coffee. After a minute or so, I leaned over the counter and handed in my key.

"Here you go," I said. "I'm checking out."

"Thank you," she said, taking the key from my hand. "I hope you had a good stay."

"I think so. I was so tired I didn't wake up to find out."

"That's good to hear," she replied. "Well, good luck on your ride."

"Thank you very much," I said and walked out the door and over to the phone booth.

I set my half-full coffee cup on top of the wall-mounted phone booth and picked up the receiver. I dropped in a couple of quarters, waited for them to clink their way through the machine, and then dialed Mo's number. It rang twice before the "ding" of the receiver being picked up at the other end cancelled out the ring tone. A deep breath from the other end of the line started the conversation. A woman's voice followed and, although soft-spoken, I knew exactly who it was.

"Hello?" she whispered.

It was Mo. I could tell even through the sleepy hoarseness of the voice. She was doing her best to sound wide awake, but not succeeding. I get it. It was 6:30 in the morning, after all. Which means Mo had likely only been asleep for about four hours, five max. She's always been a night owl and isn't at the top of her game in the earliest hours of the day. She purposely scheduled most of her college classes in the afternoon and evening so she could sleep in and go to bed late, or early, the semantics of that depending on how you look at it. She would even do her homework late in the evening, sometimes around midnight and much to the dismay of her neighbors. Problem was, she was a drama major and took several dance classes. Like any other class, homework was part of it, and she had to practice her dance choreography somewhere. The kitchen seemed to be the most appropriate place, being the only non-carpeted section of her school apartment. When the syllabus called for tap dancing, she serenaded the entire complex with her studies.

"Hey, Mo," I replied gently, answering her soft voice in kind. After not talking with her last night, hearing her voice was a welcome start to the morning.

"Hi, Matt," she continued, her voice scratchy but excited. She sounded just as groggy as I felt when I answered the hotel phone this morning. She continued in a whisper voice, "I'm sorry I wasn't here when you called last night. I had to meet up with some of my castmates to practice."

"It's okay. I just wanted to let you know I made it to Santa Barbara in one piece. Barely, but I made it just fine. I have a crazy story about the day's ride, but I'll tell you all about it when I see you tonight," I said, elevating the word "tonight" an extra octave to add emphasis.

"I know. I can't wait to see you. Pricilla told me you called. Are you alright? What happened yesterday?"

"Yes, everything's fine, Mo. It was a long day, that's all. There were a couple tire blowouts in the morning. I got rerouted because of a fire. But nothing I couldn't handle. I made it, and that's all that matters. I promise to tell you about it tonight. Okay?"

"Well, that sucks," she said sleepily. "Yeah, that's fine, Matt. I'm excited to see you."

"Me too, Mo. I've been thinking about you so much over the past couple days. I can't believe we'll be together tonight."

"I know. I can't wait. Please be careful," she said, her voice drifting.

"I will, Mo." I paused, and her voice didn't fill the void. I imagined her lying on her bed in her darkened room, eyes closed, the phone propped against her ear with the assistance of her pillow. "Well, I need to get on the road. I have a lot of miles to cover today," I said excitedly.

"Be careful," she said again, dreamily. "See you tonight."

I knew she was tired, and it was time to let her get back to sleep. *I wonder how much of this she will remember.*

"I will. See you soon. Bye."

"Bye."

I hung up the phone and took another long sip of coffee, then tossed the remainder in the trash. I walked over to Jezebel and pulled her away from the wall, straddled the top tube, and slipped on my still damp and foul-smelling helmet. I pulled on my dry gloves and, because it was still too dark to wear them, slid my sunglasses into one of my jersey pockets. Then I pushed off, turning west onto State Street toward the beach. The final day had begun.

CHAPTER TWO

A s expected, the ride down State Street was rough. I'd done a decent job of loosening up the tightness in my muscles that morning, but even with that, I had to take it slow for a while. It was going to take a few miles for these overused muscles to get warmed up for the day's long ride. If everything went as projected, *hardy har har,* the ride from Santa Barbara to UC Irvine should be a flat one, as I planned on following the coastline the entire way. So, I shouldn't be tortured with much climbing.

Regardless of the terrain Jezebel and I would encounter throughout the day, my legs would do so much better navigating all of it if I dumped some food down my gullet. A short jaunt down the street from the hotel brought me to a McDonalds. *Well, would you look at that? Lucky me.* Normally I would pass by such a place, but the primal urge to put food in my belly was rapidly rising to a state of overwhelming necessity, and with the smell of breakfast in the air, the urge to stop was almost irresistible. So I rolled Jezebel into the sparsely occupied fast food joint without any complaints and had me a hot breakfast. Not ideal, but I needed fuel and I was starving, especially since I opted for sleep instead of dinner last night. In hindsight, I still think it was the best decision.

After stuffing my face full of fast food sustenance, I hopped back on Jezebel and continued down State Street on a full belly. My ass and legs protested, but they slowly warmed up to the fact that we were riding today whether they liked it or not.

State Street, usually a bustling commercial thoroughfare, was still mostly sleeping, vacant of the usual glut of cars and countless people. Currently a ghost town, it allowed me greater access to the road than I've had over the past two days. Apart from a few restaurants and coffee shops catering to the early risers of the world, most of the stores were closed. It was Monday, so a few businesses were warming up for the start of the week. Through several shop windows, behind large signs flipped to "closed," I could make out shifting silhouettes of people inside preparing for the wandering customers the afternoon would likely bring.

Setting aside the clickety-clack sound of a homeless man's shopping cart wheels against the wide red-brick, palm tree–lined sidewalk, the town hardly made a whisper. The calmness of the early morning allowed the city a chance to breathe, providing an atmosphere of ample space for its charm and true character to shine before the hustle and bustle of mid-day settles in.

Home to the UC Santa Barbara Gauchos on the west side and quiet, high-end mountainside living in the east, I consider Santa Barbara a coastal beach town, one sandwiched between the Santa Ynez mountain range to the north and one narrow, seemingly never-ending beach to the south. Traditionally laid out with Spanish-style adobe buildings in various shades of white, all topped with red tile roofs and embellished with arched doorways and ornamental ironwork, the area reflects a significant part of the region's rich Spanish colonial history.

It's downtown, upscale by design, balances the interests of prosperous clientele, tourists and a constantly rotating college crowd. Lined with an endless supply of high-end shops, fancy restaurants, wine tasting rooms, and contemporary breweries, State Street is a West Coast tourist's dream. During the warmer months, thousands of people take a break after laying out on the soft, sandy Mediterranean-esque beaches of this "American Riviera" and stroll up and down the spacious sidewalks lining both sides of this main downtown thoroughfare. Visitors, serenaded by street musicians and entertained by magicians and portrait artists, maneuver around traveling panhandlers and leashed-up dogs to partake in the sumptuous fare.

After dipping under Highway 1 through the State Street underpass, I coasted easily until reaching East Cabrillo. East Cabrillo runs the entire length of the Santa Barbara beaches, eloquently lined with five-star hotels, time-shares and resorts, most located on the south side Stearns wharf. Three dolphin sentries kept guard over the wharf's entrance, silently greeting me as I rolled up. They stared down with smiling faces permanently etched in copper; green from age and exposure to the elements. Satisfied I wasn't there to steal any of the amazingly good fish and chips sold at the end of the creaky wooden pier, they let me pass without incident and I turned left, following the road south.

Riding through Santa Barbara's downtown reminded me how much I loved this place. I hadn't spent much time here in my childhood, but I'd become enchanted with it over the course of my few short visits. Mo actually got accepted to UC Santa Barbara but decided to attend UC Irvine instead, where she was welcomed to compete on their springboard diving team. The decision was a natural one for her, a "no-brainer" by any reasoning, but man, this place would have been nice too. Irvine is a great city, but visiting her in this town would have been the best. Besides, if she'd attended UC Santa Barbara, I would already be done with my trip! We could have been laying out on the beach today, eating some of those addicting fish and chips for lunch. Maybe we could have even rented a couple beach cruisers. They're so comfortable. Oh, well. *Enough fantasizing, Matt. Time to ride.*

Leaving fantasies behind, I stood up on the pedals and allowed gravity to assist in picking up speed along the wide, flat, and recently street-cleaned road, then sat down to enjoy the passing scenery. *I wish all roads were this nicely paved, don't you, Jezebel?* We rolled smoothly, parallel to softly crashing waves under a pristine and cloudless sky, the spokes of Jezebel's wheels whistling softly into the quiet morning as we passed hundreds of towering palm trees on our way out of town. I chuckled unbelievably at the surrounding spectacle and shook my head. It's a little absurd, this place . . . perfectly absurd might be a better way to put it. A little too perfect? Nah. Not here. This tiny spot on a map was something experienced only in dreams for many, a fantasyland of sorts. And I may have believed I was in such a state if the throbbing discomfort in my legs wasn't there to remind me that everything I was experiencing was all too real.

Thinking briefly about the condition I was in not twelve hours ago under the same clear but darkening sky, suffering in the still-visible mountains of the Santa Ynez, made me shudder. They looked so big from here, so tall. *Did I really pedal over that monster . . . in the dark?* The contrast between these two moments in time was downright glaring, almost confusing, like watching oil burning on top of water. It's impossible to make out the oil through the flames, so your mind sees only burning water and knows it can't be so. But there it is anyway, real as it ever was.

The previous night was quite real, no doubt about that. The experience now just a memory, *more like a nightmare really,* another seed planted in my garden of memories. Lost in this memory for only a moment, I pedaled resolutely down the coast. Pushing through calm coastal air down quiet and uncrowded streets was a welcome start to the day. I relished in the pleasant humidity. I was content. Content knowing today was the day I'd been waiting for, working so hard for, the day I was finally going to see Mo again. And that was going to make all my self-inflicted hardship a worthwhile investment, turning my discomfort into pleasure. The excitement pushed me forward. *So long, Santa Barbara. 'Til next time.*

On my way out of town, as the road came to an end, I passed by grassy picnic areas lined with palm trees and park benches, several housing a lone visitor lying prone and asleep across their length, possessions scattered on the ground around them or in acquired shopping carts and large bags. None stirred as I passed. To them I must have been like a ghost passing in the night, silent and fleeting. The long grassy park ended after a mile, and I passed the Santa Barbara Zoo on my left and said goodbye to the American Riviera. I turned left and merged back onto Highway 1. Finally, back on my road to Mo.

CHAPTER THREE

The next few hours on the bike were quiet, peaceful, and fast. Concentrating solely on pedal cadence made me happy and really helped move things along. I put out so much energy the previous day—with all the climbing in the mountain passes and unplanned mileage—that I was relieved to find the road mostly flat and the riding stress free.

Filling space in my periphery for the first few hours of the day were mountains to my left and the Pacific Ocean to my right. Highway 1 separated them from each other, like a parent pushing apart bickering siblings. Not the worst way to spend a morning. Traffic was light, so I kept the pace high, well aware of the approaching jungle that would slow me down. An urban jungle, mind you, but one just the same. In a matter of hours Highway 1 would change dramatically, leaving behind the tranquility of the secluded coast and dumping me into the heart of the jungle to test my skills, and luck, at maneuvering Jezebel safely through traffic-congested Los Angeles.

After passing through the densely populated town of Oxnard, then speeding through hundreds of blinking green rows of vegetable fields surrounding the town, I was back riding along the narrow strip of land between the great Pacific and the mountainside. It was here when hunger set in . . . again. *Imagine that.* It came on like an earthquake, as unexpected and sudden as the real thing. I was over the continuous consumption of PowerBars, and downing yet another water bottle full of Cytomax was as exciting as drinking a bottle of warm, flat soda. At this point I was consuming them only when necessary.

The thought of eating another piece of wrapper-encased food had little gastronomical appeal. What I really craved was a full-sugar Coca-Cola, a big fat burger, with cheese of course, and a bucket of fries. *Jesus, isn't there anything else you want to eat on this trip, Koehler? They make other food, you know.* At a time of day when many people are enjoying the final sips of their second cup of coffee, I was already coveting my next meal. The thought of it mentally paralyzed me, preventing me from thinking about much else for a while. Choices were slim out here on the lonely highway, though. Nothing for miles, I presumed, at least nothing as far as I could see. And that was pretty far at the moment. No buildings of any sort lay between Jezebels' front wheel and the horizon, and I wasn't sure where the next food stop would be, so I tried to suppress the rolling pangs of hunger and keep the pace high while the road was clear. It wasn't easy, but I'd become pretty good at "sucking it up."

Lucky for me, relief wasn't too far away. Almost as though I'd wished an eating establishment into existence, another forty-five minutes down the highway a restaurant appeared as if the ocean threw it out of the sea and set it down on the eastern side of the highway. Appropriately named, "Neptune's Net" lay nestled into the hillside halfway between Oxnard and the steep seaside town of Malibu.

I pulled up about 11 a.m. The restaurant was open and serving food, evident by heavenly aromas of fatty goodness and barbecue rising from the kitchen smokestack. When my nose caught a whiff of it, my saliva glands tingled with anticipation and my stomach growled with envious wanting. *Okay, maybe that's a bit of an exaggeration, but it sure smelled good.*

As I rolled up, I gazed across the highway at the restaurant and could see a few groups of people seated at picnic tables underneath a covered patio. The parking spaces outlining the front of the restaurant were painted into the wide sidewalk, small and thin, obviously reserved for the constant circulation of motorcycles that stopped by every day. Half of them were already occupied with a variety of models: loud Harley-Davidsons, quiet BMW-style cross-country bikes, and a few lightning-fast Japanese-made crotch rockets.

A man driving a Harley-Davidson finished parking his bike in one of the spaces just as I pulled up. I observed him from across the highway as he shut off the loudly puttering engine of the shaking beast between his legs, kicked the stand out, and awkwardly removed his large body from the bike. He was what many would label the stereotypical Harley rider: white, about a hundred pounds overweight, grey beard, salt and pepper hair pulled back from a receding hairline into a long, straggly ponytail. He proudly sported a black leather jacket with a mosaic of patches sewn onto it, dark blue jeans over black boots, black wrap-around sunglasses, and black leather fingerless gloves. *Like me,* I thought. *Only mine have gel pads sewn into them. Ha, I win!* Oh, and no helmet, of course. That level of respect for one's skull wouldn't jive with the reckless abandon persona he was putting out there for all to see. Neither would having his brains spattered all over the pavement, but, hey, let's not upset the children with such crazy talk, huh?

He walked away from the bike toward the front entrance of the restaurant and I watched him go. He waddled as he moved, all the while managing a well-choreographed swagger of confidence. He yanked his pants up as he stepped. His keys, hanging from one of his belt loops, jingled with every step and yank. *Who needs that many keys?* Huh. Well, to each their own, I guess. It's what makes America such an awesome place. *'Merica! God bless it all.*

I unclicked my shoes from the pedals as I coasted up to the restaurant, stopping just shy of the short wooden stairway leading up to the seaside-facing patio. I dismounted and leaned Jezebel's frame against my leg while pausing to remove my helmet and gloves, then stuffed the gloves in one of my jersey pockets and hung my helmet from Jezebel's aerobars. Picking Jezebel up by the top tube, I slung her over my left shoulder and started walking toward the stairway.

The stairway was short, only a couple steps, and there was a man sitting still and quiet on the lowest one, off to the left side. His head hung unsupported between tucked-in knees, exposing the top of what looked like a large faded tattoo on a suntanned neck. Dirty hands dangled lazily from the ends of his arms, which were resting on his knees at the elbows. His brown hair, unkempt and of average length, looked like it hadn't been washed in a while. The black pants and green jacket he wore appeared several sizes too big for his thin frame and were out of place on such a warm afternoon. *Why is this guy wearing a jacket? It's too hot for that.* Lying on the sand-dusted pavement between well-worn untied running shoes rested a white sheet of paper with some kind of writing scribbled on it. I approached the stairwell, raising Jezebel high in the air to avoid any possible issues, and started to shuffle past.

"Excuse me," I said, emphasizing "me" more than "excuse."

It was said more as a polite gesture than a request for him to move, at least that's how I intended it. I just wanted him to be aware of my presence, awkward as it was. I would feel pretty awful if I hit him with Jezebel should he raise his head up from between his knees as I stepped by.

Without lifting his head from between his knees, he wailed into the sandy ground.

"Free speech!" he screamed, dragging the words out so long he needed to take in a breath between words.

Spittle sprayed the paper lying on the ground beneath his face, and bits of sand blew away with the quick exodus of breath from his mouth. His neck muscles tensed with the effort, and both shoulders contracted inward like he was shivering from cold. His hands and arms didn't move from their propped position on his knees, however. That seemed weird.

The intensity and aggressiveness of the unexpected outburst startled me, and I stopped walking. Taking a step back in consternation, away from the stairwell and out of arm's reach, I paused for several seconds before saying anything else. Without ever lifting his head, he appeared to relax, returning to his slumped posture. Silence. Like nothing had even happened. *That's crazy.* I looked around the sparsely populated area and, not seeing anyone else too concerned about what just occurred, tried to pass by him again.

"Excuse me, sir, I just need to get by you here real quick," I said softly.

His reaction was similar to before: aggressive, loud, and angry. Only this time, again very aggressively, he picked up the piece of paper lying on the ground between his legs, flicking sand into the air as he did so, and held it up in front of him at arm's length, pointing it in my direction and hiding his face from my view. Or maybe he was hiding mine from his. I'll never know. His movements from behind the sign, unpredictable at best, made it clear he'd sat upright while raising his makeshift sign into the air. On the side facing me he had written "First Amendment" in bold black lettering. *First Amendment? What the hell?*

"Free speech!" he screamed again. "It's MY right to keep you from seeing MY face. It's MY First Amendment right!" The last word continued until his lungs ran out of air. This seemed to be a thing he liked to do, drag his words out.

This second outburst attracted more attention than before, and a few passersby on the sidewalk in front of the restaurant turned their heads and stared. A few people sitting at one of the patio tables on the outdoor landing peered over the railing to see what was going on as well. I didn't know what was wrong with this guy, and it appeared like nobody else did either. Was he on drugs, drunk, disturbed? Who knows? But he was starting to make me a little nervous. I decided to try one more time.

"What the hell, man? I just need to get by. I'm not going to bother you," I said.

This, as it turned out, was not the best thing to say to a guy showing aggressive tendencies, especially when he was just a few feet in front of me, but that's what came out of my mouth. I took another step back, anticipating more of the same behavior. And, sure enough, another outburst ensued.

"Free speech! First Amendment!" he screamed again. This time the words were spoken in a normal speech pattern, but just as obnoxiously and loudly as before.

He was shaking the sign at this point, still using it to block my view of his face. He wasn't doing a great job of it, though. I could see part of his head and face around the edges of the paper but didn't let him know this, of course. His eyes appeared to stay closed for long periods, several seconds at a time, and he was definitely angry about something, or someone. I just hoped it wasn't me. He looked like a guy with a tendency to be a loose cannon with a short fuse.

Woah. This guy is legitimately crazy, I thought, and started looking around for another way into the restaurant.

One of the servers saw what was going on and came over to the stairs. She placed her hands on the wooden railing nearest the top of the stairs and leaned over the edge.

"Sam!" No response. "Hey, Sam! Stop it!" she yelled. The stairway was only three steps high, so we were all pretty close to one another. The server appeared to be in her mid-forties and gave off an aura that she'd been working there for quite some time. There was no fear in her voice at all. *She knows this guy. She called him by name. What the hell? One of her regulars, maybe? Ha, ha, ha.* "Go on," she continued. "Get up and go across the street." She picked her right hand up off the railing and made a shooing motion with it. *A lot of good that's going to do considering he has his back to her,* I thought. "Quit bothering our customers Sam. Shoot. I keep telling you to not sit here, and I'm getting tired of it. Now go. Get out of here."

Sam, as I now knew him, without saying a word or freaking out, dropped his head from behind the sign, then lowered the piece of paper to his side. He stood up quickly, keeping his head down, and flicked the jacket's hood over his head in one motion using only his right hand, his left hand preoccupied with keeping a death grip on that First Amendment paper.

Now that he was standing, I didn't know what to expect. So I lifted Jezebel off my shoulder and brought her back down to the pavement, taking a few steps back in the process. I made sure to keep a safe distance away with Jezebel standing guard between us. *Sorry, Jez.* Then, promptly and without any further confrontation, he started walking away from the restaurant, pulling on his baggy pants as he staggered down the street and dragging his untied shoes across the sand-dusted pavement. I turned to watch him go and heard him scream "Free speech" again from under his hood. It was muffled by the fabric, but I could tell he was using the same aggressive tone as before. After watching him shuffle down the road until I felt he was a safe enough distance away, I turned back to the woman who had come out and rescued me.

"Woah," I said, amused. "That was a little crazy." I probably sounded more confused than anything. "You obviously know this guy. Is this a regular thing for him?"

"Ugh," she said, frustrated and with a shaking head. "Yes, unfortunately. He does that all the time." She lifted her hands from her waist and, bending over slightly, waved them up and down in unison in front of her in a sign of aggravation, like she was juggling two platters of food in each hand. "I wish he would stop, or find another place to bother," she continued. "He comes by here at least once every couple days. It's so frustrating. He's good at finding a place to hide until he freaks out on someone. No offense, but I'm glad it was someone like you and not a family with small children this time. I don't need to tell you how bad that went."

"Geez," I said, glancing back to make sure he was still walking away. He was, so I turned back to the server, still standing at the top of the stairs. "None taken. And, yeah, if I had kids with me and he pulled that kinda shit, things wouldn't have gone very well."

"I don't think he means any harm, but he's intimidating and scares some of our customers, especially the children," she said.

"Ya think?" I said in agreement.

"Sorry about that."

"Not your fault, but what's his deal? Do you know?" I asked, taking a few steps toward the stairwell.

"I have no idea. The only thing he says is 'First Amendment' and 'free speech.' Everything else is a bunch of mumbling. I'm sure there's a few mental issues going on there, there has to be. Or drugs. I don't know." She leaned her head to the side and shrugged her shoulders in bewilderment.

"You're tellin' me," I said, agreeing again. "Crazy."

"Anyway. Enough of that for now, right? You need a table? He didn't change your mind about eating here, did he?"

"Oh, yes, please. I'm starving," I said, happy to change the subject. "And no, as hungry as I am, it would take a lot more than that to change my mind about putting some food in my belly."

"Okay. Well, let's find you a place to sit then." She gestured for me to come up the steps by swaying her left arm from her waist to her head. "Come on up."

I lifted Jezebel back up to my shoulder, carried her up the stairs, and set her down gently. I looked around at the mostly empty patio and was surprised to find it smaller than it appeared from the street.

"Mind if I sit over there in the corner and lean my bike against the wall?" I asked, pointing to an empty bunch of tables at the north end.

"Go for it. Do whatever you need to do. I'll be right over to take your order," she said, smiling.

"Great. Thanks."

She walked away toward the back of the restaurant and out of sight.

I rolled Jezebel between wooden picnic tables over to the end of the covered concrete patio, its surface worn smooth along the high-traffic areas from decades of foot traffic. You could trace the paths taken by servers and guests over the years just by following the shallow off-color indentation along the surface between tables and benches. Sand filled in pits and cracks in the floor, merging land and sea in a Picasso of disorderly mosaics. Of the few guests that were seated, you would think a guy pushing a bicycle through a restaurant would garner some attention, but nobody gave me a second look.

I got Jezebel comfortable against the bench and sat down next to her. I had the entire table to myself and took advantage of the rest to rub out my tender quads and calves again. Every little bit seemed to help. Maybe it did nothing, but it felt good nonetheless.

A few moments later the server I spoke to earlier came by and laid a menu down in front of me. I noticed her nametag immediately, and it made me smile: "Maureen."

"Oh good, you found a seat, for you AND your bike," she said warmly.

"Yes, I did. Thank you."

"Sure thing. You came at good time. Lunch rush hasn't hit yet." She dipped her head and leaned over the table, lowering her voice a bit. "And, uh, sorry again about that whole scene back there."

"It's all good. No worries."

"Thanks," she replied.

"Your name's Maureen?" I asked inquisitively, abruptly changing the topic.

She corrected me quickly. "No. It's Cathy."

I looked down and nodded at her nametag. "Looks like you grabbed the wrong nametag then," I said under a raised eyebrow. Actually, I raised both eyebrows. Who am I kidding? I'm nowhere near talented enough to raise one eyebrow at a time.

She shrugged, offering up an irritated eye-roll.

"Yeah. I forgot mine at home, so I had to borrow one. 'Mr. Neptune' doesn't care what name is on it, only that we wear one. Can't go on the floor without it. Manager's rules. You know."

"Huh." I cut in with a smirk. "Yeah, I know, all right. Try dealing with a few uptight Marine Corps drill instructors for thirteen weeks. There's a lot of 'manager rules' to deal with in that organization too." I raised a finger from the table to accentuate the next point. "And they don't even tell you what all the rules are. Then they get angry when you don't know what to do when you break them. There's a lot of figure-it-out-as-you-go-along kinda shenanigans that take place."

"Ha ha. All in good fun though, right?" she said jokingly.

"Not exactly, but sure. I guess you could say that. It's all by design, anyway. Depends on your perspective too, I guess. Well . . . I only asked about the name on your tag because I'm riding down to visit my girlfriend at UC Irvine. Her name is Maureen, too, but everyone calls her Mo."

"Aww, that's sweet!" she said, smiling. "I hope she's happier to see you than the free speech guy."

That brought some laughter to the table, from both of us.

"Yeah, me too!"

"Well, you must be starving with all the riding you're doing. What can I get you to drink?" she continued as the laughter died down.

"You're definitely right about that. Oh, I'm pretty sure I know exactly what I want to eat already. I've been thinking about it for the past twenty miles."

"That's a long time to be thinking about lunch."

"Well, it's either that or choke down another energy bar and some Gu packets."

"Ugh. I don't even want to know what a 'Gu packet' is. It can't be good if it has a name like that."

I answered anyway, giving the simplest answer possible. "Basically, it's pure sugar. Think . . . syrup in a squeeze tube."

"Okay," she said, wrinkling her nose in playful disgust. "Yuck. Better you than me. Well, let's get a real meal started for you then. What'll ya have?"

she asked commandingly, putting pen to notepad.

"Cheeseburger with bacon. Can you do that? I didn't even look at the menu."

"Oh, sure. Of course. You sure you don't want to look the menu over for a bit? We got a lot of great things on there, especially if you like fish."

"I bet you do. But you know what it's like when you have a craving for that one thing on your mind and nothing else will do?"

"Yep. Definitely familiar with that feeling."

"That's where I'm at right now with the burger."

"Alright. No problem," she said, scribbling the order down.

"That comes with fries, yeah?"

"Sure does, or onion rings. Whatever you prefer."

"Fries, please. Crispy if you can."

"I can do that."

"Awesome. And the largest Coke you got, I definitely need one of those," I added.

I handed the menu over.

"We make the best shakes north of Malibu here, too, just to let you know," she said suggestively, sliding the menu out of my hand.

"I'm sure they're amazing, but I think I'll just go with the Coke for today. Thanks."

"You got it. I'll be right back."

"Thank you."

Cindy walked away, incognito "via nametag," and I continued the rubdown of my legs after removing my shoes and setting them on the patio next to Jezebel. After several minutes of massage, I stood up, walked between the empty picnic tables, and rested my forearms on the wooden railing.

I gazed out over the parked motorcycles and black highway pavement, far beyond the shallow, raised sand bank on the west side of the road, which was presumably there to deter people from running across the highway to the overlook and mostly empty beach.

A late-morning breeze was blowing in from the water, and it carried with it the salty smell of the ocean, picking up a hint of the unmistakable sweet aroma of unburned fuel as it blew across the street and motorcycle parking spaces below me. From my perch on the restaurant patio I couldn't make out any of the white sand or wave breaks along the narrow, seemingly endless beach, but I did catch a glimpse of it earlier as I rode in from the north, pausing across the highway from Neptune's before traversing over to meet Sam and enjoy an early lunch.

Slim by Southern California standards, the beach was intimate, and the sand appeared light and pillowy under the midday sun. Sluggish waves bumped quietly against the driftwood-laden beach. The water was calm, and sunlight twinkled off miniature peaks of unbreaking waves just offshore. A lone paddleboarder, in no hurry to get where he was going and oblivious to everything happening on land, slowly coasted across my view, gracefully gliding along the smooth surface a few hundred feet beyond the break. Peering deeper into the horizon, I thought about the whale that "fired the start pistol" at the beginning of my journey two days prior, kicking off this whole crazy adventure. *I wonder where he's at right now?*

Drifting thoughts of my journey's beginning led, inevitably, to thoughts of Mo. After the first thought bubbled to the surface, the dam broke. Recollections of our budding three-month relationship, filled in with dramatic expectations for our future together, flooded my mind. They often did when I was alone with only my thoughts to keep me company. Visions of her and the memories we'd already made were always there, saturating the gray voids of lonely hours with colorful daydreams. She was probably awake by now, and I wondered what she might be doing. It was Monday, so she was probably getting ready for one of her classes. Drama, dance, or musical theater would be my guess. She, for sure, slept through "breakfast time" and was now most likely thinking about lunch, or maybe something lighter, like brunch. I selfishly hoped she was thinking about me as well and was excited for my visit.

Three days. It's a long time to ride just to visit someone. But this girl was exceptional, so I didn't mind one bit. I'd fallen head over heels in love with her in the short amount of time we'd been together, at least that's what I was feeling. *Shit, you were nineteen bro; you probably would have fallen in love with a walrus if it showed you some attention.* Ha! Regardless of my age, I was smitten, and it wasn't hard to see why.

Maureen and I were similar in a multitude of ways, but different enough to keep each other interested. She was an artist, a performer mostly; I was not. I was reckless; she was calculated. I loved tomatoes and hated avocados; she loved avocados and hated tomatoes. She had lots of friends; but I was content with only a handful. Despite these differences, it didn't take much contemplation to see we were cut from similar cloth. Shoot, we met at Disneyland, for goodness sakes, the "Happiest Place on Earth." Even before we ran into each other waiting for Fantasmic! to begin, we both had Disneyland on our lists of favorite places to visit. We both intensely pursued things we truly loved, most likely a holdover from spending much of our childhood and teenage years as competitive athletes. We shared a drive for new experiences and thrived on spontaneity.

Spontaneity. Well now, that's an appropriate word for this trip, huh? Three months ago, I surely wasn't expecting that I'd be standing on the patio of Neptune's Net, gazing out at the Pacific Ocean, my legs feeling like hammered dog shit with numbness between the middle two toes of both feet, and still suffering from a slight desensitization in my nether region. All just to visit a girl I couldn't stop thinking about. *You must be crazy, Matt,* I thought. *Or maybe you're just in love, dummy.*

Thoughts of her filled the days; dreams of her filled the nights. I don't know if it was the hormones or just her personality. Most likely it was her thin smile and joyous laughter, her carefree attitude and kind heart. And let's not forget she has qualities that turn a man like me into putty. Her pale skin, dotted with constellations of angels' kisses, shined bright as the sun whenever I saw her. I could pick her out of a crowd of a thousand girls. Her light-brown hair, slightly curly, was always soft, smelling of spice and flowers, and . . . sometimes chlorine from the diving pool. A youthful life of dancing, gymnastics, and springboard diving toned and shaped her body, molding muscular legs and thin waist. Her small, perky breasts and cute painted toes tempted my lustful gaze every time. Oh man, what a woman!

Woah, Matt! Jesus, dude, chill out. There are people present.

Just before my imagination got the best of me, I was, quite rudely I might add, yanked out of my day-dreaming state.

"Food's ready there, bicycle boy," Cathy called from behind me.

I turned around to find her giggling and leaning forward to lay an overflowing plate of food on the table. I smiled shyly, pushed back from the railing, and walked gingerly back to the table.

"Sorry. Got a little lost in thought there," I said, suddenly embarrassed, like she knew exactly what was on my mind, in addition to food of course. Speaking of food, my eyes locked in and became transfixed on the arc the overflowing plate made as she lowered it to the table. "Oh yeah. That looks delicious. Thank you."

"You're welcome. And don't apologize. I get it. Getting lost in thought is a pretty easy trap to fall into around here. If it weren't for the constant incoming and outgoing of all these motorcycles"—Cindy waved an outstretched thumb in the direction of the parking lot—"it would be the perfect place."

"It's not perfect just the way it is? Looks pretty epic to me," I countered, picking up a fry that had tumbled off the crowded plate and landed on the table, then tossing it in my mouth with one quick flick of the wrist.

"Ehh. I love the place, don't get me wrong. I just don't like all the noise. I would never say that in front of any of them motorcycle riders because they're crazy about those things, but it kinda ruins the place a little for me," she said.

"Let me tell you something," I said as I took a seat. "There's nothin' like riding down the coast on two wheels, though. My bike's a little bit quieter than theirs, and a whole lot slower, but I understand the appeal."

"I suppose," she replied.

"But there are worse places to work, no?" I asked inquisitively, attempting to raise only one eyebrow again, without success.

"I'll give you that. I've worked at shittier places, that's for sure."

Still standing, I reached down and grabbed another fry, this time off the plate, tossing it into my mouth to join the other.

"Dang, these are good," I said graciously.

"Glad you like it. Well, let me know if you need anything else," she said, turning around to walk back inside the restaurant.

"Sure thing. Thanks. Could you bring me the check, please? I need to get back on the road as soon as I'm finished."

"Yep. Be right back."

I devoured the meal so quickly it didn't even have a chance to cool down. I couldn't help it. All this riding was keeping me in a constant state of hunger. The food went down my gullet so fast that I had to force myself to periodically stop and, ya know, breathe. All of it was delicious, and I was comfortably full, for the moment anyway. Most of the plate was cleared by the time Cathy came back with the check. By then I was just nibbling on the last of the fries and draining the last puddle of Coke from the bottom of my glass.

"Dang. You didn't waste any time getting to the bottom of that meal," she said with amusement, laying the check down on the table.

"Yep. I don't have much time to waste today. Got to get moving," I replied as I leaned toward Jezebel to pull my wallet out of its pannier.

"Well, have a great trip," she said, taking my empty plate with her as she walked back down the depressed path between the tables.

"Thank you . . ."—I paused for effect—". . .Maureen."

Cathy looked back, flashed me her own version of a sarcastic smile, and waved me away. She didn't say another word and slipped through an open door leading to the inside bar and dining room.

I threw enough cash down on the table to cover the bill and tip, then slid into my body armor; my basic uniform of helmet, gloves, and sunglasses. These subtle items wouldn't protect me much in hand-to-hand combat, but I wasn't swinging any swords today, so I wasn't too worried.

Oh, and shoes. I needed those too. Shoes now strapped on securely, I picked up Jezebel and walked her out of the still mostly empty restaurant. As I set her down on the sidewalk a few feet away from the steps I looked around for Sam, the "free speech" guy. He was nowhere to be seen, and I was relieved by that.

Belly full once again, I gently sat my sore ass down on the saddle and pushed off down the highway.

CHAPTER FOUR

M y end-of-day deadline put me in a cover-as-many-miles-as-you-can-as-fast-as-you-can state of mind. So I pushed on as hard as my legs, hammered dog shit as they were, would allow, keeping my pedal cadence high and maintaining a respectable speed. This worked out well for a while. Everything was moving along swimmingly . . . until I came face to face with "civilization." Progress would become a bit more complicated from this point forward.

My first run-in with significant traffic occurred as I passed through Malibu, an upscale coastal desert enclave just north of Los Angeles. A bustling cliffside town, the place fascinated me on a certain level. Comprised largely of multi-million-dollar mountain ranches, classy cliffside estates, and chic ocean-front bungalows, the town was an island in itself.

As I rolled into the outskirts of town, I could almost feel the change in the atmosphere. The closer I got to the town center, the faster its character morphed from that of a Northern California coastal laissez-faire ambiance along its perimeter to one of structure, rules, and planned indulgence.

The elevated lifestyle became readily apparent as I narrowed in on the downtown. Buzzing past grumpy Bentley and Ferrari drivers slowly meandering their way through bumper-to-bumper traffic along the PCH, I marveled at the glaring contrast between the affluent materialism here compared to the bohemian non-conformity vibe more traditionally welcomed in California beach communities. This thin strip of land appeared to attract a disproportionate amount of wealthy people and A-list celebrities than neighboring enclaves. I'm not sure if the proximity to Los Angeles elevates its appeal, or the surrounding desert environment. Maybe there's something special in the water . . . you got me. Or, maybe it just happens to be the "in" place to be . . . far enough away from Los Angeles where an escape from the craziness is only a short drive away, but not so far away that you run the risk of becoming detached from your "people." My inclination leans toward the latter. We humans are all so tribal after all, and once accepted, it's hard to separate ourselves from the camaraderie and support our social circles provide.

But hey, to each their own. People like being part of a tribe, I get it. The LA A-list tribe, evidently, fancies this small part of the California coast. That's cool. You really can't go wrong with any stretch of this coastline. *But I will enjoy whizzing by their $200,000 vehicles on my $1,000 bicycle while they're idling in traffic.*

*　　*　　*

After passing through the Pacific Palisades, the last strip of land containing anything other than concrete for a while, I slammed right into the West Coast's most notorious urban jungle: Los Angeles, the "City of Angels." Well, if there is an angel of concrete and freeways, then yes, this is it. Otherwise, the densely packed nature of the beast isn't very angelic at all. So many buildings and people concentrated onto such a small piece of land doesn't give nature, let alone the people that live there, much space to breathe. Take a few minutes and look at a photograph of Los Angeles taken from space. You'll see a large gray splotch of earth, cut up into pieces by freeways, interstates, and a few thin fingers of desert mountain ranges. It's a checkerboard of progress, the performing arts, manufacturing, and high population density.

That said, Los Angeles does have an exception worth mentioning, something that draws visitors to Southern California like nothing else, and the envy of the inland cities. It's the beaches, hands down. They're wide, sandy, stunning and always open for business. Almost the entire western border of Los Angeles County is lined with them, and I planned to follow as many as possible as I made my way through, and around, this jungle of concrete and dreams.

My strategy was to stick to Highway 1 whenever possible, even while maneuvering my way through Los Angeles and Orange County. If I was diligent, and able to stick to that plan, I wouldn't—*ahem,* shouldn't—get lost or find myself in unfamiliar neighborhoods. Realistically, I wasn't familiar with any neighborhoods in Los Angeles or Orange County yet. I was relying on the presumed accuracy of my laminated maps, recommendations from friends and family, and, loosely, the trajectory of the sun to make my way. I was basically unsure about everything between Fremont and Irvine except for UC Irvine and Disneyland. But hey, I made it this far, I could make it the rest of the way as long as I stuck to the Pacific Coast Highway. That was the most obvious choice. So that's exactly what I did. *Keep the ocean at your right and always in sight. Do that, and you're golden. You got that, Matt?*

The first city to greet me was Santa Monica. This coastal metropolis of congested streets lined with palm trees and low-level skyscrapers was genuinely welcoming in appearance and supported all forms of travel, from cars to vans to bikes and skateboards. People even appeared to enjoy walking around here too, constraining themselves mostly to wardrobes of shorts, tank tops and flip flops.

Everything was fine for the first several miles as I traversed the city along its western limit. Observing the unfolding scenery with child-like fascination, I slowly began my mental assimilation into the Southern California beach vibe. *Easy enough when the weather is close to perfect and your hanging out next to an epic beach, bro!* It felt like I was riding through the middle of a movie set. So much so I wouldn't have been surprised if a bullhorn-carrying movie director came yelling at me to get out of his scene. But nothing like that happened, it was all as real as it could be.

I let the coastline lead me all the way to the Santa Monica Beach Pier. Here, the highway abruptly cut inland, leaving the beach behind for a while. I really didn't want to go inland though, and my maps clearly showed a safe coastal "off highway" alternative. I considered this, and didn't take long convincing myself disobedience wasn't always a bad thing. I was known to break a few rules from time to time, including my own, and now was one of those moments when it made all the sense in the world. I wasn't leaving the beach, not yet anyway. My maps made it clear I was going to be pulled away from it soon enough anyhow. I wasn't worried, but the mantra kept chiming in: *Keep the ocean at your right . . .*

So, I took another not-so-dangerous "off highway" adventure for several miles, allowing the "concrete bike path in the sand" to lead me through the bohemian haven of Venice Beach. This short furlough along the sandy seashore allowed me a glimpse of what big-city beach life was all about. Skaters, cyclists, runners, walkers, roller-bladers, and people-watchers alike shared the crooked path with me, while meatheads lifted heavy weights at Muscle Beach under the mid-day sun. Tattoo shops shared real estate with burger joints, clothing stores, and ice cream parlors along the Ocean Front Walk. Musicians, street performers, and exotic animal handlers injected unique excitement and energy into the do-what-makes-you-happy ambiance of the area, livening up the atmosphere as they competed for tourists' attention and money. A new reality set in as I realized the California coast had officially taken on a new persona. I bid farewell to the relaxed nature of the NorCal beach scene. This SoCal beach scene was a whole different animal.

Lost in the unfamiliar novelty and newness of it all, I got distracted, and without realizing how far I'd traveled, a dead end at Marina Del Rey stopped me from continuing along the beach. Unable to go any further, unless I felt like going for a swim, I pulled out my maps to see what happened and where the hell I was. *Lost already. I leave the highway for a couple minutes, and look what happens.* Luckily, I wasn't too far from the PCH and the ocean was still at my right, so, for now I didn't have much to worry about. All I needed to do was find my way back to the PCH and everything would be fine. After a little backtracking, and about a mile's ride east, I met up with it again. Back on the highway, my trek into the jungle continued. Even though city borders in this area were tough to ascertain at times, I was soon leaving Santa Monica, my "gateway to SoCal," and rolling further into the heart of Los Angeles.

The highway widened a few miles down the road, and I was graced with a larger shoulder. I appreciated this, but as with most conveniences, it came with a price. Few things of value are given freely, after all. This was one of those tit-for-tat situations with its own set of challenges. The widening of the highway came with more cars. And with more cars came more stoplights. More stoplights led to more people, and even more cars, and more busses, and taxis, and bicycles. All of this led to more debris in the road shoulders. And with more debris, people, and vehicles, my chances of having an accident increased exponentially.

Naturally, the further I pedaled into the heart of Los Angeles, the higher my anxiety climbed. I had expected this and mentally tried to prepare myself for it, but I was already missing the serenity of the open coastline I'd left behind. And there was more craziness ahead, craziness that involved the convergence of airplanes, automobiles, a tunnel . . . and a cyclist. LAX was destined to keep things interesting.

I was trying to avoid having to maneuver through one of the busiest airports in the United States. My plan, instead, was to ride underneath LAX. Yes, you read that correctly. Unless I went "off highway" again into unfamiliar territory and added miles, crazy traffic-congested miles, to my journey trying to figure out a way around the airport, I would need to suck it up and stay on the PCH, following it through an underpass that tunneled under half of the runways at LAX. Yes, THE Los Angeles International Airport. Did I mention it was one of the busiest airports in the United States? That meant there would not only be flocks of airplanes taking off and landing, but there would also be herds of frantic people driving their cars around the airport, many loaded with tourists not familiar with the area and people late for departing flights.

Call me crazy, but I was pretty confident that people riding bikes would be the last thing on their minds to look out for. I really wasn't looking forward to relying on their distracted inattentiveness as part of my safety plan. This is predominately what stresses me out about Los Angeles, or any large city for that matter. There are just too many people in too small of an area for me to feel comfortable riding my bike through it. I'm sorry, I'm just not into crowds. I'm more of an "open space" kind of guy.

Having little choice other than a roundabout detour through the surrounding cities of Westchester, Inglewood, Lennox, and Hawthorne, I prepared myself for the inevitable ride under the runways. I carefully pedaled Jezebel toward the mayhem, the smog-shrouded sounds of screaming jet engines, honking cars, and the constant hum of commerce and indulgence.

Barring getting lost, everything would turn out just fine, right? *That's not going to happen if you just follow the highway,* I reminded myself. And to do that, I had to swallow that jagged pill and make it through the underpass of LAX.

*   *   *

And so I did. Before entering the "tunnel beneath the tarmac," I pulled Jezebel safely behind a guard-railing along the side of S. Sepulveda Boulevard, next to the tunnel entrance. I removed my sunglasses and slid them into my right jersey pocket. It was dark in there, and I knew I wasn't going to need them until I emerged from the other side.

Cars, lined up bumper to bumper, creeped through the shallow underpass, half entering, half exiting. I'm not a fan of traffic—I don't know anyone who really is—but seeing the tunnel was going to be full of slowly moving vehicles made me feel a little more secure. Periodically, when the traffic came to a temporary full stop, I would catch questioning glances from seatbelt-confined passengers. A cyclist pulled over on the side of the road at the entrance to a tunnel must be an odd sight to behold, even in Los Angeles, where you're bound to see anything. Or maybe it was just a welcome distraction from boredom. Who knows?

Above me, jet engines roared to life, pushing massive airplanes down long runways and into the sky. I could almost imagine the passengers being thrown back into their seats with the rapid acceleration. A short time later, after a momentary squeal from landing-gear tires, the whine of thrusters thrown into reverse would loudly assist bringing landing planes to a halt.

I leaned over the railing and peered into the dark tunnel, realizing almost immediately there was no emergency lane available to ride in, and no shoulder to speak of either. *Wonderful.*

To get through this without hitting the wall, curb, or other vehicles, I would need to follow a very narrow walking path, most likely designed as a maintenance worker access path. Not the safest option for a cyclist, but it was the only option I had. Well, I guess I could have merged into traffic with all the others and slogged along with them, but what would be the fun in that? And I had already gone over the other options a few times. No thanks. *I'll enjoy one of the only advantages I have when riding a bike in the city . . . being able to zip right past stopped traffic, thank you very much.*

So, I rolled into the tunnel, slowly and cautiously, keeping as far to the right-hand side as I could. Instantly, everything fell into shadow, like I was slipping into a dream. Having entered the tunnel from bright sunlight, my vision suffered for a moment. But my eyes adjusted quickly to the dimness, and I was soon able to make out the details of the concrete tunnel and the nearby cars. I stayed in the saddle and pedaled deliberately past the congested traffic, keeping my hands near the brake levers and my elbows plastered to my sides. *Watch out for those car door mirrors, Matt. They will ruin your day.*

Avoiding sudden movements, I followed the narrow path around the multiple maintenance vehicle turnouts. Hundreds of bulbs, strung up like Christmas lights high on the tunnel ceiling, filled the concrete cavern with sulfur-yellow light, illuminating several graffiti-stained walls. Interestingly though, the deeper I rode into the tunnel, the more artistic and colorful the markings became.

All of my apprehensions were soon laid to rest as I exited the tunnel. I was back under the sun in no time, like nothing had happened. I shouldn't have been so nervous. I mean, the tunnel has been around for a long time, and I'm sure I wasn't the first cyclist to ride through it successfully. I had spent enough time in the tunnel that my eyes burned from the sudden onset of bright afternoon light, and I squinted to beat back some of its intensity. The roar of jet engines continued, and the honking of cars kept me diligent—and my anxiety elevated. *That was a little crazy,* I said to myself. *I just rode my bike underneath an airport runway. What? How many other airports in the world can you do something like that?* I pulled over for a moment, slid my sunglasses back onto my face, and then continued west on the PCH.

CHAPTER FIVE

G rowing up, the word "highway" conceived visions of the open road and camping. Vistas of never-ending tracks of land pushing up valiantly against boundless skies shaped my childhood imagination, most likely aided by RV camper advertising too. The advertising wasn't necessary, though. During our summer breaks from school, many three-day weekends were spent camping at notable locations throughout the western states, mostly state and national parks. Inevitably, we traveled the highways to reach many of these places, and that's all the advertising I needed.

The highway offered a precious and unique gift, one I didn't much respect in my younger years. It provided access to the bountiful natural richness of the Pacific Northwest, teaching me more about nature and the outdoors than I could ever learn in a classroom. A lot of it flew by in a blur, messily laid out before me through the fingertip-smeared windows of a station wagon pulling a pop-up-tent trailer. Yosemite, the Grand Canyon, Bryce Canyon, Zion National Park, the Four Corners, the California Gold Country, the Painted Desert, Monument Valley, the redwood forests of the west, the deserts of the southwest, the coastline of the great Pacific Ocean, and various lesser-known state parks, just to name a few. Before the highways were built, many of these destinations would be difficult—and dangerous— to visit, so I am thankful the highways are there.

Far-fetched as it may seem, and pardon the cliché, but sometimes the drives were better than the destination itself . . . as long as all four of us kids could stop arguing long enough to enjoy the ride. Once the sticker books were filled, and as my interest in trying to color within the lines of my

Spiderman coloring book waned with every swerve of the car, the only thing left to do, besides picking a fight with one of my siblings, was stare out the windows at the passing landscape.

Even as a child I marveled at the openness of the western plains, the densely packed forests of the Pacific Northwest and the majestic mountains of the Sierra Nevada. And what of the roads that led us there, the highways carved into the landscape allowing access to these treasured places? So starkly divergent to the surrounding natural environment one could view them as absurd, yet perfectly placed. I remember thinking about this often, and asked myself questions about it, many times. *Why is this road here, and not over there? How in the world did they carve a road into the side of this granite mountain? What happens if we drive over the cliff? What did they do with the trees they removed to make this road?* Ah, the curiosity of a child. Innocent, but relevant. Some of these thoughts still baffle and entertain, all these years later.

*   *   *

Journeys through red-painted deserts and river-carved canyonlands, salty-air trips along the windy and rugged Pacific coast, and engine-busting jaunts through the endless forests of the glacier-carved Sierra Nevada, stand as icons for the highway experience. Some towns, like Las Vegas, one of the most famous cities in the western United States, exist only because of the highway and creative irrigation plans. Oh, and mob money. Yes, a little of that too, for sure.

Freeways, on the other hand, are a whole other animal. Built out of necessity for the burgeoning population of the cities they serve, they're designed for convenience and efficiency, their fundamental objective being to move as many people through an area as quickly and, dare I say, safely as possible. Millions of vehicles flood these thoroughfares every day with the primary goal being to get only from one place to another. Freeways do have their place, and they serve their purpose well, but there's little glamor in them, little prestige.

People don't necessarily say, "Let's take a drive on the freeway today!" unless the final destination is somewhere of interest. Even then, it's still just a means of getting there. Highways, on the other hand, at least in my adolescent imagination and childhood memories, are a place where the scenery, not the road, takes control. They offer mystery, anticipation, and adventure; food for the inquisitive spirit. Think of the intrusion as if the natural environment granted humans permission to carve a highway through it, but refrained from allowing much else. *You can look, but please don't touch.*

Maybe a little town here, and one over there. But for the most part, and for what it's worth, I still believe such a vison holds up. Even with the ever-increasing population of the United States, the humble highways are still the main arteries that feed interstate travel, leading passengers on self-paced adventures throughout the country that can only be experienced by using them.

So, after following the mostly wide-open Highway 1 along the Pacific coast for two solid days, I found it moderately confusing to ride that same highway through such a crowded place like Los Angeles. Gradually, Highway 1 had taken on similar characteristics of a freeway as it cut through the City of Angels—merely a road connecting interesting places. But not all was lost. At the same time, it managed to hold on to some of its highway charm, clinging to a unique "Southern California mystique," an exclusive character of the area that's taken on a life of its own since the days of 1960's cinema. Reminiscent of an era when movies regularly romanticized the blooming surf culture of California, the Pacific Coast Highway, and all it's possible adventures, was an irresistible draw for America's youth. They came west in droves, turning romantic escapades of escape and intrigue into real-life experiences. Some came for a short while, some never left. And for those that stayed, a foundation of identity was laid that exists to this day . . . one built of ocean waves, sand, and sunshine.

Notwithstanding the highway's nostalgic qualities, its jaunt through Los Angeles played tricks on my mind and seemed somewhat unqualified to carry the name "highway." But alas, maybe it's not so unique in this regard. It's actually quite similar to Highway 5, just east of here, connecting Northern California with Southern California via the Great Central Valley. This state-long highway begins and ends its journey through California in similar fashion, sandwiched by mountains in the north and the south, while leisurely slicing the state in half through the Central Valley, where tree orchards, vegetable fields, cattle feed lots, and otherwise open pastureland partition the vast landscape into quadrants unique to The Golden State. But in certain locales, like the San Francisco Bay Area, Los Angeles, and Orange County, it takes on the presence, and purpose, of a freeway, contrary to the nature of its surname.

*   *   *

The miles covered on the PCH from LAX to Redondo Beach were, as expected, snarled in traffic. To make matters even more dangerous for me, bike lanes and emergency pull-outs were mostly non-existent. Multiple times

I was forced to maneuver around temporarily, and illegally, parked cars. Some even double-parked in the middle of the right lane, forcing traffic to find a way around them. *Fuck me and everyone else, right? Don't worry about the bottleneck you're causing. We'll be fine, just fine.* But hey, their flashers were on, so that's cool, right? My choices were limited. I was reduced to putting my safety even more at risk by jetting out into traffic to swerve around them or hopping up onto the sidewalk to find other means to keep moving.

And then there's the bane of every cyclist's existence: traffic lights! These untimed tri-colored strobes disrupted any gathered momentum at almost every intersection. Stop, go, stop, go, stop, go. Not the way I liked to ride. If I was riding a beach cruiser with fat, squishy tires, it might be cool, but not when pushing a bike down congested city streets on top of skinny high-pressure tires. Bikes like Jezebel are designed to keep moving, not constantly start and stop. My body wanted to keep up the pace too. Every time I had to start pedaling after the light turned green, my quads and calves groaned with disapproval. *We're almost there, guys, promise. Just keep it up for another few hours. Only one more county to go.* I was only a few hours into "the jungle" at this point, but I already longed for the open stretches of Highway 1 I left behind after hitting Santa Monica, where it was not uncommon for me to ride for a solid hour, many times even longer, without having to stop once.

Pedestrians presented legitimate dangers, as well. I had to keep an eye out out for these crazy animals too, especially after being forced up onto the sidewalk by double-parkers. On more than one occasion, I would be riding past a long line of stopped cars, whizzing by as they waited for the red light to change, and someone with a death wish would jet out from the middle of the stopped traffic and right in front of Jezebel. Apparently, jaywalking is a thing in Los Angeles, even though thousands of crosswalks exist. Luckily, I didn't hit anybody. I'm sure it would have been "my fault" if I did too. A few close calls came to pass, but nothing serious. Only a few choice words exchanged after a couple encounters, both spoken and via sign language, but they all ended there. Maybe that's just part of what makes Los Angeles, well, LA.

"Where do you live, man, Los Angeles?"

"Los Angeles? Na, man, I live in LA! City of fucking angels, dawg. Shit. Get it right. What's wrong with you?"

"Oh. Pardon me, Mr. LA."

"Man, you better be check yourself. You talk like that to the wrong person around here, you might get yourself in a whole lot of trouble."

No matter if someone calls this place by its true name or alias, many who reside here do whatever they deem necessary to get where they want to go in life, even at the expense of their personal safety. I guess I can sympathize with that mentality. I mean, look what I'm doing. Nobody forced me to ride Jezebel down the coast to visit Mo. In fact, many tried to deter me from doing so. I could have done it faster, safer, and cheaper on an airplane, or even in a car. But thank goodness I chose otherwise. Ignoring the physical discomfort for a moment, this was turning out to be the ride of a lifetime, granting me experiences I will never forget.

I carefully made my way through the crazy traffic and breathed a sigh of relief as I rolled into Redondo Beach. I turned off the highway past the Redondo Beach Pier and merged onto the paved bike path lining the relatively short beach. What a mentally rejuvenating jaunt along the waterfront this was. My focus had become fractured with all the city distractions, and this brought everything back to center. My stress level plummeted, and I relaxed, settling into a mellow, low-stress pace while I had the opportunity. With the beach came the calming rhythm of waves. As each one slipped back into the ocean, a little bit of the anxiety I was swimming in went with it, and breathing came easy.

For the most part, my ride through Redondo Beach mirrored that of my trek through Santa Monica and Venice Beach, complete with a snake-like bike path that wove itself along the border between sand and pavement, where I was joined by a multitude of people engaged in various fitness activities. In lieu of tattoo shops, bohemian-style boutiques and seaside bodybuilding facilities, multi-story homes and upscale apartment complexes lined the beach here, with balconies on every level, built skinny but deep. Hotels staked their claim to the valuable coastline as well with tall buildings sporting top-dollar rooms facing west toward white sand beaches and the mighty Pacific.

Southern California beach culture took on a noticeably different vibe than the beach culture along the waterfronts of Northern California. Here, in Southern California, people were everywhere. The bike paths running alongside the popular SoCal beaches supported all sorts of physical activity: running, walking, rollerblading, roller skating, yoga, dancing, you name it. Even panhandling was popular. It was October. For most of the northern hemisphere that means long pants and a light sweater, maybe even a beanie. But not here in SoCal. The uniform of the day was swimsuits, at least along the beach, and watching people slather on sunscreen wasn't an uncommon occurrence. On one hand this made sense as the temperature hovered in the mid 80s. But on the other hand, I was saying to myself, *Really? How can the weather be this warm and beautiful in October? It just doesn't seem right.*

My thoughts and observations made for good company on this

delightful detour from the highway, but made for slow cycling. I could have flown by this section of the map in a quarter of the time just by following my own rules and sticking to the highway. *Follow the highway, Matt, and you won't get lost!* But I longed for these diversions and their beautiful distractions from the crowded streets, so I ignored my own advice for the second time. I couldn't help myself. I took in as much of the SoCal coastal grandeur as I could during the brief, rebellious escapade, knowing I wouldn't be able to enjoy this level of distraction for the next several hours.

CHAPTER SIX

A fter arriving at the southern edge of the beach, near Miramar Park and Burnout Beach, I angled back onto the main roads. A short time later I rejoined Highway 1 with my next checkpoint of Long Beach on my mind, working hard at dodging careless pedestrians and avoiding collisions with cars. It seemed there were a lot of inattentive drivers and a few drivers that didn't think tax-paying cyclists had any right to be on the road at all. *Read your California Driver's Manual, dude. Cyclists are vehicles, too, and have every right to the road that you do, whether you like it or not.*

Regardless of my intent and resilient effort to ride carefully and safely through the city streets, cars frequently sped past my left shoulder so closely I couldn't help but think it was intentional, especially when the threat was accompanied with a middle finger salute in their rear-view mirror. People with bigger balls just leaned out the open passenger side windows and yelled, "Fuck you, man! Get off the road."

Ego bruised but carefully controlled, I forced myself to dig deep into what little restraint I had to keep myself out of trouble. For the most part I kept my cool and continued the ride, hiding my frustrations behind sunglasses and concentrating on my goal, never letting my hands come off the handlebars to return hand gestures. Exhaustion helped to subdue the temptation to respond in kind to these transgressions. To comply with my impulses would only make things worse. I wasn't out for confrontation anyway. I was just out for a bike ride. The self-preservation aspect of keeping quiet was important too, because you know, whether the car hits you or you hit the car . . . you lose. I didn't feel like losing, especially when I was mere

323

hours, just one county, away from seeing my girl. My road to Mo was almost finished, or just beginning, depending on how you looked at it. I preferred the latter idea and kept that on my mind as I carefully meandered through the streets of Torrance, Lomita, Wilmington, and Long Beach. Maureen was way better at avoiding confrontation than I was, and I did my best to harness some of that restraint. *Offer honey, Matt, not vinegar.*

Crossing the San Gabriel River, I rolled into Seal Beach breathing another sigh of relief. I paused on the side of the road to take a break, polish off another bottle of water, and chow down on one of my last remaining PowerBars. I made it through the congestion of Los Angeles without getting myself killed, hurt, or lost. I even got through it without a single flat tire. *Way to go, Matt.* How the hell that ever happened, I'll never know. I was beside myself, and pleasantly surprised. But my sighs of relief weren't only a personal affirmation for what I'd left in my wake, but indicative of what lay ahead. Starting from this point forward, and all the way into Newport Beach, where I would turn inland for several miles on my final stretch to UC Irvine's main campus, I'd pass through the Orange County coastal towns of Seal Beach, Sunset Beach, and Huntington Beach. Still sticking to the famously scenic PCH, I'd ride all the way to the finish line following the edge of this ever-changing coastline, gobbling up unofficial checkpoint markers with every fancy beach sign I passed . . . all the way to Mo!

I was so close. My body hurt, almost everywhere, and my heart ached to feel her against me and hear her voice in my ears. *Sorry, Jezebel. You've done good, girl. I'm just tired of riding you.* I couldn't wait to give Maureen a giant, stinky hug after she opened up her apartment door when I arrived. She would probably be all pretty, smelling good and looking sexy. I, on the other hand, would most definitely not smell good or look anywhere near handsome. I definitely wouldn't look sexy. But whatever, we'll get over it. I'll take a shower, and all will be forgiven. *Okay, Matt, enough fantasizing, just get there already. You need to stop doing that shit. Really, man, let's go!*

For the third and final time on this trip, the sun was setting on me, but it wasn't so low in the sky to cause me any worry that I would get stuck riding after dark again. I had a lifetime fill of that experience last night. *Last night. Was I really riding down the western edge of the Santa Ynez in the dark last night? Seems like forever ago.* What a contrast between then and now. Last night the setting sun sparked fear and uneasiness; tonight it was an acclamation, a hanging lantern offering hope and a pleasant perspective about what was to come.

I didn't need to use the sun as a timepiece today, an essential strategy of daylight management over the past two days. The concern of running out of daylight on today's ride had passed. Tonight, I owned the privilege of viewing the sunset for what it truly was, a beautiful and wonderful thing, a colorful goodbye to the day and a trailing descent of welcoming for the moon and stars. There were no more mountains ahead of me that would make the setting sun an element of worry. No more risk that I would ride dangerously unprepared into the darkness like last night. Barring a tragedy, I was pretty much guaranteed Maureen's welcome embrace and a somewhat comfortable college apartment sofa to sleep on tonight. Everything was turning out okay. I was happy with my expectations for the evening and content with the condition I was in, physical discomfort aside, of course.

The sun's gradual descent toward the golden hour made the ride along the beaches a pleasant experience. These rides are seldom unpleasant, but at this particular time of day the experience can be a bit overwhelming. Filtered light bathed the coastline in the soft amber hues of autumn, casting slowly lengthening shadows of palm trees across the highway, their shape on the pavement stirring up memories of the Fourth-of-July sparklers I used to write my name in the sky with during Independence Day celebrations as a kid. The scene before me was stunning, appearing oddly purposeful; calculated even . . . like a moving painting . . . everything exactly where it needs to be and each color chosen with intention and meaning. Sometimes it's difficult to argue that certain things were made for no other purpose than to be exactly that, something beautiful.

If my estimations were correct, I had about another hour and a half of riding before rolling into Newport Beach, and another fifteen-to-thirty-minute ride from the coast to Mo's apartment at the University. Thanks to several hours of remaining sunlight, anxious urgency wasn't on the menu, only the "urgency of love." *Really? Dude, just get on with it, will ya? Get movin' before you lose yourself.*

Point taken. I pushed off and continued down the highway. I couldn't wait anymore. The excitement of riding next to the beach again almost made my legs forget how exhausted they were . . . almost. That forgetfulness came back full circle to pressing reality as soreness flared up the second I started spinning the gears again. All of the stop-and-go through Los Angeles didn't help things, that's for sure. On a good note, the beach, the shimmering ocean, and the early-evening sun—and the knowledge that I was almost at the end of my three-day journey down the coast—helped alleviate some of the discomfort. In fact, it made everything feel better. And yet, there was this looming suspicion that I was going to miss it when it was all over.

I would miss it all: the adventure, the scenery and the way I interacted with it, the unexpected developments, the people I met, the unknown, everything. But I also took solace in the fact that even though this this trip was coming to an end, it was merely a prelude to another adventure, another journey. One I hoped would be far more exciting and long-lasting. A journey with a yet-to-be-constructed path and an unknown destination. The only thing certain was its beginning, and that was because it had already begun. This journey would not be roamed alone—*no offense, Jezebel*—but would be traveled in tandem with this new girl, if she would join me. I didn't know where it would take me and I was nervous about the future, but I was willing to go along for the ride. What if the flames of desire faded with time, or one of us got pulled away by the temptation of another? What if we were forced into a long-distance relationship where separation strained our attraction for each other? Yes, the chance is there. But what if none of that happens? What if it all works out, even when the inevitable challenges of human partnership pushed against us? There was only one way to see . . . stay the course and heal from the bumps you hit along the road. Those always end up being the best trips anyway, right? The challenging ones . . . ones that carry with them the risk of hefty pitfalls, but opportunity for substantial rewards.

The best part about these journeys are the similarities they share with the highways I love so much; seemingly never-ending, infinitely adventurous, and stocked full of surprises. All highways end, as will all of my journeys and adventures, eventually. *Time is the ultimate thief, remember?* Some journeys last longer than others, but each one follows the same trajectory—they are finite and full of unknowns; two reasons why life is so valuable and should be cherished. None of us are getting out of this life alive . . . and that's all the more reason to make the journey to our final destination a lively one. Everyone's experience is unique, and every person will travel a different number of miles along their personal highways. The number of miles we travel on the highway of life is not what's important, though. Well, it's not what's *most* important, anyway. The quality of adventures we experience along these miles should be the goal, not how long it takes us to get to the end of the road.

There will be pauses along the way, rest stops where reflection is necessary. But don't be weary at rest. Sometimes . . . some may argue most of the time . . . these breaks provide the necessary opening where thought, preparation, and ingenuity are given a chance to bloom—an opportunity to slow down and assess where we came from and where we're going—time to choose another highway if we determine it necessary. There's always another one available if you have the courage to steer.

Eventually, when our ultimate journey comes to a halt, all we have is what we took from it, the treasures we found along the way. These we leave behind for others to cherish, build upon and learn from. My journey was just beginning, and I was determined to take this highway adventure as far as it would let me, all the way into the sunset of my life. I hoped this beautiful girl would join me all the way to the end of it.

*   *   *

I continued south, pedaling slowly, merging onto the bike path as soon as I could. The Huntington Beach Bike Path began at the south end of Sunset Beach, running parallel and adjacent to the PCH. I would follow this path into Newport Beach, all the way to the mouth of the Santa Ana River, where the path turns due east to follow the riverbank into the distant hills. Even though the bike path was only closer to the water by a few measly yards, at most, it was where I needed to be. And I was just far enough removed from the highway traffic, light as it was at this point, that I could push it out of my mind and pretend it wasn't even there. In an odd way, following the path in lieu of the road made me feel more like I was part of the community. Not like I was masquerading as a local or anything, but not like I was just some tourist passing through either. Admittedly, I was harboring idealistic illusions of being accepted as an honorary member of the local SoCal beach scene, but that would take time. At the moment, these feelings were embarrassingly inaccurate. There was no hiding the fact that a tourist was exactly what I was. All it took was one quick glance at Jezebel, with all the travel gear hanging from her frame, and me in my funny, tight-fitting outfit to understand that we were in fact visitors; passing through on our way to "somewhere else." Southern California beach town locals, for lack of a better term, are used to travel-through vagabonds though, so no one gave me any heed or shot me any who-the-fuck-are-you stares.

Regardless of my self-imposed rule to not leave the highway, do bike paths really count as disobedience? I couldn't help myself. Just like a marathon runner will shift toward the side of the road to give out high-fives to the fans on his, or her, final mile to the finish, sacrificing precious time in the process, I wanted to give myself a high-five for a job well done by enjoying the view from the most picturesque place I could find at the moment, riding along the beach.

*   *   *

I moderately increased my pedal cadence with every passing palm tree, settling into a speed that wouldn't freak anyone out, but fast enough to pass most people by. Not too fast, not too slow, I politely weaved in and out of the trajectory of joggers, dog walkers, and fellow cyclists. And speaking of cyclists, I was quite an awkward-looking one in these parts. Of all the cyclists

I passed, none had traveling gear attached to their bikes. I was a lone wolf in a sandy wilderness. In fact, most had nothing on at all, with the exception of board shorts and sunglasses, and maybe a bikini top.

Beach cruisers were the popular bikes of choice among the beach-goers, which made perfect sense considering the company I was keeping. I'll admit, that made me jealous for a moment. *Sorry, Jezebel, they look so comfortable and relaxing. Just look at those fat tires, cushy seats, and high handlebars.* But I wasn't completely alone out there on my touring bike with skinny tires. A few road cyclists joined me on the path this evening, squeezing the most out of an after-work sunset ride before the sun punched its timecard for the day. We greeted each other with silent head nods as we whizzed past in opposite directions.

Sand was everywhere. No surprise there, really. Pushed by the gentle autumn onshore breeze, ghostly fingers of it danced across the path's concrete surface in front of me and came to rest in the gaps between blades of freshly cut grass, planted in long patches between the eastern border of the bike path and the PCH. These patches of decorative vegetation also embraced palm trees and various other tropical plants. Occasionally, even a bench would appear among them. Dog walkers frequently used these areas too, leaving plenty of evidence behind. Some of the wind-blown sand settled into the street gutters along the highway as well, where it stayed hidden until the streetsweeper came to whisk them away. And let's not forget my bike chain. Sand was in there too, plenty of it. No longer did my perfectly aligned chain glide smoothly over the sprocket teeth with merely a whisper. Now it grinded against the teeth with a low rumble, unhappy with the bits of sand stuck to the grease that lubricated its joints. No big deal. I expected as much. I was next to the beach, after all, and I had been riding alongside it for most of the past three days. In fact, I was getting so accustomed to the presence of sand that it felt kinda awkward when it wasn't there.

CHAPTER SEVEN

A t the end of the Huntington Beach Bike Trail I rejoined the PCH before riding over the Santa Ana River overpass and into Newport Beach, the route leading me on a tour of the inland side of Newport Bay. Flanked on both sides by high-end car dealerships, classy hotels, countless seafood restaurants, and perfectly manicured sidewalks lined with palm trees and freshly cut lawns, the place smelled like money and bustled with success. Small gaps between buildings on the highway's west side gave me fluttering peeks at Lido Isle, one of two man-made islands residing within the boundaries of the bay. While crossing the overpass spanning Lower Newport Bay, I intermittently took my eyes off the road to watch a local crew team row by under the bridge, the shell pulsing silently through the water with every coordinated pull of the eight-man crew. The only sounds emanating from the boat were the barely audible gurgle of disturbed water as all sixteen oars surfaced in unison and the sharp voice of the coxswain calling out commands.

Here the streets were wide and clean, with plenty of room in the bike lane for safe riding. I quickly pedaled out of range of the coxswain, his rhythmic chirping quickly swallowed up by the passing roars of luxury European sports cars and the puttering of boat engines maneuvering small vessels and large yachts through the shallow bay and around Balboa Island. My eyes were drawn in all directions. There were so many distractions; so much to take in. Every street corner and opening between buildings had something interesting to look at, from elegant street signs to painted ocean-themed murals to postcard-worthy views of the bay. This high-class Orange

County coastal lifestyle was foreign to me, and boundlessly fascinating. It would have been wonderful to pedal around for a while and check it all out, but I had other things on my mind. There would be plenty of time for the touristy stuff later in the week when Mo and I had some time to hang out.

Before my sugar-deprived brain even had time to fantasize about all the fun I could be having on one of the boats in the harbor, what I'd been waiting for this whole time suddenly materialized, almost out of nowhere. I'd been on the lookout for it, knowing it was creeping up on me, but seeing it written out on a street sign made it all too real. Just like that, Jamboree Road came into view, the point on my journey where I would leave the Pacific Ocean behind and head east toward the city of Irvine. Admittedly, I was so engrossed in the newness of my surroundings that I almost rolled right through the intersection. If I did, it wouldn't have taken me too long to figure out the mistake. I knew if I ended up in Corona Del Mar, the next town, I'd gone too far. But I wouldn't have been very happy about such a mistake, that's for sure. If so inclined, I could have turned right at this intersection and taken a little bike tour around Balboa Island, maybe a short sunset cruise through the bay, enjoyed some fancy ice cream, or something cool like that. Tempting, but maybe later.

Oh my God! Am I really here? Was the only thing going through my head.

From this point on I would leave the highway behind, for good this time. I was done with it, turning my back to it, at least as far as this journey goes. Once I turned east at this intersection, I wouldn't be searching for a way back to the beach a few miles down the road, I wouldn't be "sticking to the highway" anymore, and I wouldn't feel lost when it wasn't in sight. The rule had served its purpose, and I had arrived just as I said I would; in three days' time.

I paused for a moment of reflection at the Jamboree/Highway 1 intersection. The significance of this name quite glaring. The word jamboree means "a celebration," and that's exactly what I was experiencing. Alone in my excitement, the celebration was a quiet, personal one. There was no fanfare or screaming, no champagne or caviar, no red carpet . . . and that was just fine with me. Over-the-top exuberance isn't my style anyway. I'm perfectly content with the self-satisfaction that comes with the accomplishment of personally set goals. I was celebrating myself for one hell of a three-day ride down the Pacific coastline, and I was celebrating the fact that I was finally going to be reunited with the woman I was quickly falling in love with.

It felt somewhat surreal standing here at the final turn of this three-day challenge, straddling Jezebel and polishing off my final bottle of fluids. Cars flew through the intersection in all directions after receiving their "green blessing" from the streetlight, the drivers all none the wiser to my happiness. I was consumed by the happenings in my own bubble, just as they were with theirs, so I get it.

Over the past several days I'd labeled this revered highway of intrigue and imagination many different things—some noble, some . . . not so much. They ranged from: my lonely friend, my road to Mo, the PCH, THE highway, just to name a few. A couple times I even labeled it a real son of a bitch, and at the time I wasn't lying. But this lengthy, sometimes lonely, stretch of pavement showed me beautiful things and gifted me a life-enhancing experience, bestowing on me memories I will not only plant in my growing garden of memories, but surely carry with me all the way to the grave. For that, I will always be grateful. Even with all the pain and discomfort I endured over the past three days—most the result of my lack of preparation, inadequate training, and prideful attachment to mission accomplishment—I did not regret even one mile, not one pedal stroke. I'd reached the dog leg on the route, the final eastward bend. UC Irvine was just up the road. *Bring it on, bitch! Let's finish this.*

Time to move. Time to finish. Time to see her again. *Nice work so far, Jezebel. You've done great, girl! Just a few more miles, my faithful friend.* I clicked back into the pedals and merged into the left lane, turning left as soon as the light went from red to green. Pedaling due east now, I cruised past the Newport Beach Country Club, the tall office buildings at Newport Center, the Big Canyon Country Club golf course, and one of the countless gated home communities in the area, all the way to University Drive. This distance covered about four miles, but it might as well have been forty. That's what it felt like, anyway. The closer I got to Mo, the longer the miles seemed to stretch out.

Turning right on University Drive, I rose out of the saddle and pushed down hard on Jezebel's pedals. For a short while I followed the San Diego Creek, a popular getaway location for people who find it necessary to leave the office for a "fitness lunch," its popularity enhanced by an adjacent two-lane multi-sport trail. Appropriately named "Mountains to the Sea Trail & Bikeway," it was centrally located near office buildings and residential homes alike, attracting all walks of life outside at some point during the day. Although the trail name was long-winded, I remember thinking the name of the creek was somewhat odd. *San Diego Creek? A little too far north to have a name like that, don't ya think?* Ah. Who cares? There weren't enough miles left in this journey to ponder such things.

With the sun and the early-evening breeze at my back, I followed my long shadow up the gradual incline toward the heart of the campus, passing by carefully planned neighborhoods on my right, with open space and protected wetlands on my left. True to the calculated reputation of the Irvine Company, these neighborhoods boasted high-dollar apartment complexes lined with landscaping so perfectly manicured even Walt Disney would be proud. *And just look at all those pools!*

I found myself amused watching my silhouette dance on the pavement as I pedaled out of the saddle, and it made me realize something interesting; this was one of only two times I actually saw my shadow directly in front of me this entire ride. The sun, having only crossed my path from left to right for most of the past three days, had only painted my shadow on either side of me, pointing it westward in the morning and eastward in the evening. The predictable late-evening breeze was also an unfamiliar feeling as it was at my back, pushing with me instead of against me, a welcome change from the crosswinds and headwinds Mother Nature forced me to deal with over the past three days.

The fascination with my dancing shadow soon became a fleeting glimpse of irrelevant entertainment as I approached the turnoff for California Avenue. As I leaned right and made a wide, sweeping turn, various university buildings came into view for the first time. The student apartment complexes, where Mo lived, were currently out of my field of view, blocked by a large roadside berm lining the north side of the avenue.

The university looked like a typical college campus from this vantage point, if there is such a thing. Tall buildings surrounded by large parking lots saturated the heart of the campus. Ample student housing apartments lined the exterior limits, bunched into small communal enclaves of student life where large, grassy knolls cut with intersecting sidewalks filled the open spaces between buildings.

California Avenue led me around the western border of the university in a long, sweeping arc. At the top of the hill, about halfway down the avenue, the roadside berm leveled off and I finally caught a glimpse of the finish line, unknown to everyone except me. After cresting the summit, Campus Village, Maureen's student apartment complex slowly came into view. My heart, already pounding with exertion, jumped with excitement. I couldn't believe I was here. After three long days, I had finally arrived.

One more turn, Jezebel.

I arrived at the intersection of Bison Avenue and California Avenue soon after sighting the apartments and made a left-hand turn. I didn't even bother to stop at the red light. There were no cars there, so I just rolled on through. I was panting from all the hard pedaling, so I sat back in the saddle and slowly coasted into the village, savoring the moment and giving my cardiovascular system a chance to settle down. I didn't want to be panting like a dog when I saw her for the first time today, especially since I already smelled like a wet, salty one. That, and my weathered physical appearance, would be plenty for Mo to deal with. Nervous excitement replaced rapid heartbeats when I saw her tiny teal two-door Geo Storm parked at the edge of the Campus Village parking lot, glistening in the early-evening sunlight. As I rode by, the sun hit its recently cleaned windows and daggers of fleeting light flashed across my eyes. I was wearing sunglasses, thank goodness, but instincts led me to turn away from the bright glare. Even with the flinch, a small green dot followed me around for a short while, making itself known every time I blinked.

*　　*　　*

I slowly rolled up to the grassy knoll in front of her door and gently squeezed Jezebel's brake levers for the final time until I came to a stop. The last stop. My road to Mo had come to an end. *Well . . . that's a wrap, Jezebel. Can you believe it?* To some, this may not seem like such a big deal, but to me, it was a moment of self-respect, the end of long personal endeavor. And in a small way I was looking for some form of validation of my efforts. I shot glances at several students as they walked by but got nothing of substance in return. No surprise there, really. *What, no clapping? No pat on the back? No welcoming party? Come on, people, can't you see what I've been through?* I said to myself in jest. To them I was just another guy on a bike, one of hundreds on campus, probably on my way back from class or something. *Relax, Matt. Mo will be excited to see you.*

Disengaging from the pedals, I straddled Jezebel and stood in the middle of the square patch of grass in front of Mo's apartment door. My gloved hands went to my waist, and I hung my head to stretch tight muscles in the back of my neck. With my head bowed, I caught myself in a trance-like state, gazing down at the cycling computer between the aero bars. My total trip miles glared at me from the bottom right corner of the display. *Four hundred and thirty miles. Wow, Jezebel. We did good.*

Who would have thought someone like me could tough out a ride like that? I guess I did, otherwise I wouldn't have done it, right? A thin smile of relief, satisfaction, and, dare I say it, pride formed on my face. Jezebel's black and blue top tube rested between the inside of my swollen thighs. The cream-colored sidewalls of the emergency tire I picked up in Cayucos, dirty after two days of hard riding, contrasted sharply against the bold colors of Jezebel's frame, reminding me of yesterday's challenges. *Black and blue*, I snickered to myself, spawning a brief moment of reflection about Jezebel's ironic color palette. *Well . . . isn't that appropriate.* When the colors of your bicycle frame remind you of how you feel, you know something ridiculous went down.

Three days ago, I set out on this journey with all the confidence in the world that I would make it here. I knew I would. I had no doubt about it, regardless of my lack of physical readiness for the adventure and the few moments of mental exhaustion I experienced on day two. *The mind can override all things, right? That's what some of the toughest people in the world always say, so it must be true, no?* The real reason I persevered and succeeded, my motivation for it all, was pretty obvious. It happened to be the woman waiting for me on the other side of this door. She kept me going. She wasn't running away from me, but even so, it felt like I was chasing her, and I was liking it. I'd had girlfriends before, but found it easy to let them go when it became obvious the relationship wasn't going anywhere special. I'd never "chased" one . . . but I'd also never been with a woman like Maureen before either.

Now that I was here, my goal met, it felt surreal and strangely unfinished, just like when I graduated USMC bootcamp. A lingering feeling of incompleteness hung in the air, like there was still more to do, miles left to ride. But I was here. My leg muscles protested this misplaced thought of deficiency, silently twitching with excitement at the finality of the moment and ready for rest. Now, I just needed to see my girl. *Hey, we've arrived. Relax man.*

Good idea. *You first, Jezebel.* I swung my right leg over to the left side of Jezebel's frame and gently laid her down in the grass, looking like a dog lying down on its side after a long run on a hot day. Her job was done.

I lifted my head and found myself staring at Maureen's front door, almost in disbelief. If this was a 1980s Hollywood movie, Mo would come bursting out of the front door. As my face lit up with happiness, she would run full speed toward me, in slow-motion, of course, stopping only after her arms were wrapped tightly around my neck. *"Freeze frame! End scene. That's a wrap, folks!"* Alas . . . life is not a movie, and nothing like that was going down at all.

Is that really the front door to her apartment? It was. And it was finally time for me to walk up, stand on the welcome mat, and knock on it. *But first, let's see how presentable I could make myself.* I sat down in the grass and removed my shoes, helmet, and gloves, laying them down next to Jezebel. I thought about pulling my T-shirt out of my pannier and switching it out with my jersey, but I just couldn't do it. I needed to see her right away. What was I even doing sitting in the grass anyhow? My heart wouldn't let me wait any longer. I forced myself up and started toward the door, wincing with the effort, my quads protesting yet again. The grass hadn't been mowed in a while and, bathed in the evening shade of the buildings, it felt cool and damp. My socked feet rustled through the tall blades, sounding like paper ripping beneath my feet. *Grass stains be damned!* Then a subtle, funny little thought crossed my mind. *No sand.* There was no sand in this grass.

A duality of emotions surfaced as I walked toward the door, nervousness and excitement building exponentially the closer I got. *Don't get all weird, Matt, she knows you're coming today.* Confidently, nervously, I stepped on the welcome mat and rapped my knuckles loudly against the door. Feeling weirdly awkward, I crossed my right hand over my left as I let my arms hang loosely in front of me. What the hell else was I going to do with them? My heart pounded with anticipation as I waited for the door to open. It was the first time over the past three days it thundered like this without the catalyst of extreme physical effort. Several seconds past with no answer. I thumped on the door again, this time adding a little more gusto, hammering with the meaty part of my right hand. Nothing . . . only silence from inside the apartment.

Ah, man. You've got to be kidding me. How can she not be here right now? I was frustrated, for sure. All this time, all these miles, and then nothing. *Well, shit, Matt. Let's see. Shall we discuss this? It's Monday. And it's dinnertime for most Californians right now. So, that means she might be eating somewhere. Oh, and if you didn't know already, which you do, Mo's an evening girl, so maybe she's out running around doing stuff. Did I mention that it's Monday? That also means classes are in session, which, alternatively, means she could also be in class.*

Damn. Common sense can be a real face-slapper, if you know what I mean.

Well, it is what it is. *Let's make the best of this, shall we?* I turned away from the door and stared out across the quad, taking a few seconds to think about what I could do while I waited for her to show up. It didn't take long for something to come to mind. This was my chance to clean up a little. *Great idea. You stink, man.* I walked slowly through the thick, sand-less grass over to Jezebel, still looking like she was taking a nap in the warm evening sunshine. *Go ahead, girl, you deserve it. But don't mind me. I need to get a few things.*

CHAPTER EIGHT

I freshened up with what little I had available. I slid my jersey over my head in one well-choreographed motion and dropped it inside-out in the grass, then, using the remaining water in my water bottles, spent a few minutes washing dirt and grime from my face, shoulders, arms, and head. With the bottles empty, my skin still glistening from the washing, I slipped into a somewhat fresh-smelling T-shirt. It wasn't date-night worthy, but it was better than the jersey. Now I felt moderately presentable. With nothing better to do I lay down on my back in the grass, cupped my hands behind my head, and relaxed. A sky void of clouds spilled out before me, allowing unencumbered views of the impending twilight. To the east, above the ridgeline of the distant desert hills, the inland sky had begun its cyclic fade to dark blue, and to the west, above a glaringly white horizon, pastels of crimson and gold gently welcomed the evening. I absorbed the day's final rays of autumn sunlight with pleasure, pushing away the temptation to treat myself to a short nap. I kept diligent surveillance of my surroundings, hoping I would catch a glimpse of her walking by, but I saw nothing. For a while. And then I heard her scream.

"Matt!? Matt!"

My eyes were closed, but my attentive ears heard the call. *So much for diligent surveillance.* Maureen's loud and distinguishable voice bellowed from the other side of the grassy knoll, reverberated off the buildings, and filled the otherwise muted quad. To me it sounded like music, the song I had been waiting to hear for three days. There weren't too many people walking about, but everybody in the vicinity turned and looked in her direction as if she was

337

calling out to each and every one of them. *Huh, they can't all be named Matt. Quit looking, people, that's my girl!*

I sprung to my feet as fast as my exhausted legs would allow, suddenly not giving a shit about the beautiful sunset, and lumbered forward in her direction. Even from across the quad, I could see the excitement in her face, and I hoped she was able to see the same in mine. After three days of only dreaming about her, to let another moment go by without casting my eyes on her radiant face would be too much. My chapped lips widened, and a smile so large it hurt stretched across my face.

She was moving quickly too, clumsily striding in my direction with a small canvas bag awkwardly swaying uncontrollably under her left shoulder while a pair of tap shoes dangled lazily from the first two fingers of her right hand. She wore an oversized loose-fitting Zot-squad T-shirt over short, leg-hugging black dancing shorts. Shoot, she might as well have been wearing a formal dress as beautiful as she was.

The gap between us collapsed rapidly, our eyes locked as we closed in. We came together with a thud, right in the middle of the quad, and embraced tightly, her arms around my neck and mine around the middle of her back. She briefly lowered her left arm and let the shoulder bag, as well as her tap shoes, drop to the ground somewhere in the grass behind me. Our reunion must have been comical to the onlookers. Two hormone-laden college students over-reacting at the sight of each other. But who gives a fuck about the onlookers? We surely didn't. Only we knew the underlining story behind the meeting, and that made it special; a moment shared between us, and only between us. The only thing missing was some slow-motion photography and a Cyndi Lauper song playing in the background as we melted into each other's arms. By the time her left arm was back around the nape of my salty neck, we were already kissing passionately, right there in front of God and everybody.

We soon parted, smiling, happy, content, and relieved; lost in the moment and oddly speechless. Everything else fell away, and we accepted the moment for what it was, a loving reunion of hearts.

Mo let out a mousey squeal, and we kissed again. Both of us feeling the need to breathe a few moments later, we parted again, and I pulled her in close. She had her hair pulled back in a ragged ponytail, and I could tell she'd been dancing. Her pale freckle-dotted cheeks were rosy and flushed from excursion, her skin clammy and cool. I didn't care, not one little bit. In fact, I found it beautiful and endearing, like everything else about her. Maureen is always the most radiant when spellbound by something she loves, and right now she was glowing in whatever had her in shackles. Today it was dance. Or maybe even me. I could only hope for the latter. I pressed my face into the cradle of her neck. As I did, some of her ponytail-bound hair spilled over the left side of my head, and I breathed in deeply as I held her tight. She smelled of spice and flowers, just as I remembered. Unfortunately for her, I surely did not.

We pulled away once more and stood there smiling at each other. She dropped her arms from around my neck and let them fall to her sides. I mimicked the motion but took my time doing so, sliding my hands over her shoulders and down her arms, stopping at the exposed skin of her upper arm below her shirt sleeve. I squeezed her gently and rubbed the surface of her skin with my raw thumbs.

"Damnit, Mo, I've missed you so much."

Maureen sighed, filled with excitement.

"Me too, Matt. I'm so happy you're finally here," she said, rising up on to her toes and then quickly rocking back onto her heels.

I let out a snicker at that. How right she was. *Finally here. Yes, yes. Finally.*

"Me too, Mo. Dang it, it sure is good to be here. After all those miles, man, you are such a beautiful thing to see.

"Ahh. Thanks, buddy," she replied sheepishly.

"Four hundred and thirty miles. Can you believe that shit? That's a long way to go . . . just to see you," I said, my tone increasingly sarcastic.

"Hey! Watch it, pal . . ." she replied, playfully poking me in the center of my chest. "Or you can hop right back on that bike over there and pedal back home," she said, playfully.

"THAT bike?" I replied, pretending to be insulted. "She has a name, you know."

"Oh really?" She asked, her voice swimming in a pool of exaggerated intrigue.

"Yeah, it's Jezebel, thank you very much."

"Hmm. Fine, you and Jez over there can just turn around, if you won't play nice. How's that sound?"

"Oh God." I rolled my eyes in exhaustion. "No. Please don't make me do it. I just couldn't do that again right now."

"I still can't believe you rode your bike down here." Maureen looked at Jezebel lying in the grass. I followed her gaze. Poor thing looked a little beat up. She was dirty, salty, and had mis-matched tires. Some of her handlebar tape was even starting to rip away from the end of the handlebars. "I still remember having to go pick you up at the Golden Gate Bridge when you tried to ride your bike to my house. Remember that?" she replied, laughing. "You were shivering when I got there."

"Ha!" I huffed. "Oh, yeah. I won't be forgetting that anytime soon. That was . . ."—I dragged out my response—" . . . probably not one of the best decisions I've ever made. I'll chalk that one up to some kind of testosterone-induced delirium."

"Oh, sure. And testosterone had nothing to do with THIS bike ride?" she replied, emphasizing "this" while raising a quizzical eyebrow and using the first two fingers on both hands to make the universal quote hand gesture as she said "testosterone."

"Well, I don't know." I shot a quick glance into the heavens, then brought it back to her eyes. "Maybe a little bit." I snickered. "But that doesn't matter. It was all about you, anyway."

"Mmm, that's sweet," she said sarcastically, sliding her hands around my waist again. She smiled.

"I've been thinking of you so much over the past three days," I said sheepishly. "You might not have known it, but you pushed me through a lot. I would have stopped several times if I didn't have you to think about. Especially yesterday. God, yesterday was not, let's just say, an ideal riding day." I paused and smiled at her. "Your pretty face kept me going."

She just stood there, silently looking at me in the fading evening sunlight. She lifted her right hand from my waist and gently ran her fingers through my short, greasy hair and over my salty face. Her left hand dropped and grabbed mine.

"How are you feeling? You okay?" she asked, her facial expression slowly changing from exhilaration to concern.

"Yeah. I'll be fine." I laughed light-heartedly. "In a couple days or so."

Mo frowned playfully.

"I'm sorry, Matt. You must be a little sore, huh?"

"You're sorry? Shoot, I'm sorry. I know you can smell me. I mean, I can smell me, and I know I smell like shit," I replied, scrunching up my nose.

"No, you smell like sweat, and a lot of it!" She laughed, mirroring my nose-scrunch to accentuate the point. "Nothing a shower and a visit to the laundromat can't take care of."

"True, true. Ah man, I do really need a shower. Be thankful I was able to find a hotel room last night. Imagine what it would be like if I didn't get a shower at all over the past three days."

Maureen crinkled her nose again.

"And, as luck would have it, I still have quarters left over for the laundry machines."

I conjured up a pathetic puppy-dog look and, rooting around for some kind of "earned sympathy," engaged in some exaggerated theater even she would be proud of. I let go of her hand and, bending over gingerly at the waist, gently rubbed the top my inflamed quads.

"What are you doing?" she asked.

"But my legs, Mo. Oh, they hurt so bad." They did hurt, but I was milking it, putting on a bit of a show, so why not take the exaggeration to a ridiculous level? "I just don't know if I can bend over far enough to fully clean up." I grunted with fabricated restraint. "I think this is as far as I can go. " I scrunched up my face and attempted to raise an eyebrow for full effect. But alas, I failed again. Both went up in unison. "I might need some help."

"Oh, pa-leze. Spare it, will ya?" She laughed.

I put on a wicked grin.

"You can't blame a man for trying, right?"

"Well . . ." she paused and raised her hands, placing them on my dungy forearms. This brought me back to a full standing position. "Maybe, just maybe, I can help you out with that," she replied, slathering on her own serving of youthful exaggeration. "As an act of charity, and in the interests of human dignity, of course," she added, smiling. "I can't have my boyfriend running around with me all dirty and smelly."

"If you insist, Miss Maureen," I replied eagerly, playfully, then dipped into a casual bow. "My queen."

"That's right. And don't you forget it."

She cocked her head to the right and pressed my nose flat with her finger, shooting me a sexy glance. *Damn, this girl is fine! What the hell is she doing with me?* I thought. *Shut up, Matt. Just roll with it, bro.* And damnit if that look didn't get me every time, so adorable and seductive. It gives her a power over me that I haven't been able to shake to this day.

Putty in her hands, man. You're just putty in her hands.

Yes, I know. Leave me alone. I'm cool with that.

*   *   *

So, there we were, standing together in the center of the UC Irvine campus. With waves of golden light brilliantly glistening in Maureen's eyes, the sun was calling an end to the day, and to my journey. But this was far from the end for us. As a matter of fact, our fairy-tale union was just beginning. We were in love, there was no doubt about that. We both felt it. Mo, happy and relieved that I made it to her safely. Me, also happy about all that, but enthusiastic about so many other things. A fearless future, an exciting outlook, an expectation of great things, and a loving companion to join me on a new adventure.

Our summer romance brewed into a whirlwind of fun and excitement, and I couldn't wait to see where it was destined to go. I was hopeful about our budding relationship, confident in what the future had in store for us, and feeling blessed that we were given an opportunity to plant a garden of memories together that will last a lifetime.

Over the past three days, on my road to Mo, I felt all kinds of love; love for Maureen Denise Marks, love for cycling, and love for the California coast. But most of it was for her. Maureen was the circle that encompassed everything else in my life. She's an embodiment of true optimism and always there offering an embrace that will warm your heart, even when everything around you is cold. Thoughts of her pushed me through the most challenging moments of the ride, and dreams of her filled my peaceful sleep.

Months had passed since we first met in that magical place called Disneyland, but it was only the dawn of things to come. Our relationship was young, blooming and already filled with adventures. But right then, at that special moment we shared on the grassy knoll under a typical Southern California sunset, what we had was far from typical. I knew that, and I think she did too. The magic surrounded us, and I was confident it would help us build a life together. I wanted . . . needed, to be with this woman forever.

It was time; time for me to leave the highway I was traveling on alone and find another one, one that Maureen and I could travel together.

We found it, together. And we are still on it to this very day, making plenty of pit-stops along the way, sometimes changing course but always planting more seeds in our garden of memories.

THE BEGINNING...

Leaving Santa Barbara shortly after sunrise on day three, via State Street.

The "Sentries of Stearns Wharf" seeing me off for my final day of riding.

Us standing on "our spot" about a year after meeting there.

Mo standing next to her Geo Storm in front of her apartment at UC Irvine.

The waters,
they sing their own songs
and dance to their own rhythms.

At times, the music is loud and the dancing chaotic.
but the waters are more content at peace,
when the music they make
is comforting, and their dancing smooth.

As are the waters, so is love.
Without turbulence,
there is no knowledge of calm.

I choose to suffer the beatings,
taken from the chaos,
only to coast smoothly into the still waters,

With you. Forever.

ABOUT THE AUTHOR

Matthew Koehler lives in Santa Rosa, California with his wife, Maureen (Mo), and their two daughters, Athena and Haven. Still an avid cyclist, Matthew enjoys cycling the backroads of California's wine country and coastal redwood forests; always looking for new cycling routes and interesting adventures. Connect with him on Facebook as **Matthew Koehler** and on Instagram as **mattkoehler**

Mo, an enthusiastic knitter, keeps herself busy making garments for herself, family and friends.

Disneyland still holds a very special place in both their hearts, and they visit "The Happiest Place on Earth" as much as possible.

You can follow along with their combined adventures on Instagram at **mattrides_moknits**.

This is Matthew's first book.

Made in the USA
Middletown, DE
29 June 2021

43300872R00213